PRAGMATICS OF PSYCHOTHERAPY

Pragmatics of Psychotherapy

A Survey of Theories and Practices

WILLIAM SCHOFIELD

Foreword by
Sol L. Garfield

Transaction Books
New Brunswick (U.S.A.) and Oxford (U.K.)

Library of Congress Catalog Number: 87-13926
ISBN 0-88738-174-X
Printed in the United States of America

Library of Congress Cataloging-in-Publication Data
Schofield, William.
   Pragmatics of psychotherapy.
   Bibliography: p.
   1. Psychotherapy. I. Title. [DNLM: 1. Psychotherapy.
WM 420 S367pa]
RC480.S248   1987   616.89′14   87-13926
ISBN 0-88738-174-X

To the
Psychotherapists of the Future
and to
Their Teachers

Contents

List of Figures

Acknowledgments

Skill and effectiveness in the practice of a clinical profession are the end products of three sources of personal influence and inspiration: 1) teacher/ authors, mentors, and supervisors; 2) clients and patients; and 3) colleagues. It was my great privilege to be closely associated for over 25 years with the late Professor Starke R. Hathaway and to have the opportunity as student, assistant, and colleague to know his thinking about and observe his practice of psychotherapy. It would be difficult to characterize what kind of psychotherapist Starke was; clearly he was anti-theory in the sense of having an abhorrence of lining up with any one school, and this led to his being perceived as anti-dynamic. He might have labeled himself an eclectic. His relative disinterest in any general conceptual elaboration and his reluctance to offer formal seminars on therapy were balanced by his willingness to have his therapeutic work observed directly, and by his famous case conferences. In both his formulation of the idiosyncratic dynamics of the individual case and in his incisive interventions Hathaway was a master therapist.

My thinking and work as a therapist have been influenced by Professor Paul E. Meehl with whom I have enjoyed nearly 40 years of collegial association. To Paul I am indebted for encouraging a receptive attitude toward and recognition of the validity of certain psychoanalytic concepts, and a sensitivity to unconscious dynamics. Moreover, as he has for untold numbers of clinical psychologists, he instilled in me a respect for the limits of clinical acuity and judgment.The close-hand observation of the Hathaway–Meehl intellectual tensions served as a good innoculant against monotheistic infection by any one psychotherapy theory.

It is obvious that I have been greatly influenced by those psychotherapists who have enriched the literature by their seminal writings and by those researchers who have addressed the "what," "why," and "how" of psychotherapy. Foremost among these have been Sigmund Freud, Carl Rogers, Albert Ellis, Jerome Frank, and Hans Strupp.

A famous psychoanalyst has been credited with the observation that there are two types of patients: those we help and those from whom we learn. My own experience is that *every* client is at least potentially a teacher from whom we may acquire a newly broadened perspective on the dilemmas of being human, although the lessons learned from those we fail are more painful. I am grateful for the circumstances of being a medical school and university hospital psychologist and, thus, having not only the opportunity to practice but the time to think about that practice, and about the role of the psychotherapist as a teacher and as a social agent.

I am indebted to my colleagues in the Department of Psychiatry and Psychology at the University of Minnesota for providing a stimulating and supportive environment for my studies. Two of these warrrant a special note of appreciation. Burtrum C. Schiele, M.D., professor emeritus of psychiatry, was one of the first to encourage me by both referring cases and being always available for consultation, and ready with sage observations. Over some four decades of collegial association, he referred a number of patients who contributed significantly to my clinical experience.

Alan H. Roberts, Ph.D., formerly of Minnesota, and now Director of Behavioral Medicine at the Scripps Clinic of La Jolla, California, has been a valued colleague, confidant, and professional correspondent. I recall especially his astute contributions to the weekly case conferences which we co-chaired for psychology interns.

I must also note in passing the significant stimulus provided by the late Ned Twing, Ph.D., in encouraging me to expose myself to the stresses and rewards of leading group supervisory conferences. These training conferences have found a natural extension in my informal weekly case consultations with junior colleagues for whose clinical stimulation I am most grateful: Drs. Kate Hathaway, John Hung, and William Robiner.

I am very appreciative of the courtesy of Robert M. Schwartz, Ph.D. and Nan R. Presser, Ph.D. for their permission to reprint material from their publications.

I am especially pleased by Professor Sol Garfield's cordial acceptance of the invitation to provide a Foreword.

Katherine Sarkanen has been the epitome of gracious efficiency in attending to the intricaces of manuscript preparation and in adjusting to my less than crystalline script.

Mary E. Curtis and the editorial staff of Transaction Books have conscientiously saved me from infelicities of phrase.

Finally, I am deeply indebted to my wife, Geraldine Bryan Schofield, and to my daughter, Gwen Star Bernal, and her family, who together afforded me the "mini-sabbatical"—the retreat of long days of uninterrupted solitude that made possible the completion of the work.

Minneapolis, Minnesota
June, 1987

Foreword

I am pleased to offer some comments as a foreword to this volume on psychotherapy by William Schofield. It is not the typical book on psychotherapy that either espouses one exclusive theoretical orientation or presents a quick tour of a dozen different schools of psychotherapy. It also is not a "how to do therapy" primer. Rather, it is a book that presents the reflections and judgments of an individual who has thought seriously and deeply about the field of psychotherapy, its theories, techniques, and therapists. As the author, himself, comments about the book: "It does not address in any detail the intervention techniques associated with any one or several of the major approaches to psychological intervention. Rather, it is intended to stimulate an appreciation of the particular role and limitations of psychotherapy in our culture at the present time. It seeks to provide the reader with a guide to 'how to think about' psychotherapy in all its rich complexities" (p. 115).

In the current era of psychotherapy where we are witnessing a proliferation of psychotherapeutic schools and orientations, an increasingly diverse group of mental healers, a visible popularity boom for psychotherapy, as well as a clear emphasis on accountability, it does appear worthwhile to consider the role and limitations of psychotherapy in our culture. Professor Schofield does indeed carry out such an appraisal and performs it in a socially sensitive manner.

The author's discussion of the varieties of psychotherapy leads him to conclude that in actuality there are a relatively small number of patient pathologies that respond to psychotherapy and that a few major orientations have been developed to treat these pathologies. Thus, psychoanalysis, client-centered therapy, rational-emotive therapy, and behavior therapy have been developed in this light. Each of these may be most appropriate for certain types of problems and the well trained therapist needs proficiency in each of these forms of psychotherapy. In contrast, followers of one form of psychotherapy are capable of dispensing only one type of therapy and may be mainly effective for the type of pathology that the therapy was devised for originally. This view of therapies resembles that presented by Donald Glad[1] some years ago, but the implications for training and practice are more specifically spelled out by Schofield.

The more recent emphases on integration and eclecticism in psychotherapy also receive attention and appraisal, as does the important issue of common and specific therapeutic factors. Schofield takes a more critical attitude toward eclecticism than I do and is inclined to equate their level of effectiveness with that of those who are followers of only one therapeutic approach. "If they (eclectics) practice an essentially casual, therapist-personal albeit nondoctrinaire form of eclecticism that does not vary much in form or content from case to case, their clients are likely to be subject to as much Procrustean stress as the clients of therapists who hew to the theory and constructs of a particular school" (p. 72). His reasoning here is that in both instances every client is likely to get the same type of therapy regardless of the problem presented. In contrast, Schofield emphasizes selecting the form of therapy that best fits the type of pathology manifested by the client. This is a view that most therapists, particularly eclectics, would probably agree with. However, each would ostensibly mean something different. In Schofield's view, selecting the appropriate therapy would mean assessing the client in terms of cognitive, affective, and behavioral difficulties and then using one of the primary therapies mentioned earlier. The eclectic would select whatever procedures were deemed appropriate, regardless of their theoretical origin.

A number of the items discussed by the author are clearly suggestive of the need for research to clarify the issues raised. How specific are the different therapies? What are the relative importance of technique, theory, common factors, therapist personality, and therapist skill? Despite a significant increase in research in recent years, we have few solid answers to such questions. Furthermore, as the author points out, there are no rule books that tell the therapist when and how to use specific interventions. Even with the recent appearance of training manuals, therapy is not automatic and is conducted by varying and variable humans.

Schofield has designated his emphasis on training in several major schools of psychotherapy as pragmatism and has attempted to differentiate it from eclecticism. "The pragmatic therapist can be thought of as practicing *selective* as contrasted with *generalized* eclecticism" (p. 148). However, as the author points out, pragmatism is not necessarily antithetical to eclecticism. Both differ from the emphasis on just one theoretical approach. How the therapists of the different persuasions actually would differ in practice remains for future researchers to investigate. What may be more important are the emphases made by Schofield against providing unneeded therapy, against unnecessarily prolonging therapy, and on

tryingthe most conservative approaches first. Individuals can find sufficient topics of importance that are worth thinking about in the present
book.

Sol L. Garfield
Professor Emeritus of Psychology
Washington University, St. Louis, Missouri

Note

1. Glad, D. (1959). *Operational Values in psychotherapy: A conceptual framework
   of interpersonality*. New York: Oxford University Press.

Introduction

Given a field of human endeavor with a modern history of some 75 years, and an accumulated literature of essays, research studies, theoretical papers, books, and clinical reports which is massive (albeit of highly variable quality) and when three generations have been at work on a problem and have left an extensive record of observations, hypotheses, theories, laboratory investigations and field applications, is it not likely that all the truly rich ore has been mined, that all the critical questions have been recognized, and that appropriate and adequate answers are pretty well in hand? Can there be left anything truly new and freshly enlightening to be said? Is it not likely that both the domain of general theory and that of associated technology have been clearly established, and that any subsequent offering is likely to entail either rather esoteric refinements of the essential axioms or insignificant modifications of procedural techniques? And after three-fourths of a century of scholarship, what is the likelihood of discovery when the essential phenomena under study begins when one person says to another "I am distressed" and entails the verbal exchange between these two persons until such time as the first person says, "I no longer suffer," or "I can now cope alone with my problem"? There are considerations encouraging a belief in the possibility that another piece of work, while not totally original nor inventive, may contribute a meaningful, useful and fresh conceptualization.

"Nature guards her secrets jealously." If one is in touch with the realm of science there is ample evidence that humans are not within sight of that time when they will run out of questions about the world they inhabit. Practitioners of the so-called "hard" sciences, with the great investigatory leverage provided by their instruments and the associated precision of measurement those instruments afford, and with the apparent lawfulness of the universe they seek to explore, continue with unabated initiative and imagination to find persisting mysteries and perplexing questions. The guarding of nature's secrets is a function of complexity, intricacy, subtlety, and interactionism—and the advantage to the scientist afforded by the general lawfulness of natural phenomena is balanced by the sobering recognition of Heisenberg's principle of indeterminancy—the fact that some methods of observation/measurement can influence the observed so

1

that it is always perceived, to some degree, in other than its natural condition. We cannot know Nature as *it is,* but only as we *know it to be.* This gnostic restriction does not prevent science from ardent and effective pursuit of an ever-expanding understanding of our world, an understanding which has been significantly if only partially validated by man's increasing ability to predict and, to some lesser extent, to control.

Can we find in the undiminished vigor of the hard sciences some support for a belief that psychology has not exhausted the potential for meaningful inquiry when we turn to a "softer" phenomena—personality, social interaction, and the dynamic mix of these in the process of psychotherapy? No—not if we accept the view of many: that the essential dimensions of personality are fewer and simpler than those of the physical world; that all possible combinations of such dimensions generate a finite and relatively small number of "types;" and that the quality and process of interaction between all possible pairs of such types likewise constitutes a highly manageable field for inquiry. According to this view psychotherapy is subject to rather early exhaustion of meaningful inquiry. This tends to be the view of many—especially "hard science" types—but also of many lay persons whose conviction about what their common-sense tells them is frequently inversely related to their direct experience. Much of the plethoric literature on psychotherapy would be characterized in the words of a late colleague, as "grinding nothing down to a fine point."

Are the critical elements entailed in a continuing communication between two humans less complex, intricate, subtle and interactive than those discovered (and discoverable) in the physical realm? And does not Heisenberg's principle present greater problems for the observer of human behavior? If in fact the elements and dimensions entailed in conversation with therapeutic intent (Schofield, 1986) are readily identifiable and their critical interactive patterns easily recognizable, how does it happen that psychologists have yet to generate a unified, general theory of personality (or instrumentation for personality measurement), that we do not have satisfactory measures of social intelligence, and that we are more than a little embarrassed when asked, as we are frequently, to appraise motivation, for example, of an applicant to medical school?

The possibility for discovery and progress, for imagination and initiative in the behavioral sciences, is not limited by any inherent lack of complexity. Simple minds find only simplicity where others detect "a blooming, buzzing confusion." A reductionistic urge is the frequent bedfellow of intolerance for ambiguity.

"There is nothing permanent except change . . . . you cannot step twice into the same stream." (Herecleitus) If each personality is the unique product of a complex interaction of unique genetic endowments as these unfold and are developed in response to a necessarily uniquely perceived and introjected chain of experiences, how can any profound verbal exchange between two such personalities be other than a fully unique event, hence not replicable, and hence not a proper base for any generalizations either about persons or about interpersonal communications, such as those which are the essence of psychotheapy? If this be the case, might it not account for the extent of the literature in this field and the fact that each "new" discovery seems almost totally additive rather than corrective, not serving to displace, at least in part, previous "truths?" If one holds to the "uniqueness" postulate, no therapist ever would be justified in offering generalizations from his or her unique observations of unique interactions. But every psychotherapist, regardless of his or her special professional identity (as a psychologist or psychiatrist) has had some education in scientific thought and carries a more or less conscious and deliberate commitment to be on the lookout for recurrent phenomena, regularities, patterns and, furthermore, to communicate these as soon as he or she is confident of an adequate evidential base.

The uniqueness postulate has never had an impressive consensus of adherents among psychologists, especially students of personality. Significant theoretical and methodological contributions have come from the nomothetic (statistical or normative) school (Cattell, 1965) and from the idiographic (clinical) school (Gordon Allport, 1961). The generality versus specificity argument in regard to personality traits has been almost continuous and seems only recently to be moving toward significant rapproachement through acute insight into the role of methodological procedure in supporting one or the other. (See Bandura, 1977, and Mischel, 1973)

The fact that each object and event is unique in and of itself does not prevent one from observing at appropriate levels of generalization that there are meaningful repetitions of Nature, and that properly restrained generalizations can lead to useful expectations. Adequacy of observation and restraint in inference is critical. Each of the blind men could give accurate descriptions of their "grasp" of the tail, the trunk, the leg of the elephant—the absurdity rests not in their respective inferences as to "the nature of the beast" but in the very encouragement of such inference from a restricted observational base.

Viewed in this light, every thoughtful explorer of the phenomena of neuroses and their alleviation by therapeutic conversation who has offered a "discovery" should be credited with a piece of the "truth." They may be faulted only if they imply that their insights encompass the "whole truth and nothing but the truth," and at once forgiven in recognition that this is a common and very human failing. We are encouraged in the conviction that the whole truth is knowable, and properly humbled by an appreciation that "Nature guards her secrets jealously."

These considerations of the rich complexity of the phenomena under study and of the limitations of the human observer encourage one to believe that there is still a possibility for meaningful contribution. Beyond that, hesitation as to whether one is justified in placing yet another volume into an already ponderous and still expanding (perhaps too rapidly?) library is reduced by explicit recognition of what one is *not* attempting.

The following pages will not offer any new theories of psychotherapy, of personality or of psychopathology generally, or of neuroses specifically. They will not propound a new school of therapy, or a specific new technique of psychotherapeutic intervention. In brief, no discoveries are claimed.

The literature on psychotherapy is superabundantly devoted to theory propagation and to elucidation of process, to concepts of etiology and techniques of intervention. With a very few notable exceptions (such as London's *The Modes and Morals of Psychotherapy*, Glad's *Operational Values in Psychotherapy*, Ford and Urban's *Systems of Psychotherapy*, Prochaska's *Systems of Psychotherapy: A Transtheoretical Analysis* and Margolis' *Psychotherapy and Morality*), the literature on psychotherapy promotes dominant theoretical constructs and the associated conventions of practice of the writers. Attempts at a comparative morphology or a systematizing of views and procedures have been rare, and have had little effect on the training of psychotherapists. Even these attempts, valuable and much needed, have neglected the problem posed by the cultural relativity of definitions of neurosis and have assumed the social legitimacy of all psychotherapeutic endeavors.

What is attempted in this volume is a focus on a mode of thinking about psychotherapy. In particular, there will be attention to psychotherapy as a *social* process, on individual, dyadic psychotherapy as an inherently social process. The reader will be encouraged to think as much about the "why" as about the "how" of psychotherapy.

This work arose from a conviction that at this time there is a need for a philosophy of psychotherapy, and it seeks to examine the social process of therapy in the context of basic philosophical questions of social values and social goals.

This volume is addressed to all mental health workers. It draws heavily for its substance and recommendations from the published work of psychologists, psychiatrists, and social workers—the three professions that have a primary and highly visible role in the delivery of mental health services. It seeks, however, to provide an overview and orientation for that broad panoply of service providers who work directly with individuals who are psychologically confused, demoralized, or distressed. These include, but are not limited, to all those workers who provide personal counseling and who, by virtue of their special roles, have the opportunity to provide a significantly positive experience for their clients: school counselors, educational and vocational counselors, rehabilitation counselors, chemical dependency counselors, speech pathologists, genetic counselors, home service nurses, and others. Given the recognition that a very large portion of persons seeking medical attention have complaints that are psychogenic or whose physical disorders are complicated or exacerbated by attitudinal and emotional factors, general physicians and medical specialists, including dentists, can benefit from awareness of those psychological elements by which the effectiveness of prescription and intervention can be augmented or lessened by attention to or neglect of those interpersonal forces present in every communication with therapeutic intent. In brief, the potential for meaningful, psychotherapeutic impact is not limited to mental health specialists. The overview offered in these pages should encourage all personal service clinicians to have less awe and more understanding of the field of psychotherapy and, if nothing else, more comfort and skill is making appropriate referrals.

The perspectives offered in this essay are intended especially for those preprofessional students who are contemplating a career in the mental health arena, or who are already in the early stages of professional study, and whose goal is to become competent psychotherapists. As future or present consumers of graduate curricula, they should benefit from an awareness of the options available to them and be alert that their graduate school preparation does not prematurely and inappropriately circumscribe their stimulus for flexible thinking. The skillful practice of psychotherapy requires a breadth of *education* which is antithetical to a narrowness of *training*. Chapter 8 in particular addresses these issues.

The analyses offered in this volume are relevant for lay readers whose interests in psychotherapy arise from a variety of sources: the taxpayer who contributes to and the legislator who allocates funds for training of therapists and for research into and delivery of mental health services; administrators/directors of graduate programs that train mental health professionals; philanthropists who support private training institutes; and curious lay persons who would like to better understand the divisiveness among professional therapists.

Finally the perspectives presented may be helpful to potential or present consumers of psychotherapy. For the former there is some guidance in how to appraise their experienced discomfort in respect to the need for psychotherapy and how to evaluate the appropriateness of possible therapists. For the latter, there is a guide to some of the potential sources of dissatisfaction or frustration they may feel in their present therapy experience.

References

Allport, G. (1961) *Pattern and Growth in Personality*. New York: Holt, Rinehart & Winston.

Bandura, A. (1977) "Self-efficacy: Toward a unifying theory of behavior change." *Psychological Review, 84*, 191–213.

Cattell, R. B. (1965) *The Scientific Analysis of Personality*. Baltimore: Penguin Books.

Ford, D. and Urban, B. (1963) *Systems of psychotherapy: A comparative study* New York: John Wiley and Sons, Inc.

Glad, D. (1959) *Operational values in psychotherapy: A Conceptual framework of interpersonality*. New York: Oxford University Press.

London, P. (1964) *The Modes and Morals of Psychotherapy*. New York: Holt, Rinehart and Winston, Inc.

Margolis, J. (1966) *Psychotherapy & morality: A study of two concepts*. New York: Random House.

Mischel, W. (1973) "Toward a cognitive social learning reconceptualization of personality." *Psychological Review, 80*, 252–283.

Prochaska, J. O. (1979) *Systems of psychotherapy: A transtheoretical analysis*. Homewood, IL: Dorsey Press.

1

Principles of Pragmatic Psychotherapy

Psychotherapy is an area of professional service delivery, it is a field of academic theorizing, and it is a focus for both clinical and laboratory research. It is a subject for vital discourse among and between public representatives (such as consumer advocates and journalists), clinical practitioners, personality theorists, and researchers. Over the last eight decades, these participants very slowly and to a very limited extent, have reached agreement on some general principles.

The essence of the process of psychotherapy, at least that part of it most readily accessible to observation and recording, is in the process of communication between (at least) two personalities. With the complexity of the dimensions that compose the multifaceted phenomena of personality, it is obvious that any interaction between two personalities, extended in time, will certainly be no less, and possibly more, complex and variable.

This complexity of the phenomena of psychotherapy is a source of perplexity for patients and would-be patients, for clinical providers of therapy, and for those who seek training to become psychotherapists.

However, variation is not limitless. Those major predispositions and proclivities, aptitudes, aspirations and assumptions by which the individual copes, adapts, and achieves are the dimensions that, when inadequate or distorted, become explanatory of his or her failure and psychological maladjustment. (See chapter 2)

The equipment for success is the equipment for failure and the work of psychotherapy uses this same equipment, uses the potentials and limits of the components of personhood, to assist the maladjusted and disturbed individual to gain equanimity and effectiveness. The real constraints on variation in the number and functional range of the psychological components of adaptation impose upper limits on the number of possible, meaningfully different *forms* (classes, types, syndromes) of psychopathology, that is, of nonphysical, nonorganic illness. This fact of limited but

7

real variation provides the basis for understanding the evolution of psychotherapy.

There are a limited number of forms of basic psychological pathology—ways in which the human can become emotionally distressed, cognitively confused or conflicted, and maladjusted. Awareness of these core pathological processes has arisen from the keen perceptions of clinicians who have observed specific forms of psychic dis-ease (primary patterns of symptomatology).

Observation of the manifest forms of neurotic pathology has led to persistent and fruitful efforts to tease out the underlying predisposing and precipitating etiological factors.

From the evolving understanding of matrices of the etiology–pathology interrelationships, clinicians have moved on to the proposition of distinct methods of treatment. Each system (theory) of etiology–pathology therapy has had a coherence resulting from the sometimes accidental and sometimes predetermined homogeneity of the clinical disorder and distress confronted by the theory founder.

Motivation for the construction of new "schools" has had several sources. Sometimes this has arisen from the clinical observation of previously unrecognized forms of pathology, or has derived from changes in preponderant clinical syndromes arising at least in part from broad cultural influences. It may be surmised, for example, that the gradually increased pervasiveness of knowledge of Freudian psychology in the populace, as a result of improved educational levels, has had a role in the decline in cases of "classical" conversion hysteria, (for example, sudden loss of sensation or muscular control, as in a "glove" anesthesia or paralysis of a hand). Similarly, those conditions of modern life in developed nations (the loss of exploratory frontiers for all but the elite few, the technologically fostered expansion of leisure, and the nuclear threat of a close-to-now end to all of human existence) have provided a nourishing medium for the insidious infection of a philosophical anomie, leading to the recognition of "existential neuroses."

Some of the motivation for the formulation of new systems has been stimulated by the reluctant recognition of therapeutic failures. Such acknowledgement has sometimes encouraged an awareness of a form of pathology previously unrecognized. At times it has led primarily to experimentation with a new focus of intervention and the discovery of specific techniques which might or might not be consistent with the theory on which the original treatment was formulated. The question of whether the role of relaxation is "necessary and/or sufficient" in systematic desensitization and biofeedback is illustrative. (See chap. 4).

Sometimes the spur to the development of new (antagonistic) systems has come from intellectual dissatisfaction and criticism of existing theories, or the need to develop a therapy that could be rationalized on the basis of a more general theory (with supporting data) of human psychology. Thus, much of academic psychology's general rejection, or at least ardent skepticism, of psychoanalysis arose from the apparent nontestability of major Freudian hypotheses.

The fervent competition of theory versus theory and technique versus technique has had two outcomes, one highly desirable and one of questionable value. On the positive side, it has led to increasing efforts to clarify and refine theoretical formulations and, even more usefully, to refine research methodology so that the determination of locus, nature, and relative efficacy of specific interventions can be known more precisely. On the other side, it has led to a seemingly limitless proliferation of the literature, especially of the "how to" variety, that overwhelms the clinician who is conscientiously motivated to "keep up." For some there is the promise that the "psychological penicillin" has been discovered. For others there is the implication that one must continuously add to the armametarium of techniques. Must the professionally proper therapist be a theoretical purist, or must he or she be a skilled technician whose multiplex interventions are dictated by an incohate empiricism? Is there a choice between the Charybdis of a monolithic theory and the Scylla of a conceptually unstructured eclecticism? Is the greatest good for the greatest number (and with greatest efficiency!) accomplished by the Procrustean therapist who fits every case to his or her framework, or is it accomplished by the Siva-like multi-armed technician who may focus on symptoms to the neglect of pathology?

Tenets of pragmatic therapy

The therapist who practices within a pragmatic framework accepts the following basic assumptions:

There are a limited and small number of primary forms, types or modes of psychopathology. (see Chapter 4.) There are a limited number of *differentiable* ways in which humans can become and be maladjusted. The limits on forms of pathology reflect the functional interactions among genetic factors, biological equipment, and the experiential possibilities provided by the individual's development and status in a particular culture and time. While the *contents* of pathology may be highly varied, the forms are strictly limited by the basic response (adaptation) possibilities of the individual. (It is not possible to spit and swallow simultaneously!)

There are a limited number of significant and valid concepts of etiology of the basic forms of psychopathology.

For each of the basic psychopathologies there is a major treatment of choice, that is, an approach to intervention that is addressed specifically to the underlying pathology and is not determined primarily or exclusively by the contents (symptom complex) of the presenting complaint.

Where established, the treatment-of-choice consists of modes of intervention of proven efficacy in attacking the core pathology.

The pragmatic psychotherapist accepts responsibility to be *knowledgeable* and *skilled* in the basic modes of psychotherapy.

Principles of Pragmatic Practice

The work of the pragmatic psychotherapist is guided by a few basic principles. In brief, these encompass assessment; the *decision* to treat or *not to treat;* choice of a particular therapeutic approach; the regular monitoring of patient progress; and the seeking of maximal relief, improvement, or recovery for the patient in the shortest possible time.

Assessment

The pragmatic therapist uses the initial consultation to answer a number of questions. (For discussion of assessment methods, see Chapter 6.) Foremost among these is the question of whether the applicant is a legitimate candidate for psychotherapy. (Refer to chapter 3). The pragmatic therapist does not uncritically assume that every consultee, by the simple fact of showing up, is truly in need of help. The therapist carefully evaluates the nature of the presenting complaint, the client's attitudes about his or her "symptoms," and the expectation as to their probable future course if untreated. The assessment process is attentive to the expressed goals of the client; where these are vague or poorly articulated, the therapist assists the client toward a focused statement of what is desired. Is the client seeking: relief from depression, freedom from anxiety (generalized fearfulness or specific phobias); enhancement of self-esteem; establishment or improvement of interpersonal relations with significant others; the extinction of self-injurious or self-destructive behaviors; reduction of attitudinal conflicts or clarification of values and priorities; improved productivity or efficiency; assimilation of a significant loss or disappointment; verification or invalidation of a "self-diagnosis," and knowledge of what is "normal"? The therapist is alert to possible erroneous self-diagnoses for which a single, educational consultation may suffice. When, as is frequently true, the client presents multiple areas of disturbance, the therapist's assessment establishes priorities; which problem area demands primary attention?

When the applicant appears to be a valid candidate for psychotherapy, the therapist seeks a functional diagnosis of the core pathology, which may or may not be identical with the client's presenting complaint. Also, the therapist assesses the quality and extent of the client's matrix of social support and extratherapy sources of corrective experience. Finally, the therapist appraises the strength of the applicant's motivation for help in relation to the initially expressed goals. Is the applicant seeking (appropriately or not) a "quick fix"? Is the applicant seeking, under cover of a goal of self-understanding, the socially modish experience of being "in therapy"? Does the applicant who erroneously requests intensive psychotherapy really have a valid need for brief counseling? Does the applicant for prescriptive, authoritative advice and direction really require a corrective interpersonal experience?

Decision

From the beginning of an initial contact with a prospective client, the pragmatic therapist makes it clear that a course of treatment is not automatically assured by the mere fact of the consultation. After the careful assessment indicated above, the therapist makes a deliberate decision to offer or not to offer treatment. The therapist's decision to treat is expressed explicitly and firmly as just that, and in a manner that elicits clearly from the applicant a complementary decision, that is, the *decision to change* and to do that work of therapy necessary to accomplish the change. This provides a final check on the applicant's motivation. The therapist should be hesitant to accept the candidate whose side of the contract has the note of passivity and non-decision implied in "I am ready to *let* you *try* to help me". The ethical practitioner who knows that his or her appointment calendar is completely filled, preventing any likelihood of adding another case, will make this fact clear to the prospective candidate and indicate that at best only a single session consultation may be available; this can be done best by letter or phone call following the candidate's initial contact.

If the therapist's decision is not to accept the applicant, this is conveyed with deliberate care and thoughtfulness so as to be optimally beneficial to the applicant. The possibility of such benefit from a single (or at most two or three) sessions arises when the applicant has misjudged the significance of self-diagnosed symptoms, is failing to make use of corrective resources within his/her social community, has insupportable expectations of what therapy is or can provide, or is a suitable candidate for a form of intervention that the therapist/consultant does not practice. In the latter instance, for example, if the applicant is desirous of hypnotherapy (an element of self-diagnosis!), and the consulting therapist thinks this might be an appropriate intervention that he or she does not practice, it is professionally responsible to provide two or three suitable referrals. Unlike the monolithic therapist, the pragmatic therapist is not tempted to "convert" the client's pathology to fit the therapist's preferred mode of practice. (See Chapter 5).

When the decision is to accept the applicant for therapy, the essential elements of the decision are conveyed to the client in a manner that begins the therapeutic process. This communication includes acknowledgment of the legitimacy (validity) of the patient's complaints, recognition of a form of therapeutic intervention appropriate to the patient's problems, and the therapist's expectation of being helpful. The latter should not imply a guarantee of cure, but rather an indication of a reasonable probability that the client will experience benefits, conditional upon his or her compliance with the therapeutic contract.

Choice of Therapy

Part of the decision process for the therapist rests upon the assessment of the primary or core pathology that the patient presents. This assessment essentially dictates the primary mode of intervention. (See Chapter 5). This aspect of the therapist's decision to treat should also be communicated to the patient, as it provides the framework for specifying the respective responsibilities of therapist and patient, elements of the explicit contract. (See Chapter 6).

Monitoring

There are philosophical or value orientations within some schools of therapy that favor a passive stance on the part of the therapist with regard to responsibility for the patient's progress. The rationale for such passivity is somewhat varied from school to school. It may be argued that the patient must take primary responsibility as part of the essential motivation to work for gains. It may be argued that for the therapist to take an authoritarian-parental role, or teacher-like role to issue "grades" for the client's behavior, is antithetical to the prime goal of therapy, that is, to help the client toward independence and self-sufficiency. It may be argued that since the essential pain of the client is intrapsychic he or she alone can judge and report salutary changes.

Two movements have significantly challenged the passive (potentially self-serving?) stance of therapists with regard to responsibility for the monitoring of patient progress. The first of these was the development of behavior therapy. This approach not only requires explicit behaviorally defined goals of therapy but entails specific criteria by which both the client's baseline status is determined and his or her subsequent progress can be measured with precision. The public nature of the criteria affords the client data for self-reinforcement and renewed or sustained effort as progress is demonstrated. Further, they inform the therapist as to whether the intervention program is working and may provide the basis for alterations in the therapeutic plan. The behavior therapist accepts a clear responsibility to monitor therapy progress.

The accomplishments of the behavioral approach together with economic pressures for the development of short-term therapies (even within the psychodynamic framework), have fueled the second movement that has fostered the principle of the therapist's responsibility to continually evaluate the client's response. The growing role of third-parties (health insurance underwriters) in covering the cost of mental health services has led to concern for cost containment, or quality assurance, and in turn to the development of systems of peer review. Such reviews require the service provider, the therapist, to provide evaluations of the client's response, especially to support requests for continuation of insurance covered services (Bent & Shueman, 1987; Chestnut, Wilson, Wright, & Zemlich, 1987; Schofield, 1987).

Apart from these recent forces, the pragmatic therapists in acceptance of their inherent role as sanctioned agents of the community (see Chapter 2), take responsibility for monitoring the effectiveness of their efforts.

Termination

A passive stance in regard to the responsibility for monitoring client progress is consistent with the same irresponsibility with regard to termination of therapy. Such passivity undoubtedly accounts in considerable measure for the very prolonged treatment of some (but not all) cases. It is easier for the therapist, other things equal, to continue with old, familiar, and "comfortable" cases than to struggle with the uncertainties and exigencies of new ones. The predictability (and absence of disruptive surprises) of long-term cases may more than compensate for the stress of professional ennui. Similarly, there are forces that support the willingness of the patient to wait passively for official dismissal by the therapist. Prominent among these are those attitudinal predispositions of the patient to accept a status hierarchy and assign to the expert both authority and responsibility for evaluation of the response to treatment (see chap. 5). Equally significant is the natural reluctance of the patient to sever a relationship that has achieved the qualities of the ideal therapeutic alliance, especially when many of those qualities parallel those of an ideal friendship (Schofield, 1970, 1986). This latter motive is of particular relevance if the therapist is unaware of or indifferent to the fact that the client has assigned to him or her the role of "best friend" or when, because of the client's neurotic isolation from social resources, the therapist functions as an only (substitute) friend—serving as intimate confidante and confessor.

The pragmatic therapist is sensitive to these forces that may lead to unduly prolonged treatment and accepts responsibility for assisting the patient toward termination at an optimal point. The power of the forces suggested above to delay optimal termination is reflected in their inclusion in the *ethical* codes of professional organizations and state regulatory bodies.

> Psychologists terminate a clinical or counseling relationship when it is reasonably clear that the consumer is not benefitting from it
>> —Ethical Principles of Psychologists, American Psychological Association, 1981

> A psychologist shall terminate a professional relationship with a client when the client is not likely to benefit from continued professional services or the services are unneeded.
>> —Rules and Regulations, Minnesota State Board of Examiners of Psychologists, 1982

Given the pathology–process model presented in chapter 4, the pragmatic orientation to psychotherapy requires that the therapist be knowledgeable, experienced, and skilled in a small number of basic modes of psychological intervention, that is that the pragmatic therapist will be an effective and efficient generalist. It requires the therapist to be competent in assessment and differentiation among the core forms of psychopathology. It requires that the therapist be well informed and practiced in the forms of intervention (therapies-of-choice) that are empirically (and theoretically) associated with the effective treatment of each of the basic pathologies. The pragmatic approach assumes that the therapist will treat different clients (problems) in different ways, that some clients may receive unimodal treatment while others may require a sequence or combination of therapeutic modalities.

Apart from the general principles outlined above, there are basic elements of attitude and expectation germane to the conduct of pragmatic therapy. The therapist provides an atmosphere of acceptance and support essential to help the client to move out of a state of demoralization. The therapist encourages an appropriate degree of hopeful expectation (and related motivation) in the client by the communication, reasonably explicit, that "I have *deliberately* accepted you as a client because you do have a problem with which I can be helpful." The responsibilities of the therapist are explicit; "I will conduct our sessions (keep them on track), but *you* are responsible for the *agenda*." It is made clear (and consistently monitored) that the client is to *think* and to work between therapy sessions, to test, experiment, and validate outside of the treatment room the learnings acquired there.

Ethical Principles for Pragmatic Practice

The pragmatic therapist works with a continuous awareness of certain guidelines of a specific professional ethic:

• I need not and must not accept every applicant and referral.

• I recognize that some problems are essentially untreatable within the limits of present therapeutic knowledge. I recognize that some clients may be accessible only to limited benefits from a palliative, supportive relationship. If I do not have the time resources nor the personal disposition to provide such support, I will make assiduous effort to direct the applicant to potential sources of such.

• When, by deliberate decision, I accept a client, it is because I am confident that I can provide the necessary therapeutic methods and relationship.

• My basic goal is always to assist the client toward increased self-sufficiency, toward functional interdependency with social resources, toward mature decisions and responsibility for self.

• I will work with continuous concern for effectiveness and efficiency to help the client *as soon as possible* to that psychological condition in which he or she will neither need nor desire to continue treatment.

• When and if my efforts are unsuccessful, or the client's program is unduly slow or irregular, I will look first to myself (to my assessments and my choice of treatment method) to account for the difficulties rather than attributing them to the client's resistance or lack of motivation. In such instances, I will acknowledge my errors to the client and provide the rationale either for discontinuing treatment or changing the method of treatment.

These elements of a pragmatic orientation to the conduct of psychotherapy have stringent implications on the selection and training of therapists. These will be examined in chapter 8.

References

Bent, R. J. & Shueman, S. A. (1987) Health care delivery, peer review, and the role of APA: History, administrative experiences, and empirical issues. *Professional Psychology: Research & Practice, 18,* 102–106.

Chestnut, W. J., Wilson, S., Wright, R. H. & Zemlich, M. J. (1987) Health care delivery, peer review and the role of APA: Problems, protests, and proposals. *Professional Psychology: Research & Practice, 18,* 107–112.

Schofield, W. (1970) The psychotherapist as friend. *Humanitas, VI,* 211–223.

Schofield, W. (1986) *Psychotherapy: The purchase of friendship.* New Brunswick, N J: Transaction Books.

Schofield, W. (1987) Health care delivery, peer review, and the role of APA: Overview and update. *Professional Psychology: Research & Practice, 18,* 117–118.

2

The Structure of Psychotherapy

Essential Elements

Individual psychotherapy is a process of communication between two persons. One of the participants is a supplicant who brings a complaint. This may be a circumscribed symptom (such as chronic headache, or fear of automobiles), an emotional distress (such as persisting depression following a personal loss, with multiple physical and mental symptoms), or chronic psychic tension (such as anxiety, persistent self-criticism, dissatisfaction with achievement or life circumstances, or conflict and lack of comfort in relationships with others).

The other participant is a therapist/expert (not necessarily an expert therapist!) whose basic qualifications to offer psychotherapeutic services have at least a minimal validation through the therapist's credentialed membership in one or another of several professional disciplines, namely, medicine, psychology, social work, the ministry, or nursing. "Psychotherapy is an activity in which one member of the dyad attempts to relieve his or her distress; the other member of the dyad attempts to facilitate this process using a variety of interventions" (Watters, Rubenstein, & Bellissimo, 1980).

In all psychotherapeutic relationships, there is a contractual element. This may be more or less formal, sometimes written. Even if informal, there is at least an implicit acknowledgment of certain expectations as to the respective behaviors and commitments of the supplicant and the therapist. These include an understanding as to the physical setting for sessions, the length of sessions and their frequency, and the cost and mode of payment by the service recipient. These structural elements usually are understood in the initial consultation. There may be several sessions before both participants have a mutual understanding and agreement as to their respective roles (e.g., the degree of activity on the part of the therapist, the responsibility of the client for the "agenda" of each therapy session, and the limits on physical contact and on between-session communications).

The term *supplicant* is used in this introductory statement to emphasize that the person who consults a therapist brings a problem, symptom, or complaint and is a petitioner for help. As such, it is best if the therapist views the supplicant initially as an applicant for extended psychological help and does not assume from the act of petition alone, that he or she is a suitable candidate (see chap. 3).

The term supplicant has no established usage in referring to persons who seek psychotherapy. It is a concept that subsumes the more common designations; *client* or *patient*. In the didactic and research literature, there is some tendency to use *patient* and *client* interchangeably. With some consistency but no explicit convention, the term *patient* is applied to individuals with more serious, more incapacitating or dysfunctional complaints and the term *client* for those with less serious and less long-standing problems. Persons seen in a medical setting, even if receiving exclusively psychological treatment by nonphysicians, are customarily (and thoughtlessly?) referred to as patients. In contrast, the recipients of services at a student counseling center or clinic are typically identified as clients. In a degree far short of unanimity, it is a general practice for certain professionals, notably physicians and clinical psychologists, to refer to their cases as patients, and for other professionals, notably counseling psychologists, family therapists, and marriage counselors, to identify cases as clients. Because of the status/prestige connotations associated with the practice of medicine (and related terms, *clinic* and *treatment*) there is a pull on all psychotherapists, regardless of their professional identity or work setting, to refer to all their cases as patients. The pragmatic therapist is sensitive to the role/image impact of labels, to the differential implications about dependency and passivity of the term *patient* in contrast to *client*, and will use these, if at all in communication with his consultee, differentially and sensitively. Thus, the same therapist may have some "clients" and some "patients." Accordingly, the two terms will be used interchangeably in this text, but not as semantic equivalents. (On words as therapeutic tools, see chap. 6.)

Another essential element is the privilege held by the supplicant to have his or her communications held in strict confidence.[1] This provides a degree of confidentiality greater than the supplicant is likely to assume concerning communication even with family members. This element, plus the stability of place, time, and frequency of the sessions, makes for a special experience of intimacy that affords a profound satisfaction of the human need for relationship. This satisfaction may in degree sometimes surpass that of spousal, parental, sibling, or other familial relationships, and may approach (but never attain) that of the ideal friendship.

Definitions

Psychotherapy:

Mental treatment of illness, especially of nervous diseases and maladjustments, as by suggestion, psychoanalysis, or re-education. (*Webster's New International Dictionary of the English Language*, 2nd ed., 1967)

Treatment designed to produce a response by mental rather than physical effects, including the use of suggestion, persuasion, re-education, reassurance, and support, as well as the techniques of hypnosis, abreaction, and psychoanalysis which are employed in the so-called deep psychotherapy. (*Dorland's Illustrated Medical Dictionary*, 26th ed., 1974)

To be noted in these two general definitions for the public is the shared inclusion of the terms *suggestion, re-education,* and *psychoanalysis*, implying a continuum from more superficial to more profound therapeutic modalities, from weaker to stronger. Notable also is the inclusion of such methods as suggestion, persuasion, and reassurance, which are either denigrated, eschewed, or considered taboo by many therapists (for discussion of the implications of these professional biases, see chap. 6).

In the technical literature of psychotherapy, is there found not only greater specificity but some semblance of agreement and uniformity in definition? For comparative analysis of the definitions provided (and many texts do not offer formal definitions) three questions are appropriate: (1) What is the substantive *focus* of attention (or how is the treated "pathology" conceptualized)? (2) What is the *process* of therapy (or what is the essential medium of therapy)? (3) What are the goals (or the desired end products) of the process?

Figure 1 presents the results of such an analysis applied to a selection of texts on psychotherapy. Examination of the figure indicates some author-to-author agreements on one or more of the elements, but variation exceeds uniformity. Focus may be placed on the feelings or on the thinking of the client. The process is seen by some therapists as resting on the experiencing of the therapeutic relationship, by others as instructional and reeducative. For some therapists the goal is for the client to achieve understanding of self, for others it is conflict reduction or personality growth. The suggested differences among therapists in their conceptualization of psychotherapy may be more apparent and superficial than phenomenally real, more semantic than substantive. But these conceptual

FIGURE 1

Comparison of Elements in Definitions of Psychotherapy

Source	Therapy Focus	Therapy Process	Therapy Goal
Bandura	deviant behavior	stimulus control; response contingency	adjustment
Berne	ego states	transactional analysis	mastery of internal conflicts
Colby	patient's verbal productions	interpretation	understanding
Dollard & Miller	conflict reduction	learning through reinforcement	normality
Ellis (1962)	patient's ideas, thoughts	rational confrontation, instruction	rational life philosophy
Frank	feelings, attitudes behavior	rituals	relief of suffering
Frankl	predicaments	I-Thou encounter; paradoxical intention	achievement of meaning
Perls	immediate situation	creative adjustment of the self	reintegration of dissociated parts
Rogers (1942)	patient's self	acceptance and clarification	changed self-image; conflict reduction
Strupp (1960)	difficulties in living	patient-therapist relationship; interpretation	resolution of conflict
Thorne	psychological state; life situation	client-centered; distributive	self-understanding; life management
Wolberg	emotional problems	patient-therapist relationship	symptom removal; personality growth
Wolpe	unadaptive behavior	learning	changed habits
Yates (1970)	abnormal behavior	deconditioning; reconditioning	behavioral change

contradictions and factious formulations have yielded more literature and less enlightenment. Over 30 years ago, an unidentified conference participant offered the following definition, which in perspective is less "facetious" than its original characterization: "Psychotherapy is an unidentified technique applied to unspecified problems with unpredictable outcome" (Raimy, 1950). A current paraphrase would be: Psychotherapy is a variety of techniques applied to a variety of problems with a variety of outcomes. In recent times there have been real concern and attempts to seek reasonable uniformity and generality of practices and their conceptual bases.

These are identified as efforts toward "rapproachement" or "integration" (Garfield, 1982; Goldfried, 1982; Kendall, 1982; Messer & Winokur, 1980; Yates, 1983). Rapproachement and integration may be improper goals if they prevent recognition of a meaningful differentiation, one that acknowledges the *real* but *limited* variation in the types of psychological disorder or distress that are responsive to appropriately differentiated modes of psychological intervention (see chap. 7).

Could the apparent divergences suggested in the figure be reduced if the authors were surveyed with a series of yes or no questions?

- Is the successful recipient of psychotherapy a different person at the end of treatment?
- Are the differences manifest in the way the recipient thinks, or feels, or behaves—or some combination of these?
- Do the changes in the recipient result from a process of learning (of new attitudes, new perceptions of self and others, new skills—or some combination of these)?
- Is the essential role of the therapist that of a facilitator of the learning process (by acceptance, instruction, coaching, modeling, interpreting, scheduling, and rewarding—or some combination of these)?
- Can the specific learning needs of the recipient be discerned early in the therapy relationship?
- Can selection be made of a most efficient mode of facilitation of the recipient's learning needs?

It is highly likely that there would be a nearly unanimous positive response to these queries.

Structural Analysis

The conduct and process of a conversation with therapeutic intent between two persons is determined and constrained by what each of the participants brings to the discourse. It is broadly agreed that the therapeutic exchange is an interaction between two personalities. The elements of personality (perhaps better, "personhood") germane to the exchange are rarely fully explicated. Rather there is an emphasis on a few of the personality dimensions of the therapist and patient respectively as of central importance.

Figure 2 outlines significant personal elements that the two participants bring to the therapy setting. It points up parallels in their respective "luggage," although the contents of similar bags may be in some instances much alike and in others very different.

FIGURE 2

Structural Components of Psychotherapy

	THERAPIST	PATIENT
General Components	Perceptions	Perceptions
	Cognitions	Cognitions
	Attitudes, values, biases	Attitudes, values, biases
	Tempo	Tempo
	"Style"	"Style"
Specific Components	Experience—history: personal history; experience as therapist; Theoretical orientation	History—experience: personal history; experience as client/ patient
	Patient "preferences"	Therapist "preferences"
	Therapist "expectations"	Patient "expectations"
	Preformed rapport	Preformed rapport
	Objectivity	Subjectivity
	Therapy skills	Symptoms, complaints, problems, conflicts

General Components

With respect to perceptions, the sensory acuity of the two participants may be intact and active or variously impaired or neglected. Each may be more of less aware of and attentive to changes in the voice quality of the other. The therapist may elect a physical setting that enhances the possibility to observe not only the client's changes in posture and physical activity, but also more subtle physical cues of emotional or affective states. The orthodox, behind-the-couch analyst chooses not to observe the blushing or blanching of the analysand, which may or may not accompany some periods of blocking in the course of free association. Similarly, the patient may or may not be attentive to changes in the therapist's posture or tone of voice by which the latter intends to convey contextual meaning to what is spoken. The therapist may be more or less attentive to subtle changes in the patient's dress and appearance. The patient may or may not observe and comment that the therapist appears "tired." Individual differences in the two participants' habits and skills of perception can significantly influence the communication process.

The respective perceptions of the therapist and client are processed by each of them, that is, they are thought about, as are the explicit verbalizations of each. The therapist seeks to understand the client so as to assist the client toward understanding. There is a process of continual inference leading to working hypotheses that are tested by communication to the client. Likewise, the client brings a certain level of cognitive ability to the communication process and a capacity to understand the talk of the therapist. The therapist has an apperceptive mass of theory, concepts, associations, and experience to apply to the observations of the behavior and productions of the patient in arriving at a formulation—diagnosis, etiology, pathology, prognosis, and indicated therapy. Finally, the therapist needs the cognitive ability to translate his or her understanding into language that can be clearly comprehended by the patient. In brief, all other considerations aside, the therapist must be a skilled listener/observer, and an expert communicator. In many cases, part of the patient's therapeutic gain is a result of an increase in his or her communication skills.

Figure 2 indicates that both the therapist and the therapist's client bring to their interaction individual constellations of attitudes, beliefs, biases, and values. Although many of these elements may be irrelevant to the therapeutic process, and in fact never explicitly enunciated by either participant, some of them may be quite focal. They may play a prominent role in contributing to the client's distress, conflict, or frustration, and they may significantly influence the therapist's capacity to achieve an empathic response to the patient.

An *attitude* may be defined as an acquired predisposition, an habitual readiness to respond rather automatically and in a consistent fashion to certain stimulus situations or to certain abstracted categories. The individual who says, "I do not like to ride buses" is expressing an attitude, as is the person who says, "I like to talk to strangers." Likes and dislikes, interests, preferences, attractions, and aversions are restricted, specific attitudinal sets, readiness to respond in a specific way, that do not usually either facilitate or impede therapy significantly. However, the discovery by therapist and client that "we have something in common" can contribute to the early phase of rapport. This possibility is encouraged by the therapist whose room is self-revealing through photos, artwork, or other "personabilia," an indirect, passive self-disclosure. There are two schools of thought on this. The older, traditional view—stemming from psychoanalytic theory—required that the therapist be *impersonal*, a "persona raza" so as to facilitate the projective processes of transference deemed crucial to the process of therapy—hence, the orthodox stance of the analyst behind the couch and out of view of the patient. (Given this rationale for a practice, it is striking to note how very much the office in which Freud conducted therapy spoke of himself!) Another more recent view argues that the therapist must be forthcoming, real, and genuine (Rogers, 1957) and that self-disclosing behavior by the therapist encourages openness and growth by the patient (Curtis, 1981; Jourard, 1961).

While accumulated experience may have led to Freud's rationale for the therapeutic facilitation of the "hidden" therapist, he was honest enough to admit that he had initially adopted his behind-the-couch position because of his reluctance to face the direct scrutiny of patients for long sessions. With respect to the question of whether therapists should reveal their "little attitudes," the skill of the work rests upon accumulated experience that enables wise judgments as to when it is best to respond to a client's personal question with a direct, honest answer and when to reply with, "Why do you ask?" The latter is too frequently the unthoughtful, reflexive response of the inexperienced tyro, or of the older therapist who conducts therapy by rule rather than by reason.

Of greater import for psychotherapy are those broader categories of attitude that have been studied by psychologists, sociologists, anthropologists, and economists because of their relationship to the choices made and the behaviors engaged in by individuals. Notably studied have been the attitudes of specific demographic groups toward God, law, money, and sex. Psychometric theory and method have provided an approach to the measurement of a wide range of attitudes—from mind-sets toward monotheism to those concerning freedom of the press, state lotteries, and abortion, for example. At the core, the study of attitudes has emphasized the locus of the individual in a space defined by parameters of religion, politics, and economics. Attitudinal assay permits identification of individuals as basically religious or irreligious, conservative or liberal, capitalistic or socialistic. It is important for the psychotherapist to be sensitive to the attitudinal stances of the patient (the "assumptive world," Frank, 1961, p.20), because the patient's attitudes may be the cause of conflicts or frustrations, and they may render the patient more amenable to certain approaches and less so to others. The achievement-accumulation-oriented person who is suffering from a restricted perspective on the sources of personal reward may receive only first aid rather than treatment from a therapist who happens to share achievement-accumulation as a primary goal.

Over the eight decades during which the field of psychotherapy has evolved, one of the general precepts to which the great majority of therapists has ascribed, regardless of wide divergences in their "school" identities, has been the requirement that they be nonjudgmental. The therapist is expected to make no moral ethical judgments on the "goodness" or "badness" of the supplicant as reflected in the latter's attitudes and behaviors. Most applicants for psychotherapy do not come to the therapist for an ethical evaluation of the "rightness" of their regnant values, but rather for assistance in ridding themselves of conflicts and anxieties that impede their achievement of those very personal values. For the therapist to express a critical judgement of the patient's values is considered to be antithetical to the purpose of therapy.

There are two problems with this widely accepted dogma. The first resides in the improbability that the therapist who is fully self-aware of his or her governing values and of their divergence from those of the client can totally prevent any manifestation of that incompatibility in the therapeutic discourse. The second problem arises from the fact that some clients experience and complain of distress that arises from their unsuccessful efforts to accommodate an inherently inconsistent value structure. The value conflict may be entirely intrapsychic (e. g., between the motive for career advancement and the motive to be an attentive parent) or a conflict between personal and social values (e. g., between a value placed on solitude and a value attached to community participation). In both cases, social norms and expectations have been incorporated by the individual and contribute to the value conflict.

Attempted resolutions of these problems provide only limited reassurance to the conscientious therapist. One such resolution is to insist that the therapist be fully cognizant of his or her value structure. There is a widely, but not universally, accepted notion that the best avenue to this self-awareness is for the therapist-in-training to receive extensive personal therapy (see chap. 8). There are assumptions in this approach: first, that given full self-awareness, the therapist can indeed fully suppress any expression, even by the most subtle and indirect cues, of his or her value system; second, that proper training will move the therapist to become functionally amoral or value-free, at least in the therapy setting.

Another attempted resolution is to explicitly define the work of therapy, contractually accepted by the client, as value-free, that is, that value issues, if raised even indirectly by the client, will be promptly identified by the therapist as not appropriate for the agenda of therapy. This may entail the assumption that the therapist, upon recognizing the value issues expressed by the client, will promptly and comfortably make a referral to an appropriate ethicist-counselor (minister, priest, rabbi, philosopher?). None of these assumptions can withstand very hard scrutiny. For example, consider the fact that an amoral stance, a position of moral neutrality, is in itself a value statement. When the patient asserts a value-laden sentiment (possibly a probe!), does the therapist's silence maintain the integrity of an intended amoral stance? Or will the patient hear the silence, rightly or wrongly, as acceptance or rejection of the proposition? "Values are an inevitable and pervasive part of psychotherapy"; in therapy the value systems of the client, the therapist, and the *community* come into play (Bergin, 1980). (p.97)

Research on the process of therapy has shown that, at least for some patient-therapist dyads, the course of therapy is marked by the increasing approach of the client's attitudes and values and those of the therapist (Kessel & McBrearty, 1967). Other studies have indicated that therapeutic gains are larger or made earlier when therapist and client share certain attitudinal orientations rather than being dissimilar at the outset of treatment (Beutler, 1981; Beutler, Arizmendi, Crago, Shanfield, & Hagaman, 1983). These findings have encouraged a critical reevaluation of the concept of a nonjudgmental, value-free stance for the therapist. Rather than permitting values to be the enfant terrible of psychotherapy, there is a good argument that the therapist must be not only sensitive to the increasing role of values as conflict sources for many clients, but willing to participate in nondogmatic discourse on value issues (Weisskopf-Joelson, 1980). For those patients who look to psychotherapy to help them to "lead a better life," the therapist cannot escape the attribution of a modeling role despite any effort to refrain from explicit assertion of his or her guiding values; indeed, for many patients, the therapists functions as a "secular priest" (London, 1964). Bergin (1985) has suggested an outline of seven major value domains, each encompassing specific values (e. g., "II. Love and Relationships, C. the ability to forgive others, even those who have inflicted pathologizing experiences on oneself!"). He believes that there are predominant values that guide the work of a majority of therapists despite their reluctance to publicly claim a value stance. Thus, while some minimum degree of compatibility of therapist-patient may be a facilitating condition in many instances, a significant incompatibility may provide the essential starting point for significant therapeutic gains in other cases (Arizmendi, Beutler, Shanfield, Crago, & Hagaman, 1985).

Within the domain of values, the role of religious beliefs and allegiances has been met until recently with diagnostic biases at worst or neglect at best (Meehl, 1959, 1981). Beginning with Freudian psychology, the earliest of modern psychotherapists tended to view the patient's formal religious affiliation either as a significant source of symptom-generating repressions or as a socially acceptable sublimation of underlying instinctual drives (Houts & Graham, 1986). Freud drew comparisons between religious and neurotic ceremonials and accepted the notion that religious zeal was traceable back to erotic perverseness (Freud, 1916). As psychoanalysis has been challenged by other schools of therapy, there has been controversy as to the implications of the client's religious identification for the process of treatment. Some authorities have argued that the patient's religious values were impervious to the work of therapy (Mowrer, 1953); others have seen the patient's religion as a potential source of beliefs that must be vigorously challenged (Ellis, 1966).

More recently two trends have been noticeable. There has been increasing interest in both natural and experimental studies of the relationship of the religious orientations of therapists and clients respectively to the process of therapy (Lewis & Lewis, 1985; Wadsworth & Checketts, 1980). Also, there has been special attention paid not only to the potential problems presented by the religious dimension in treatment, but, most significantly, to the idea that the religious tenets of the patient may be a source of therapeutic potential (Bergin, 1980; Lovinger, 1984; Spero, 1985). These developments reflect the gradual awareness that increasing numbers of persons are turning to psychotherapy for what may be defined as existential (Frankl, 1959) or philosophical (Schofield, 1986) "neuroses." It has been noted that "in increasing number, patients enter psychotherapy not for the cure of traditional 'symptoms' but (at least ostensibly) for the purpose of finding *meaning in their lives* [Italics added] . . ." (Strupp, Hadley, & Gomes-Schwartz, 1977).

Finally, to be noted as general components that each of the participants brings to the therapeutic interaction are their respective tempi and "styles." In this context, *tempo* may be thought of as a complex expression of personality that is manifest in rate or speed of action, notably speech. Style is manifested in the individual's characteristic tendency to be active or passive, emotionally expressive or flat, terse and verbally restrained or voluble, favoring concrete instances or abstract generalizations in discourse. Thus, a particular therapist may be disposed to speak rapidly, often, expressively, and abstractly, while another characteristically speaks slowly, relatively rarely, with little affect, and chiefly about specifics. The tempo and style of the therapist may be a deliberate adaptation of a persona prescribed by a particular school of therapy (theory and/or technique), or it may be the individual therapist's assumption about the desirable qualities of a "therapeutic personality." It is arguable whether a therapist can successfully adopt a "presence" that may seem appropriate to a particular therapeutic approach but that is not a natural expression of the therapist's innate tempo or style. While certain treatment problems or certain phases in a treatment program may make "role-playing" an appropriate tactic for the therapist, any persisting effort to assume a "therapeutic personality" is likely to prove unduly stressful, if not impossible. Also, there is a distinct risk that patients, many of whom suffer from an oversensitivity to minimal cues in social interactions, will detect and be put off by any simulation on the part of the therapist. The work of Carl Rogers (1951, 1957), his students, and others has provided evidence that "genuineness" and "congruence" on the part of therapists may be common, active factors in some successful treatment (Patterson, 1984).

Specific Components

The second section of Figure 2 indicates further components that each participant brings to therapy. These are more specific to the therapy transaction. While the structure of these components is parallel for therapist and client, their content is quite different. In general, the personal life history of the therapist has relatively less import than that of the patient, but the nature and extent of *experience as a therapist* will contribute heavily to the manner in which therapy is conducted, as will the therapist's theoretical orientation. The identification of the therapist with a particular school or approach influences both his or her preferences for certain kinds of patients or problems as well as expectations as to how the client will or should respond to therapy. Similarly, many but not all patients come to therapy with certain "preferences" as to how a therapist will respond to their presentations and some expectations as to the course of treatment. While therapy may be facilitated when there is a "good fit" of these preferences and expectations, significant differences are not necessarily detrimental to the goals of treatment (Goldstein, 1962). It is desirable in the very earliest sessions for both therapist and patient to be forthcoming about these elements in developing their contract. This process can contribute to the important condition of rapport between the participants. To some extent there is a preformed rapport arising from the complimentary expectations of the therapist and client respectively, to be accepting and helpful and to be accepted and helped. The experienced therapist rarely finds a need to engage in deliberate tactics designed to establish rapport. The unique contribution to the components of therapy are those that reside in the reason why the applicant has sought treatment: his or her complaints, conflicts, problems, and symptoms. In presenting these, the client expresses some degree of subjectivity, a subjectivity that is expected by the therapist and responded to with objectivity.

In overview, Figure 2 indicates those elements of individuality that each participant in psychotherapy brings to the endeavor. It points up the considerable similarity in the basic equipment that each possesses with which to influence the interpersonal transaction. At the level of structural analysis, the participants are more alike than different. Recognition of this should give promise of the potential for achieving mutually agreed upon goals. For the therapist, recognition of the client's "anatomy" can facilitate careful assessment of the latter's assets and liabilities and appropriate judgment as to proper focus of treatment as well as choice of more likely rather than less likely modes of effective intervention. Given the complexity of these variables in the individuality of the therapist and client respectively, and the interactive patterning of these variables making for the unique personality of each, the probability that any particular therapist-client pairing will closely approach an "ideal therapeutic fit" is extremely small. This fact may account in considerable measure for the failure thus far of validating research to establish more than modest evidence of the effectiveness of therapy (Meehl, 1965). Tjelveit (1986) has provided a probing analysis of the ethical implications of conversion of client values in psychotherapy.

Comprehensive studies of the actual relationship of specific therapist and patient characteristics to the dynamic interaction of the therapy process are lacking. Much of the research on the "assortative mating" of therapists and clients has rested on global or summative categories that may encompass some but not all of the personal characteristics delineated above. In such research, there has been reliance on indexes of socioeconomic class to identify the relationship of the similarity or divergence of therapist and client class status to such variables as the diagnoses assigned to the client, the probable outcome anticipated, and the type of therapy recommended. The classic study of Hollingshead and Redlich (1958) was a major analysis of the relationship of these variables to the socioeconomic status of mental patients. Diagnoses, prognoses, and treatment recommendations or assignments were made by mental health professionals, predominantly representatives of the highest social classes. It was found that as the therapist-patient divergence in social class membership increased, there was a distinct trend toward more severe diagnoses (psychoses rather than neuroses) and recommendations for medical (including hospitalization) rather than psychological treatment. Subsequent studies have confirmed these findings (Abramowitz & Dokecki, 1977). Such data do not allow inference of a casual relationship, for example, that the upper-class diagnostician/therapist is biased by the implications of value discrepancies when appraising lower-class candidates for help. The findings are, however, consistent with the facts that the foundations of psychotherapy arose from experience with upper-class patients, and that lower-class patients are viewed typically as rejecting of or nonresponsive to traditional forms of psychodynamic therapy. It is not social class *membership* that causes any possible bias on the part of therapists nor resistance on the part of clients; rather it is the likely discordance in the associated personal

elements (attitudes, values, "psychological mindedness") that may preju-
dice assessment and deter psychological treatment. The danger that such
factors may inappropriately determine therapy decisions is greatest for the
physician who has ready recourse to medication rather than psychological
mediation. However, nonmedical therapists express the same relative lack
of interest in working with clients from the lowest social classes (Sutton &
Kessler, 1986). In contrast, patients seen for psychotherapy by private
practitioners (nonagency affiliated) are seen for intensive treatment over
longer periods (Koss, 1980). It is not reasonable to infer that these upper-
class patients have more severe pathology!

The Social Matrix

It is natural and customary to think of psychotherapy as a very private
business in which the only concerned parties are the therapist and the
client. Custom, practice, and the general expectations of the community
place a special mantle of privacy on what occurs in the therapy room. This
assumption of unbreached privacy for the two-party contract between
therapist and client rests upon the uniformly accepted tenet that the client
will be unable to experience maximum benefit if there is not complete
assurance that what is revealed of his or her most intimate, personal self
will be held in strictest confidence. The principles of privacy and confidentiality have deep historical roots in the professions of the clergy, law, and
medicine. It is both appropriate and necessary that psychotherapists have
insisted on the same right of "privileged communication" for their clients
as has been long established for supplicants to the clergy, clients of
attorneys, and patients of physicians.

The assumption of the principle of privacy is complemented by the
uniform commitment of the professional to the principle that his or her
attention and efforts are dedicted first and foremost, and above all other
considerations, to the welfare of the client. These dual principles serve to
safeguard the interests of the individual who seeks counsel. Laws prescribe the special circumstances in which their observance may (or must)
be violated.

Clients of the relatively new profession of psychotherapy have been
served well generally by the adherence of the therapists' commitment to
the principles of confidentiality and "client welfare first." However, the
adoption of the role of psychotherapy in the broad stream of social welfare
has perpetuated an isolation of the therapist-client endeavor that may not
always be in the best interests of either.

Two actual letters illustrate the problems and ethical dilemmas that arise
when psychotherapists are unclear about or insensitive to their responsibilities not only to their clients but also to the communities of which both

they and their clients are members. The first letter was addressed to the director of admissions of a medical school.

Dear Dr. _____:

I am sorry I cannot send you the exact letter that I sent to the Army on _____, as I only made one handwritten copy. However, I remember him very well. I diagnosed him as schizophrenia, undifferentiated type. He showed no delusions or hallucinations. He has never had a nervous breakdown, nor any psychiatric treatment. He is one of millions of schizophrenics who have no outstanding symptoms, do their work well, and function adequately.

As you know, he has a very high level of intelligence, is an exceptional scholar. He wants to be of service and to help people. He did some teaching, and considered entering the Peace Corps. He favored nonviolence. I recommended that he be rejected for the Army, as I did not think he could stand the training. The Army psychiatrist concurred, and he was made 4F.

In my opinion, he would make a good medical student, and a good doctor.

Sincerely,"

_____, M.D.

On two separate occasions, this professional apparently was motivated primarily, if not solely, to serve his client, unmindful of the implications of his recommendations for the community. How else to understand such a bald *use* of diagnosis in one instance and disregard of it in another!

The second letter was the reply received by a former client in response to his request to his former therapist that information be sent to his present therapist who believed that the work of therapy might be expedited by the previous therapist's information and insight.

"Dear_____:

It is my usual policy not to communicate about my patients (current and former) to anyone, which includes psychiatrists and psychologists. I consider the therapeutic relationship necessarily to be (and remain) a two-person situation, consonant with the overriding ethic of autonomy.

I hope this policy on my part causes no practical difficulty for you in obtaining further treatment.

Sincerely yours,"

_____, M. D.

Clearly, this therapist's concept of the "ethic of autonomy" (?) overrode any sense of responsibility to facilitate the work of his clients with other professionals!

The conduct of psychotherapy will be more responsive and responsible when the therapist is consistently mindful that psychotherapy is an inherently social process. It is imbedded in a social matrix that includes elements of definition, training and sanction of the expert, exhortation of potential clients, and financial and other supports (Frank, 1961).

Figure 3 presents a broad sketch of the continuum from adjustment to maladjustment suggesting the relative roles of social concern and social process that determine whether an individual is viewed as mentally healthy or unhealthy. The diagnostic clues of "group identity" and "isolation" are placed in parentheses to suggest that there is less than unanimity as to whether these are requisite criteria for defining either psychological health or psychological disorder. The "borderline" area is not reflective of that form of personality disorder recognized in the official diagnostic manual (American Psychiatric Association, 1980). Rather, it is intended to suggest elements of a pattern of adjustment that may or may not lead to an individual either escaping or being caught up in the social net that seines for mental illness. The wealthy eccentric who indulges in nude "air baths" (à la Mark Twain) in the seclusion of his or her private estate is unlikely to receive a professional diagnosis. The same behavior on the roof of an urban apartment building would bring intervention by the police initially; persistence and a "kooky" rationale on the part of the "health nut" would likely lead to a psychiatric diagnosis. This is why the term *criminal* is in parenthesis in the borderline domain of the chart. The same behavior that in one social context could bring the individual before the courts, in another could lead to the psychiatric clinic or hospital. This has led some authorities to decry the role of psychiatry and of the mental health

FIGURE 3

Dimensions of Definitions of Mental Health/Mental Illness

	Mental Health	"Borderline"		Mental Illness
Socially defined	Conformity	Eccentric	If severe, society is concerned	Deviant behavior
	Independence	Fanatic		Dependency
	Productivity	(Criminal)		Nonproductivity
Personally defined	Efficiency		Society may or may not be concerned	Inefficiency
	Contentment			Dissatisfaction
	(Group identity)			(Isolation)

movement broadly in interfering with, if not usurping, the role of the courts (Halleck, 1971; Szasz, 1963).

The process of therapy begins with an assessment of the patient's presenting complaint or problem. The therapist must by training and experience be able to recognize the patient's condition as falling within one, another, or several of diagnostic rubrics that are generally recognized by the profession and for which psychological intervention is an acceptable therapeutic medicine. Psychological illnesses, disorders, or distresses do not have the precision of definition, coherent and consistent syndromes of symptomatology, and supporting laboratory tests that are the underpinnings of reliable diagnoses of physical illness. Consider the wide divergence of meanings and implications between a diagnosis of "measles" and a diagnosis of "adjustment disorder." As the recognition of psychological "illness" and the practice of psychological treatment have evolved from their earliest, confined roots in medicine, the definition of what constitutes treatable pathology has become increasingly a social (or political) function (Halleck, 1971; Leifer, 1969). The official nomenclature changes in response not only to accumulated clinical experience and scientific discovery but also, and perhaps as much, to professional self-interest and social pressure. Recent time has witnessed vigorous debate as to whether homosexuality should or should not be recognized as a psychiatric disorder. The term *neurosis* was officially "voted out" of the most recent diagnostic manual adopted by the American Psychiatric Association (American Psychiatric Association, [APA], 1980; Bayer & Spitzer, 1985; Schacht, 1985; Townsend & Martin, 1983). The same manual has given the chronic use of tobacco the status of a psychiatric disorder. Beyond these relativistic and professionally grounded diagnostic styles, the mental health movement, through its broad educational efforts, has encouraged a large amount of self-diagnosis and a readiness to seek professional consultation for problems that may not be truly pathological in either nature or degree. The desirable, enhanced public awareness of mental illness and resources for response to it has not included education that would help the individual to distinguish between significant depression and lowered morale or situational unhappiness, or to discriminate disruptive anxiety from a physiologically appropriate mobilization for a normal stress experience (see Schofield, 1986, chap. 1, sec. 3). The pragmatic psychotherapist who is socially attuned and socially responsible will not casually and uncritically accept all candidates but will be sensitive to the need to, and appropriateness of, reassuring the would-be client who has made a faulty self-diagnosis.

Society's role is represented also in the fact that the therapist receives officially recognized education and training in institutions (graduate schools) that are heavily subsidized both by taxes and private endowment.

The future therapist pays only a part of the costs of his or her preparation to play a role that society requires. This investment by society in the preparation of therapists is supplemented by the social mechanism of state licensing and accreditation agencies that officially sanction the professional practice of therapy.

The privacy of the transactions in the "magic room" of psychotherapy was nearly inviolate when most therapy was on a fee-for-service basis, and the individual customer was responsible for the cost of treatment. With the gradual increase in comprehensive health insurance plans that include mental health benefits, with the rise in national concern for the rapidly rising costs of health care and the consequent attention to "quality of service" and cost-benefit analysis, psychotherapy has become but one of the health services that is subject to peer review. This has meant that both client and professional have had to agree to allow the basic facts of the course of therapy to be open to review and evaluation by external experts. Many psychotherapists have responded to peer review with a high level of defensiveness (Cohen & Holstein, 1982; Sechrest & Hoffman, 1982).

By the way in which it spells out the criteria (symptoms) for psychological illness; by the way in which it supports the training of psychotherapists; by providing the mechanism by which the therapist is licensed, credentialed, or otherwise sanctioned to offer therapy; and finally, by developing and controlling mechanisms for reimbursement—in all of these ways, the community has a vested interest in the work of the therapist. To the extent that psychotherapists are unmindful of or indifferent to the fact that they are inevitably social agents for a social process, they may underserve those clients whose distress and dissatisfaction stem in some measure from their narcissistic withdrawal from their community and their isolation from meaningful social discourse.

Finally, the pragmatic therapist attends to the question of whether the patient's symptoms and behavior have only a circumscribed, very personal effect, or whether they have immediate or potential impact on the well-being of others, such as spouses, children, parents, and employers. The therapist does not cling to one-on-one individual therapy when there are clear signs that the client's problems indicate marital, family, or group therapy as the intervention of choice.

Note

1. In the case of therapists who are licensed professionals, there may be statutory limitations on the privilege, e. g., the requirement that the professional must

report to appropriate authorities any information of abuse of children or of vulnerable adults, or of sexual exploitation.

References

Abramowitz, C. V., & Dokecki, P. R. (1977). The politics of clinical judgment: Early empirical returns. *Psychological Bulletin, 34,* 460–476.

American Psychiatric Association (1980). *Diagnostic and statistical manual of mental disorders* (3rd ed.). Washington, DC: Author.

Arizmendi, T. G., Beutler, L. E., Shanfield, S. B., Crago, M., & Hagaman, R. (1985). Client-therapist value similarity and psychotherapy outcome: A microscopic analysis. *Psychotherapy: Theory, Practice and Research, 22,* 16–21.

Bandura, A. (1969). *Principles of behavior modification.* New York: Holt, Rinehart & Winston.

Bayer, R., & Spitzer, R. L. (1985). Neurosis, psychodynamics, and DSM-III: A history of the controversy. *Archives of General Psychiatry, 42,* 187–196.

Bergin, A. E. (1980). Psychotherapy and religious values. *Journal of Consulting and Clinical Psychology, 48,* 95–105.

Bergin, A. E. (1985). Proposed values for guiding and evaluating counseling and psychotherapy. *Counseling and Values, 29,* 99–116.

Berne, E. (1961). *Transactional analysis in psychotherapy.* New York: Grove Press.

Beutler, L. E. (1981). Convergence in counseling and psychotherapy: A current look. *Clinical Psychology Review, 1,* 79–101.

Beutler, L. E., Arizmendi, T. G., Crago, M., Shanfield, S. B., & Hagaman, R. (1983). The effects of value similarity and client persuasibility on value convergence and psychotherapy improvement. *Journal of Social and Clinical Psychology, 1,* 231–245.

Cohen, L. H. & Holstein, C. M. (1982). Characteristics and attitudes of peer reviewers and providers in psychology. *Professional Psychology: Research & Practice, 13,* 66–73.

Colby, K. M. (1951). *A primer for psychotherapists.* New York: Ronald Press.

Curtis, J. M. (1981). Indications and contraindications in the use of the therapist's self-disclosure. *Psychological Reports, 49,* 499–507.

Dollard, J., & Miller, N. E. (1950). *Personality and psychotherapy: An analysis in terms of learning, thinking, and culture.* New York: McGraw-Hill.

Ellis, A. (1962). *Reason and emotion in psychotherapy.* New York: Lyle Stuart.

Ellis, A. (1966). The case against religion: A psychotherapist's viewpoint. In B. N. Ard (Ed.), *Counseling and psychotherapy.* Palo Alto, CA: Science and Behavior Books.

Frank, J. D. (1961). *Persuasion and healing: A comparative study of psychotherapy.* Baltimore: The Johns Hopkins Press.

Frankl, V. E. (1959). *Man's search for meaning: An introduction to logotherapy.* Boston: Beacon Press.

Freud, S. (1916). *The history of the psychoanalytic movement* (Nervous and Mental Disease Monograph Series, No. 25). New York: Nervous and Mental Disease Publishing Co.

Garfield, S. L. (1982). Eclecticism and integration in psychotherapy. *Behavior Therapy, 13,* 610–623.

Goldfried, M. R. (1982). On the history of therapeutic integration. *Behavior Therapy, 13,* 572–593.

Goldstein, A. P. (1962). *Therapist-patient expectancies in psychotherapy.* New York: Macmillan.

Halleck, S. L. (1971). *The politics of therapy.* New York: Science House.

Hollingshead, A. B., & Redlich, F. C. (1958). *Social class and mental illness: A community study.* New York: John Wiley & Sons.

Houts, A. C., & Graham, K. (1986). Can religions make you crazy? Impact of client and therapist religious values on clinical judgments. *Journal of Consulting and Clinical Psychology, 54,* 267–271.

Jourard, S. M. (1961). *The transparent self: Self-disclosure and well-being.* Princeton, NJ: Van Nostrand.

Kendall, P. C. (1982). Integration: Behavior therapy and other schools of thought. *Behavior Therapy, 13,* 559–571.

Kessel, P., & McBrearty, J. F. (1967). Values and psychotherapy: A review of the literature. *Perceptual and Motor Skills, Monograph Supplement, 3–V25.* 669–690.

Koss, M. P. (1980). Descriptive characteristics and length of psychotherapy of child and adult cases seen in private psychological practice. *Psychotherapy: Theory, Research and Practice, 17,* 268–271.

Leifer, R. (1969). *In the name of mental health: The social functions of psychiatry.* New York: Science House.

Lewis, K. N., & Lewis, D. A. (1985). Impact of religious affiliation on therapists' judgments of patients. *Journal of Consulting and Clinical Psychology, 53,* 926–932.

London, P. (1964). *The modes and morals of psychotherapy.* New York: Holt, Rinehart & Winston.

Lovinger, R. J. (1984). Working with religious issues in therapy. New York: Jason Aronson.

Meehl, P. E. (1959). Some technical and axiological problems in the therapeutic handling of religious and valuational material. *Journal of Counseling Psychology, 6,* 255–259.

Meehl, P. E. (1965). Discussion of Eysenck's "The effects of psychotherapy." *International Journal of Psychiatry, 1,* 156–157.

Meehl, P. E. (1981). Ethical criticism in value clarification: Correcting cognitive errors within the client's—not the therapist's framework. *Rational Living, 16,* 3–9.

Messer, S. B., & Winokur, M. (1980). Some limits to the integration of psychoanalytic and behavior therapy. *American Psychologist, 35,* 818–827.

Mowrer, O. H. (1953). Neurosis and psychotherapy as interpersonal process: A Synopsis. In O. H. Mowrer (Ed.), *Psychotherapy: Theory and research.* New York: Ronald Press.

Patterson, C. H. (1984). Empathy, warmth, and genuineness in psychotherapy: A review of reviews. *Psychotherapy, 21,* 431–438.

Perls, F. C. (1971). *Gestalt therapy: Excitement and growth in the human personality.* New York: Julian Press.

Raimy, V. C. (Ed.) (1950). *Training in clinical psychology.* Englewood Cliffs, NJ: Prentice-Hall.

Rogers, C. R. (1942). *Counseling and psychotherapy.* Boston: Houghton Mifflin Company.

Rogers, C. R. (1951). *Client-centered therapy: Its current practice, implications, and theory*. Boston: Houghton Mifflin.

Rogers, C. R. (1957). The necessary and sufficient conditions of therapeutic change. *Journal of Consulting Psychology, 21*, 95–103.

Schact, T. E. (1985). DSM-III and the politics of truth. *American Psychologist, 40*, 513–521.

Schofield, W. (1986). *Psychotherapy: The purchase of friendship*. New Brunswick, NJ: Transaction Books.

Sechrest, L. B., & Hoffman, P. E. (1982). The philosophical underpinnings of peer review. *Professional Psychology: Research & Practice, 13*, 14–18.

Spero, M. H. (Ed.). (1985). *Psychotherapy of the religious patient*. Springfield, IL: Charles C Thomas.

Strupp, H. H. (1960). *Psychotherapists in action*. New York: Grune & Stratton.

Strupp, H. H., Hadley, S. W., & Gomes-Schwartz, B. (1977). *Psychotherapy for better or worse: The problem of negative effects*. New York: Jason Aronson.

Sutton, R. G., & Kessler, M. (1986). National study of the effects of clients' socioeconomic status on clinical psychologists' professional judgments. *Journal of Consulting and Clinical Psychology, 54*, 275–276.

Szasz, T. S. (1963). *Law, liberty, and psychiatry: An inquiry into the social uses of mental health practices*. New York: Macmillan.

Thorne, F. C. (1968). *Psychological case handling*. Brandon, VT: Clinical Psychology Publishing.

Tjelveit, A. C. (1986). The ethics of value conversion in psychology: appropriate and inappropriate therapist influence on client values. *Clinical Psychology Review, 6*, 515–537.

Townsend, J, S., & Martin, J. A. (1983). Whatever happened to neurosis? *Professional Psychology: Theory, Research and Practice, 14*, 323–329.

Wadsworth, R. D., & Checketts, K. T. (1980). Influence of religious affiliation on psychodiagnosis. *Journal of Consulting and Clinical Psychology, 48*, 234–240.

Watters, W. W., Rubenstein, J. S., & Bellissimo, A. (1980). Teaching psychotherapy: Learning objectives in individual psychotherapy. *Canadian Journal of Psychiatry, 25*, 111–117.

Weisskopf-Joelson, E. (1980). Values: The *enfant terrible* of psychotherapy. *Psychotherapy: Theory, Research and Practice, 17*, 459–466.

Wolberg, L. R. (1954). *The technique of psychotherapy*. New York: Grune & Stratton.

Wolpe, J. (1969). *The practice of behavior therapy*. New York: Pergamon Press.

Yates, A. J. (1970). *Behavior therapy*. New York: John Wiley & Sons.

Yates, A. (1983). Behavior therapy and psychodynamic therapy: Basic conflict or reconciliation and integration? *British Journal of Clinical Psychology, 22*, 107–125.

3

Candidates for Psychotherapy

The previous chapter sketched the structural components of individual psychotherapy as represented by the personal elements that the therapist and client bring to the therapeutic dyad. It was also pointed out that the desirable condition of privacy and confidentiality of the therapist-client discourse can never be absolute, for it is constrained by the limits arising from the fact that therapy is a social process imbedded in a social matrix.

The need for the therapist to be aware of a deliberate philosophical stance as a social agent stems from certain realities. If certain conditions were (could be?) met, the work of psychotherapy could go on in a unique isolation from the "world out there." These "ifs" are:

- If the definition of mental, emotional, psychological, or behavioral distress, disorder, dysfunction, illness or disease were precise, objective, and generally agreed upon—
- If diagnosis (assessment, classification, identification) of specific forms of psychological (psychosocial) disorder were reliable—
- If the relative efficacy of reliably distinguishable forms or modes of psychotherapeutic intervention, applied to specific problems, were known—
- If there were no restrictions on the supply (availability) of psychotherapy—

At present, these conditions are not fully satisfied. The concept of psychological disorder (the "old fashioned" neurotic personality) is not absolute; it is relative to the degree of distress or disorder expressed by the individual, it is relative to the psychological "economy" of the individual, to his or her very personal goals (values), and finally it is relative to the goals and values of the community of which both therapist and client are members. The problem of relativity is reflected in the very wide range in the incidence of "mental illness" reported from various surveys (Dohrenwend et al., 1980). It follows that the efficacy of therapy can be measured only against relativistic criteria. The decision to treat and the measure of impact are simple when the applicant for psychotherapy presents a circumscribed symptom that is impairing occupational productivity. In this case, it is possible that something relatively simple can be made less so if the seeker for help happens upon a therapist whose theoretical stance leads to an overinterpretation of the symptoms, an extension of the field of pathology, and a consequent prolongation of the work of therapy (see chap. 5). When the supplicant is confused and conflicted by an intrapsychic imbalance of values stimulated by a situation from which withdrawal is not possible, the decision to treat, the choice of treatment modality, and the measure of effectiveness is far more complex.

Not every person who appears at the door of the therapist is a *valid* candidate for psychotherapy. This may be a purely academic notion for the therapist employed by an agency in which policy dictates that *all* applicants are to receive interventive services, for although there are guidelines under which some may be placed on a "waiting" list, none are to be appraised (and apprised) that they do not "qualify" (need) ongoing psychotherapy.

For those individuals with recourse to, and resources for, private consultations, the situation is different. Demand exceeds supply, and the private practitioner has the privilege, and the responsibility, to be selective as to who shall receive treatment. When the situation of the individual therapist is such that there are far more calls than can be accepted, the therapist can operate on a simple "first come—first serve" basis so long as the appointment calendar is filled. This avoids the problems of decision and selection. However, therapists who adopt this response are (probably unthinkingly) neglecting their responsibility as social agents.

The Nature of Complaints—Justifiable versus Expectant

The psychotherapist is presented at the outset with the reasons why the applicant is seeking help. In brief, these reasons are the "presenting complaint" and are in the form of symptoms of certain distress. The symptoms may be relatively specific and circumscribed (e.g., a fear of cats, or of high places, or of crowds), or they may be diffuse and, at least at the outset, vague and abstruse (e.g., persistent anxiety or chronic depression). The symptoms may have import primarily for the applicant, with little impact on others. They may interfere negligibly with his or her ability to carry out day-by-day functions and roles. Or, they may impinge on the welfare and function of others. Agoraphobia, a fear of public places and crowds, does not have the same meaning to a creative writer as it does to a homemaker and the head of a household.

The potential client brings not only an account of the symptoms being experienced, but also certain attitudes toward those symptoms. Most applicants are very forthcoming about their symptoms. Their underlying attitudes toward (or the meanings they assign) their symptoms may be less apparent. The discriminating therapist will be as attentive to the attitudinal foundations as to the symptom picture itself. Careful probing to tease out the dimensions of the symptom–attitude complex may enable the therapist to discern that treatment may be in some cases more effectively directed toward the patient's attitudes (expectations) than toward the presenting complaint itself.

People suffering from a particular emotional disorder or psychological distress can be divided into three groups: Those who will be quick to seek expert intervention, those who will be slower, and those who will simply "live with it." The factors that differentiate among these groups are multiple and complex. Level of education is an obvious one, as is availability and visibility of intervenors; cultural and subcultural norms and mores and the availability of social supports also activate or suppress the individual's readiness to seek relief from others and especially from sanctioned healers (Cobb, 1976; Goodman, Sewell, & Jampol, 1984; see also Chapter IX in Gurin, Veroff & Feld, 1960). There has been relatively more study of demographic correlates of seekers of mental health service than research into the individual, psychological determiners of help-seeking (Halgin & Weaver, 1986).

In the evolution of medical science, symptoms and complaints antedate the recognition and labeling of a clinical syndrome. With clinical recognition of a syndrome, it becomes possible and appropriate for the sufferer to lodge a *justifiable* complaint. The sufferer is justified in expressing the complaint because it has a publicly recognized status as a deviation from the norm. It is not yet an "expectant" complaint, that is, in the sense that inquiry, study, and experiment have brought discovery of methods by which the complaint (symptoms) can be alleviated if not totally removed.

With respect to physical ailments, the passage of a pathological condition from its status as a collection of subjective experiences of isolated individuals to that of an accumulation of cases by astute clinical observers through to, ideally, a disease whose underlying pathology and treatment is understood, is the work of physicians and medical scientists. The public supports their work, and the lay citizen is involved neither in the definition of illness nor in dictating modes of treatment. In recent time, however, we have witnessed advances in medical technology the use of which for the saving or prolongation of life is possible only through the application of resources that are in crucially short supply and that entail tremendous expenditures. Thus, with the development of kidney dialysis and organ transplantation, we have been faced with the need to establish priorities. Who shall receive treatment, and who shall not? It is here that the "privacy" of the physician-patient contract is invaded. The basic ethics of medicine no longer suffice of themselves but must be integrated with social ethics and with the prevailing value system of the community (Caplan, 1983). The patient's *justified* complaint is only a relatively *expectant* one.

For distresses ubiquitous to the human condition the evolution of complaints to the status of "justified" is much slower, irregular, and unstable. There was a time when individuals suffered poverty without complaint. Our society has taught that poverty is not only the basis for a justified complaint but for an expectant one, that is, the impoverished individual has the right to expect some relief. Mechanisms of assuagement, although they are far from adequate, are in place.

Between the ostensible pathology and symptoms of physical illness on one hand and the readily observable conditions of situational deprivation and emotional trauma on the other are found those conditions of the distressed human that are variously called "mental," "emotional," "psychological," or "psychosocial." The person's complaints may be justified or not, expectant or not. They are expressions of the way in which she or he is *interpreting* the nature of his or her "self," the nature of the immediate life situation, the nature of the world, the probable future, and the meaning of life. Those particular interpretations, personal meanings, "guiding fictions," in some cases *are* the pathology. The pathology may escape early or easy detection because they are the introjection of "expectancies" that have been socially inculcated.

Therapeutic Consultation

The psychotherapist who is aware of and sensitive to the culturogenic impact of aspects of the mental health movement on individuals with susceptibility to self-examination and self-diagnosis will be prepared for certain applicants for treatment who are not valid or legitimate candidates. Many, perhaps most, persons who present themselves are seriously distressed and in need of psychological counsel, and the work of therapy may begin with the very first session. Others, appropriately, are perhaps momentarily overly sensitized and seeking consultation to determine if indeed they need psychotherapy and would benefit significantly from it. Still others who do in fact have a justified complaint, but one for which individual psychotherapy is not appropriate, corrective, or meliorative, may be benefited significantly by a single, therapeutic consultation.

It is true with respect to the latter two classes of potential clients that the skilled therapist can readily transform the borderline or inappropriate candidates into "real cases." This is especially so for those individuals who really have no "significant other" with whom they enjoy the security of a sense of worth that comes from sharing one's innermost self. It is the case also for those who, for whatever reason, are not utilizing the resources of existing significant others. It is unlikely that the psychotherapist who "treats" these essentially normal or healthy persons will do them great harm. However, the fact of being "in treatment" with a mental health specialist cannot help but be reinforcing of their self-concept as "different," maladjusted, "neurotic," and so on. Also, it may contribute negatively to the ways in which they are perceived by family, friends, employers, and others. Such harm is less likely to ensue in those subcultures in which being "in therapy" with a "shrink" is a status symbol of sorts (see the discussion of the "Friends and Supporters of Psychotherapy" in Kadushin, 1969).

The psychotherapist who is insensitive or indifferent to the issues raised by the nonlegitimate candidate for therapy is causing harm to those valid supplicants who are being displaced from the therapist's necessarily limited roster. The psychotherapist who treats (overtreats) the essentially healthy personality is violating the cardinal principle for all sanctioned healers: *Primum non nocere* (Above all, cause, no harm).

Nonpathology and Nontreatment

In the latter half of the 20th century, all the media have contributed to the dissemination of the mental health movement. The goals of that movement have been increased public awareness of the nature, extent, and treatability of mental illness; increased facilities and resources for the treatment and aftercare of psychiatric patients, with particular emphasis on more and better resources for outpatient care; increased training of mental health specialists; and increased support for both basic and applied research on mental illness and mental health. These are laudable goals, which have been extensively supported by federal and state agencies and by private foundations. Much progress has been made; much remains to be done.

While the level of the public's enlightenment about mental illness has been raised, we are far from eradicating the connotations of stigma and the suspicion or distrust at worst or the vague discomfort at best that many people feel about "psychiatric" patients, present or former. Because of the general support that all the public media have given to the more preventive facets of the mental health movement, there has been a perhaps inevitable, undesirable side effect. Certain concepts or syndromes, loosely and vaguely defined, have become popular foci for self-diagnosis. The public at large has been overly sensitized and misled as to the significance of anxiety, depression, stress, and other conditions.

The candidate who presents a complaint of being anxious, depressed, tense, or conflicted or frustrated should not be taken into therapy simply on the basis of the complaint itself. Rather, an assessment of the complaint must be made. How severe is it? How long has it existed? How, if at all, does it affect the individual's adjustment—impair or interfere with daily coping? How does it relate to any other complaints, if there are any? What is the attitude of the applicant for therapy: what are his or her interpretations of the significance of particular symptoms; what are the expectations with respect to the future course of the complaint? What are the situational precipitants, if any, of the condition troubling the applicant?

Anxiety is not per se abnormal, nor is depression. Many conditions of change in a person's experienced psychological state are essentially acute, circumscribed, appropriate, and will be time limited, if they are not treated in a manner that amplifies the client's readiness to overinterpret their meaning.

The psychological literature is rich on the subject of "test anxiety", a topic that has been researched extensively on a primary subject group, college students. The classroom culture encourages an awareness of the phenomenon and a readiness for erroneous self-diagnosis. There is a difference between being "keyed-up," a condition of test readiness, and being in fact disorganized by extreme anxiety. It is a matter of degree that the expert is capable of distinguishing and communicating.

Consider the would-be therapy consumer whose presenting "anxiety" can be traced readily to only partially suppressed *worries,* who possibly has a chronic tendency to "what if . . ." ruminations. Drawing out the distinction between anxiety and worry, and the distinction between worrying ("what if") and thinking, that is, planning and problem solving, may be all the person requires in order to cope successfully. The chronic worrier has an habitual attitude of pessimism, a readiness to focus thoughts on future deleterious events or circumstances (probabilities) over which he or she has no control, and as a result of such focus to become fretful, tense, and, in some instances, immobilized. For such persons, the therapist best becomes a *mental hygienist* who helps the worrier to explore clearly whether there are possible preventive or preparatory actions he or she could take to avert or at least diminish the impact of the anticipated negative events. If no "acts of insurance" are discernable, the tension-inducing preoccupations must be firmly identified as functionless, fruitless worry. *Worry* is defined as the "act of . . . shaking and mangling with the teeth" *(Webster's International Dictionary)*. Chronic worriers are like the proverbial dog with a bone and do not easily relinquish the habit of "awfulizing" and "catastrophizing" (Ellis, 1962) unless they are offered something better—the opportunity to think, plan, and most important, to *choose* between thinking and worrying. While some amount of didactic repetition of the lesson may be required, eradication of the habit of worry (implemented by instruction for "thought [worry] stopping" and "channel changing" does not call for the long-term, intensive psychotherapy that is likely to be required for the individual with a pervasive obsessive-compulsive personality.) (Dengrove, 1972; Tryon, 1979; Wolpe, 1973) The pragmatic therapist is alert to the indications for brief instructive mental hygiene and will not insist on prolonged treatment of the candidate for very short-term prophylactic education.

Therapy applicants frequently present themselves as "depressed". Careful assessment may readily discern that they are not suffering a depression of clinical dimension, but rather from a state of lowered *morale* that is appropriately reactive to certain recent events in their lives (Frank, 1974, 1985). Correction of the erroneous self-diagnosis of depression together with focus on the applicants' assets for adaptive readjustment to their changed life circumstances may be all that is required.

Still another culturogenic self-diagnosis of "pathology" may occur in the person who is *by nature* an introvert. Such persons deviate from the *visible* cultural norm in that they are quiet, introspective, enjoy solitude, are not comfortable in large groups, have a distaste for noisy parties, have only a few rather than many friends, are not "joiners," and do not enjoy being the focus of attention. They are clearly deviant from the "well-adjusted" extrovert who is the predominant social stereotype, at least in our urban culture. Careful assessment will distinguish them from individuals who suffer a neurotic social aversiveness. If the introvert's personality expresses an inborn, constitutional pattern of temperament and action, and is not the result of early life trauma, rejections, and a distorted self-image, it is not ipso facto a valid basis for attempts at "reconstructive" therapy. Rather, after careful assessment, the pragmatic therapist who understands the psychology of individual differences is in a position to offer a corrective diagnosis and assurance that the introvert's personality is a genuine expression of a natural way-of-being and he or she should be comfortably accepting of his or her personality. Of course, even the valid introvert may be in a situation where some change, for example, in situation or in degree of sociability, may have occupational or other advantages. Helping the individual to make those changes is a proper goal for a course of therapy.

These are but a few examples of cases in which the therapist may be presented with fallacious self-diagnosis, and in which the therapist who accepts the presenting symptomatology and does not regularly make careful assessments of the validity of the presenting complaint may create rather than reduce pathology. They are examples of instances in which, by contrast, the therapist has the opportunity to contribute effectively to the well-being of the therapy applicant by making a therapeutic diagnosis and offering brief therapeutic consultation.

A general social force that subtly encourages therapists to be less questioning of the applicant's real need for treatment than they should be is the effect of education in making individuals increasingly ready to self-diagnose with complaints that the culture of the time generally accepts as valid (e.g., anxiety). By contrast, the increasing availabiliity of health insurance with mental health benefits affords a social mechanism whereby the therapist may be sensitized to the nonpathology of some would-be clients. The therapist's or the client's reimbursement for the costs of treatment require the former to submit an official diagnosis. A conscientious therapist, finding that the complainant's discomfort or unhappiness cannot be validly labeled under any of the recognized-for-reimbursement diagnostic categories, will experience a conflict. Does he or she simply inform the applicant that treatment will not be covered by insurance? Or does the therapist look for a least "stigmatizing," "minimal pathology" diagnosis to satisfy the system and activate the would-be patient's insurance (e.g., "adjustment disorder with atypical features")? Should the therapist's decision as to whether to accept the applicant for treatment be influenced by recognition that, at this time, the would-be patient does not have a socially *justified* complaint? The distinction between justified and expectant complaints is reflected in the fact that most comprehensive health (medical) insurance policies do not provide reimbursement for surgical procedures that are purely cosmetic (narcissistic) rather than necessary and reparative. Perhaps some later evolution of psychiatric-psychologic nomenclature will recognize the M/C/L syndrome—malcontentment: chronic and low grade—as a valid clinical entity, so that the M/C/L client's complaints are both justified and expectant.

For the applicant who does not have, or does not wish to use, insurance to cover the costs of psychotherapy (frequently out of concern that the confidentiality of treatment will not be maintained) and is able and willing to pay, the therapist may be dissuaded from any concern over the validity of the applicant's request for service. In that case the unqualified candidate is reducing the accessibility of the therapist to persons with a valid need for his or her expert services.

Philosophical Dysphoria vs. "Mental Illness"

Much of our lives are lived in a predominantly secular context. Our comings and goings, our activity and aspirations are directed by the world as we know it, by the "now" as we experience it. The modern person is largely sustained by a faith in our capacity to know more and more of *this* world and to gain increasing control over it. The pursuits of our sciences and their associated technologies are inherently secular. The creative genius of our scientists has now brought us to two polar extremes of possibility: the potential to create human life in vitro, and the potential for nuclear destruction of the world that sustains human life.

For most persons, if not continuously at least at certain points of crisis, there arises an inevitable question: What is the meaning of life? For the great majority of persons, this question, which does not permit an answer of demonstrable certainty, is managed by recourse to faith. There are those with strong faith that this life is followed by another life; they are guided in their day-to-day conduct by the promise of a life hereafter, a life that will be very much better or very much worse, depending on their here-now behavior. There are those with equally strong faith that the notion of immortality is a fiction, a myth, that the here and now is all there is, that any pleasures to be achieved and any pains to be avoided are confined to the limits of one's life span and by one's here-and-now choices.

Except for those persons who are delusional and hold to a *fixed*, immutable belief concerning matters that are unknowable, all others recognize that they are functioning on the basis of faith. Regardless of the strength of basic faith, whether it be positive (as to immortality) or negative (as to mortality), it is the essence of a faith that it is subject to test. Both the "believer" and the "nonbeliever" are subject to tests of their faith by life experiences (crises) that they cannot easily incorporate into their basic guiding assumptions about the meaning of life. They experience a philosophic dysphoria, a philosophical neurosis (Schofield, 1986). At such times their distress may become manifest through symptoms of anxiety and depression. By themselves, or with the aide of a therapist, they may attribute their emotional pain to the specifics of a recent crisis (e. g., the loss of a loved one). Such may or may not be a sufficient attribution on which to base the work of psychotherapy.

It has been the experience of many psychotherapists that they are being consulted by increasing numbers of supplicants who are suffering a failure of faith, a confusion as to ultimate values, a restless uncertainty as to final meanings. These seekers for relief are suffering from a philosophical dysphoria, not from a condition that can be properly diagnosed as a recognized "official" form of mental illness. From an existentialist frame-work, Victor Frankl (1959; 1962; 1967) has designated these disturbances in basic belief systems as "noögenetic neurosis" and has developed the techniques of logotherapy for their treatment.

The presenting picture of the philosophic dysphoric may be one of overt symptoms similar to the clinical syndrome of anxiety or depression, or a mix of both. As such, he or she may be, at least temporarily, responsive to the psychotherapeutic approaches of established effectiveness with such symptoms. However, if the underlying pathology of faith is not perceived or addressed, the patient's early symptomatic relief may be followed by a persistent demoralization and a susceptibility to recurrent episodes of heightened discomfort.

The pragmatic psychotherapist, sensitive to those changes in the human condition wrought by the advances of our science and technology, recog-nizes the possibility that the patient is suffering, at core, not from a secular blow, reversal of fortune, or substantive loss, but rather from a loss of previously unquestioned or untested "articles of faith."

Recognition of a philosophic dysphoria (or an "existential neurosis") is helped when the therapist is aware of some of its common manifestations. These are in the form of subtle attitudinal biases or value assumptions that may be revealed only indirectly unless probed for by the therapist. Among these are the following:

- Pain and suffering are to be avoided *at all costs*.
- Happiness is the only justification for living, the prime goal.
- Life *must* have a meaning (or, life is meaningless).
- Change is uncertain (the world, as I know it, will continue unchanged).
- Conviction is necessary (one cannot live today with uncertainty about tomorrow).
- Death is indefinite (improbable in the near future and not to be thought about; or, the "final solution").

There are some corollary assumptions on the part of the philosophic dysphoric who chooses to consult a sanctioned psychotherapist:

- There *is* an answer (or a program) for my problem.
- I need expert advice.
- The psychotherapist (psychiatrist, psychologist, social worker) is an expert on "how to live."

When a diagnosis of philosophical dysphoria has been made appropri-ately, the therapist faces a decision as to whether to treat, and if to treat, how. In many cases, it suffices for the therapist simply to assist the patient to an awareness of his or her underlying assumptions. From that point on, the patient may be willing and able to undertake the examination and restructuring or restoration of his or her philosophic foundation. In other instances, where there is a vacuum of values, the therapist may be disinclined to undertake treatment (instruction). Such cases present a particular danger that the therapist may be tempted to "prescribe," to provide a "faith" to the disillusioned client. If the therapist recognizes the appropriateness of a referral to a clergyman or other religious (philosophical) counselor, there is always the risk that such referral may prove to be unhelpful. There is a particular need for the therapist to be as knowledgeable as possible about the "track record" and approach of those nonsecular professionals in the community who have a reputation for working with such clients (Schofield, 1979).

The problem of referral is eased if the therapist is fortunate enough to be able to turn to a credentialed pastoral counselor, preferably one identified with the client's church. Unfortunately, the literature on pastoral counseling and many of the formal training programs serve primarily to prepare the pastoral counselor to wear another hat, and, in effect, to function essentially as a psychotherapist, not unlike the psychiatrist, psychologist, and social worker, perhaps only with the advantage of an easy preformed rapport through an apparent shared faith with the troubled parishioner (Schofield, 1979).

The Decision to Treat or to Refer

The problem presented by the philosophic dysphoric represents but one instance in which the question of whether to treat or to refer arises. It is not a question, of course, when the therapist's calendar is full and there is no possibility of accepting new cases. Absent this condition, the therapist must exercise discretion as to which applicants will be accepted and has a responsibility to do so.

The therapist's responsibility not to accept all cases that time allows rests upon certain probable conditions that are not always explicitly recognized, especially by younger therapists who are concerned with starting and building a practice. In this regard, note must be taken of the frequency with which such professionals, only recently graduated from a training program, announce services that imply almost no limit to their expertise. It is not unusual for such announcements to offer individual and group psychotherapy for children, adolescents, and adults; marriage and family counseling; couple counseling; sexual therapy; hypnosis; and psychodiagnostics. (It is interesting to note that the very last service, [i.e., assessment and evaluation] may be the only one omitted from the panoply.)

It may be appropriate for such a range of services to be offered by a group practice in which individual staff members may have a developed expertise in one or more specialty areas and with one or more age groups. It is questionable when offered by the recently certified or licensed professional unless he or she has had considerable postgraduate, supervised training or work experience in a wide range of settings and with a wide range of clientele. Professional ethics stipulate that advertisements of services be accurate, objective statements of qualifications (American Psychological Association, 1981). There is some indication that professional societies do not regularly monitor the public service offerings of their members (Thackrey, 1985). The typical "internship" training of psychologists, social workers, and other mental health professionals, usually one year in duration and in a limited clinical setting, provides a weak foundation for independent, solo practice. The psychiatrist is better off in this regard in that postmedical school residency (apprenticeship) training requires a minimum of three years, and four years for the physician who chooses to specialize in child psychiatry.

On the other hand, new therapists require a reasonable amount of general and broad experience if they are to learn about their special interests and talents as a basis for eventual specialization. The therapist working in a relatively isolated rural setting with limited professional resources readily available, or as a member of an agency with limited staff and a heavy clientele load, may not be able to enjoy the benefits of specialization and the privilege of referring applicants who are not his or her "ideal." Such "generalists by circumstance" have a particular burden to constantly broaden their expertise through reading, supervision, and advanced workshops (see chap. 8).

The therapist who does not work under these restrictions or pressures and who can be selective about clients has a resonsibility not to accept applicants who are not appropriate for his or her specialized interests, skills, and experience. However, professional responsibility demands not simply the denial of an applicant but some effort at appropriate referral. Sometimes a telephone conversation, or a letter from the prospective patient, may suffice as a basis for the therapist's decision to treat or to refer. More frequently, an initial office visit is necessary, and the conscientious therapist will make it clear that this is a *consultation*, on the basis of which there may be a mutual decision to go ahead or not with a contract for therapy. The therapist should be alert to the possibility that the preliminary consultation may be sufficiently therapeutic in and of itself.

Most recognized psychotherapy professions have formally acknowledged the importance of making appropriate referrals and of not accepting all applicants in a nondiscriminatory manner. Explicit ethical codes and rules of conduct guide the therapist with general principals such as these:

- The therapist recognizes the limits of his or her competency and does not practice outside those limits.
- The therapist recognizes when a client requires or would benefit from the resources available from other professionals or agencies and assists the client with suitable referrals to those resources.

Apart from the initial decision to refer, the therapist also has the responsibility to recognize when in the course of ongoing therapy there may be a need to terminate the therapy and refer the client to other sources. Thus, for example, in treatment of one member of a married couple, a point may be reached where further benefit, in the judgment of the therapist, requires marital counseling. Given the existing relationship of client and therapist, it would be best that the client and spouse be referred to another professional for specialized counseling.

In sum, at the initial interview the conscientious, pragmatic therapist appraises the supplicant not as a client or patient but as a *candidate* for psychotherapy. The potential therapist assesses the nature of the presented problem as it affects the candidate's personal and social functioning against the dimensions sketched in chap. 2, figure 3; evaluates the severity and duration of the candidate's distress and the latter's response (or lack thereof) to previous treatment; examines the reality (validity) of the candidate's expectations (goals); explores the strength of the candidate's motivation to change and his or her willingness to accept the conditions and make the sacrifices required by therapy. Finally, the therapist appraises the appropriateness of the candidate's pathology for one of the established major forms of psychotherapeutic intervention (see chap. 5, figure 6). Only when the findings from this appraisal are affirmative does the therapist accept the candidate and propose a course of therapy. When the decision is negative, for whatever reasons, the therapist accepts responsibility to communicate his or her decision in a manner that will be beneficial to the candidate. This may take the form of a consultation that therapeutically corrects the candidate's erroneous self-diagnosis, or of a referral of the candidate to more appropriate sources of help, that is, other therapists or agencies (Tryon, 1983).

References

American Psychological Association (1981). Ethical principles of psychologists. *American Psychologist, 36*, 633–638.

Caplan, A. L. (1983). Organ transplants: The cost of success. *The Hastings Center Report*, *13*, 23–32.

Cobb, S. (1976) Social support as a moderator of life stress. *Psychosomatic Medicine*, *38*, 301–304.

Dengrove, E. (1972) Thought-block in behavior therapy. *Behavior Therapy*, *3*, 344–346.

Dohrenwend, B. P., Dohrenwend, B. S., Gould, M. S., Link, B., Neugebauer, R., and Wunsch-Hitzig, R. (1980) *Mental illness in the United States: Epidemiological estimates*. New York: Praeger Publishers.

Ellis, A. (1962). *Reason and emotion in psychotherapy*. New York: Lyle Stuart.

Frank, J. D. (1974). Psychotherapy: The restoration of morale. *American Journal of Psychiatry*, *131*, 271–274.

Frank, J. D. (1985). Further thoughts on the anti-demoralization hypothesis of psychotherapeutic effectiveness. *Integrated Psychiatry*, *3*, 17–26.

Frankl, V. E. (1959). *Man's search for meaning: An introduction to logotherapy*. Boston: Beacon Press.

Frankl, V. E. (1962). *Basic concepts of logotherapy*. Journal of Existential Psychiatry, III, 111–118.

Frankl, V. E. (1967). *Psychotherapy and existentialism*. New York: Washington Square Press.

Goodman, S. H., Sewell, D. R., & Jampol, R. C. (1984). On going to the counselor: contributions of life stress and social supports to the decision to seek psychological counseling. *Journal of Counseling Psychology*, *31*, 306–313.

Gurin, G., Veroff, J. & Feld, S. (1960). *Americans view their mental health*. New York: Basic Books.

Halgin, R. P. & Weaver, D. D. (1986). Salient beliefs about obtaining psychotherapy. *Psychotherapy in Private Practice*, *4*, 23–31.

Kadushin, C. (1969). *Why people go to psychiatrists*. New York: Atherton Press.

Schofield, W. (1979). Psychology, inspiration, and faith. *Journal of Religion and Health*, *18*, 197–202.

Schofield, W. (1986). Psychotherapy: The purchase of friendship. New Brunswick, N J: Transaction.

Thackrey, M. (1985). Breakdown in professional self-monitoring: Private practice announcements. *Professional Psychology: Research and Practice*, *16*, 163–166.

Tryon, G. S. (1979). A review and critique of thought stopping research. *Journal of Behavior Therapy and Experimental Psychiatry*, *10*, 189–192.

Tryon, G. S. (1983). Why full-time private practitioners refer patients to other professionals. *Psychotherapy in Private Practice*, *1*, 81–83.

Wolpe, J. (1973). *The practice of behavior therapy*. (2nd ed.) New York: Pergamon Press.

4

Varieties of Psychotherapy

All professional therapists, most advanced students, and increasing numbers of the informed public recognize that psychotherapy, like a coat of many colors, stimulates diverse perceptions. Within the profession it may be perceived as a splendid product of the capacity for discovery and innovation and adaptation to the multiform needs of those to be helped. By some it may seem to have its parts neatly bordered, all held together by a common thread. By others it is perceived to be a loose patchwork, with irregular pieces, ragged edges, and even some holes. While some may view the coat's predominant color to be the "royal" blue of psychoanalysis, others see it as brilliant with the "cardinal" red of behaviorism. To all who view it, however, it is clear that it is not the product of a single tailor.

For professional, student, and informed consumer alike, the nonuniformity of psychotherapy's fabric presents puzzlement and problem. Why the variety of pattern and hue? Can one size fit all? Are there prototypes of greater simplicity from which the present Josephian jacket has evolved? And how can it fit more exactly a particular customer's needs? And if just a cuff was frayed or an elbow worn thin, would not replacement or repair be easier if the cloth were whole and not an unpredictable patchwork?

How many kinds of psychotherapy are there? There are two extreme answers. At one extreme are experts who assert that there is only one *real* psychotherapy, and that all other methods are either minor variations on the *real* therapy or approaches that lack lasting effectiveness. Historically, and not simply because it was earliest in point of time, proponents and practitioners of psychoanalysis have been prone to set it apart as the ultimate therapy and to denigrate all other methods as affording mere symptom relief. In recent time, the circle of monotheistic professionals has come to include others who profess fealty to a presumably unimodal therapy; easily recognizable among these are the behavioral therapists.

At the other extreme, the answer is that there are *many* different kinds of individual dyadic psychotherapy, each with a discernible degree of validity. How many? Some authorities have been content to differentiate as few as 2 (London, 1964; McCary, 1955), 3 (Cole, 1982), 4 (Glad, 1959); 10 (Ford & Urban, 1963), 13 (Harper, 1959), or as many as 64 "major innovative approaches to psychotherapy in current use" (Corsini, 1981, p. ix). But the log does not stop there; a psychotherapy handbook describes "250 different therapies in use today" (Herink, 1980). As practitioner, student, or consumer, how is one to comprehend these two extremes to the basic question, and how is one to assimilate the implications of as few (?) as 13 let alone 250 approaches?

Limits on Variation

Consider first the setting and the participants. Two persons converse in a private conference room. Questions are asked and responded to. Statements are made. Emotion is expressed. Hypotheses are formulated and perhaps exchanged. Observations are noted. Suggestions are proffered, explanations may be made, and specific tasks (homework) may be assigned. Each session is time limited, and the course of therapy may or may not be time limited. Some quality of relationship develops between the participants as they work toward a mutually agreed upon goal. A few general rules are observed: confidentiality, promptness, regularity, and fees.

Recall the elements that each participant brings to the exchange (figure 2, chap. 2). Allowing for the individual variation in the specifics of each element for each participant (while recognizing that not all of these individual specifics are equally germane to the work of therapy), the interaction among these provides for such a tremendously rich variety in therapist-client activity as to encourage the notion of uniqueness. If, in fact, each case of therapy were unique, there would be no possibility for the discovery of uniformities across cases necessary to arrive at either a descriptive nosology or an explanatory theory. The fact is that there are natural limits on the possible range of reliably observable, systematic, and consistent differences in the manner and content of the conduct of therapeutic conversation.

Suppose that the complete record of a therapy case were available on videotape. Suppose that a panel of judges were assigned to independently view the tape and to develop summative, descriptive, categories to encompass the activities of the therapist and client, without the therapist identified to them as an adherent of any specified "school" of therapy. Suppose that the judges later reached agreement on basic categories of description, thus arriving at reliable, independent analyses. The panel of judges could then be set to analyze other therapist-client dyads and courses of therapy.

How many such cases would have to be reviewed before the judges would cease to need to revise or extend their descriptive system?

Suppose that a separate panel of judges were to explore the summative, descriptive analyses of the content and course of another very large sample of therapy cases to answer the question: Can these cases be clustered? Despite different therapists and clients, are there detectable uniformities in the process and content of therapeutic conversation, such that a number of groupings, much less than the number of individual cases, would account for all of the cases. If the process were continued, how many cases would have to be examined before no new clusters were discovered? And, with this process of exploration (discovery) completed, how many basic groupings would have been identified? Two? Four? Sixty-four?

This is an outline of an hypothetical research project designed to answer the question: how many meaningfully, reliably discriminable kinds (schools or approaches) of psychotherapy are there? The essential methodology has been well developed (Auld & Murray, 1955; Bales, 1950; Marsden, 1971; Russell & Stiles, 1979). It has been applied to analysis of the process and course of therapy conducted by practitioners identified with a particular school. Carl Rogers and his students, identified with one school of therapy, have made pioneering contributions to this line of research (Porter, 1943; Snyder, 1945). A recent study of six different systems for coding therapist behaviors in therapy sessions determined that six modes of therapist response (questioning, informing, reflecting, advising, interpreting, and self-disclosing) reliably accounted for most therapist behaviors, and also differentiated the response patterns of individual therapists. (Elliott, Stiles, Mahrer, Hill, Friedlander, and Margison, 1987).

At a conceptual level, without the benefit of a comprehensive empirical study of the type suggested above, some reduction of the very large number of purported kinds of therapy to a more "simple structure" is suggested by overviews that group a large number of techniques or approaches into a few major categories. Examples of these therapy categories include: "reconstructive" versus "supportive" (McCrary, 1955; Wolberg, 1954); "action" versus "insight oriented" (London, 1964); "affective" versus "cognitive" (Harper, 1959); "directive" versus "evocative" (Frank, 1961). Such organizational typologies reflect the recognition of two facts: one, that the possible behavioral repertoires of the human individual impose limits on the number of dimensions or parameters that define (confine?) the interaction between two persons; and two, that many of the putative therapies are in essence only specific techniques, tactics, or strategies for facilitating or accomplishing the healing process as conceived in a broader theoretical formulation. The sophisticated ear, listening to the Rachmaninoff variations on a theme by Paganini, or the Goldberg variations of Bach, perceives the continuity of the thematic material. The three blind men were each correct as far as they could "see"; the elephant remained an elephant all the same! The developmental record of the psychoanalytic school of therapy makes it relatively easy to see the Adlerian, Jungian, and Rankian offshoots as variations on the Freudian theme. It is more difficult to separate variation from theme for the apparent proliferation of therapies that has occurred in the latter half of this century.

Something of the divergence among professionals in their conceptualization of psychotherapy is suggested by the following sample of definitions

> During psychotherapeutic interviews a therapist and a patient carry on a verbal exchange in which the productions of the patient are interpreted to him by the therapist with the goal of relieving the patient's neurotic or psychotic distress and providing him with some understanding (and hence mastery) of his psychological motivations.
> (p.v.)
>
> Colby—*A Primer for Psychotherapists* (1951)

> There is one absolutely necessary condition for real or basic personality change to occur. . . . The afflicted individual must learn to recognize his irrational, inconsistent, and unrealistic perceptions and thoughts and change these for more logical, more reasonable philosophies of life.
> (p. 117)
>
> Ellis—*Reason and Emotion in Psychotherapy* (1962)

> Certain types of therapy rely primarily on the [socially sanctioned] healer's ability to mobilize healing forces in the sufferer by psychological means. . . . Although physical and chemical adjuncts may be used, the healing *influence* is primarily exercised by words, acts and *rituals* in which sufferer, healer, and—if there is one—group participate jointly. [Emphases added]
> (pp. 1–3)
>
> Frank—*Persuasion and Healing* (1961)

Other researchers, using preformed categories to describe therapist-patient behaviors, have examined relevant questions: Do practitioners who self-identify as adherents to particular approaches (theories, "schools") of psychotherapy respond in significantly different fashion when presented with identical clinical problems? Do differences in the therapeutic behaviors of "school" representatives increase or decrease as a function of greater experience (Fiedler, 1950a, 1950b; Strupp, 1955a, 1955b, 1960; Sundland & Barker, 1962)? While these studies have found some degree of variation among presumably "different" therapists, the general finding has been one of considerable similarity in the way in which they respond to the same stimulus material and the way in which they describe the primary attributes of the "ideal" therapist. Furthermore, with increased experience, there is an apparent movement of therapists with different claimed allegiances toward greater similarity in clinical behaviors and attitudes and less dependence on theory (Norcross & Prochaska, 1983). Another basis for questioning whether or not there are indeed as many significantly different ways of performing psychotherapy as the literature suggests arises from survey studies of the "school" allegiances claimed by professional therapists (Garfield, 1982; Garfield & Kurtz, 1974, 1977; Norcross & Wogan, 1983). These surveys have found a progressive shift, namely, a decreasing number of therapists claiming to practice as adherents to a particular approach (e.g., psychoanalytic or psychodynamic; Rogersian or client-centered; etc.) and an increasing number identifying themselves as practitioners of "eclectic" psychotherapy. A majority "disavow any systematic, organized, articulate theory held in common with others" (Sundland, 1977, p. 190). Unfortunately, these surveys do not provide a clear definition of what the surveyors may have intended in providing the "eclectic" category as a choice, nor what the responders understood in making that identification of their work. Garfield (1982) observed that "eclecticism is perceived as the adherence to a nonsystematic and rather haphazard clinical approach." (p. 612) This is clearly not the connotation intended by the formal definition of *eclecticism* as "selecting and integrating that which is *best* from many sources." A study of 154 self-identified eclectic psychologist/therapists (Garfield & Kurtz, 1977) found that they used 32 different combinations of theories that "appeared to be blended and used in individually unique ways" (p. 613 Garfield, 1982). It can be surmised that the shift away from school identity may reflect the impact of experience, which is dissuasive to the practice of a "pure" therapy.

Finally, note must be made of research that has provided evidence on two basic points: One, therapists who presumably practice from very different theoretical stances are equally effective with similar patients; and two, patients who have a successful response to treatment, both in their own view and the view of their therapists, provide similar descriptions of their therapist as "a keenly attentive, interested, benign, and concerned listener—a friend who is warm and natural, is not adverse to giving direct advice, who speaks one's language, makes sense, and rarely arouses intense anger" (Strupp, Fox, & Lessler, 1967 p.117).

These general findings regarding the overt manifestations of therapists' theoretical orientations are in contrast to survey findings that, when questioned, therapists express satisfaction with their respective orientations and the belief that their theories significantly influence how they practice (Norcross & Prochaska, 1983).

The Nature of Schools of Psychotherapy

To undertake a comparative analysis of presumably different modes of conducting the psychotherapeutic endeavor, it is necessary to define the essential elements of a *school*. As applied to psychotherapy, the term *school* does not have, in all instances, the usual connotations of that term. There may or may not be a physical place or places where training occurs. There may or may not be an officially credentialed faculty. There may or may not be an accredited program of study from which formally matriculated students graduate as certified practitioners. Most of these expected definitional criteria are clearly satisfied by the established psychoanalytic schools with their several training institutes in this country and abroad. Similarly, the rational-emotive school of Albert Ellis presents the features of a formal school. In contrast, the "cognitive" and "behavioral" schools (and the cognitive-behavioral amalgam) show few features of an organized centrality. Perhaps intermediate in degree of institutional identity is the nondirective or client-centered approach founded by Carl Rogers. For purposes of comparative analysis, the existence of formal institutes and identified teachers is of secondary import. What is crucial is the substantive corpus of concepts and practices.

"School" = theory × techniques

"A theoretical orientation is a consistent theory of human behavior, psychopathology/behavior disorder, psychotherapy, and the mechanisms of therapeutic change. . . . Theories of human development and personality *per se* are desirable, but not characteristic of all orientations" (Norcross, 1985). With this structure for study, there are discernable differences in theoretical formulations and differences in recommended technique for the conduct of therapy. A theory may emphasize psychological development and personality structure, or it may emphasize etiological concepts regarding psychopathology. A theory may be relatively more biological or more sociological in its foundation. It may be highly articulated or schematically sparse. The associated techniques for doing therapy may be few in number and emphasize attitudinal "sets" for the therapist, or they may be numerous, diverse, and expressed in descriptive detail. Finally, the rational foundation for both the theory and the techniques may be supported by much or little research. However the different schools might be scored for excellence of theory qua theory or specificity and theoretical relevance of their associated practices, it must be recogized that no client is ever treated "with" a theory (Howard, Orlinsky & Trattner, 1970; Strupp, 1978). The client is treated by the techniques and practices associated with the school to which the therapist adheres, if he or she is a "purist." In this light, a "therapeutic failure" is not directly attributable to a therapy school, but must be attributed to the therapist who was a poor practitioner of the technique of that school (or made a diagnostic error in accepting the patient for *that kind* of treatment) (Chessick, 1971; Thorne, 1961).

Figure 4 lists some of the major components on which various therapy schools may be compared. The Freudian school has a clear biological emphasis in constructing human nature. Beyond that, it views pathology as arising from the individual's failure to adapt basic urges to repression-favoring social mores. By contrast, the Rogersian school sees the individual as inherently driven to positive growth, with a need only to have self-healing processes encouraged.

For the Freudian, the individual's history, and especially the period of early childhood, is of great importance. The Rogersian, on the other hand, and the "behaviorist" focus on the here and now, with any historical interest generally limited to the immediate past. Both Freudians and Rogersians prescribe a relatively passive role for the therapist, with the "locus of responsibility" for the therapy session clearly assigned to the patient. In contrast, both the cognitive therapist and the behaviorist accept an active and responsible role in directing, instructing, prescribing, coaching, and modeling. With respect to techniques and tactics, the behaviorist school has by far the largest and most distinctly explicated armamentarium of specific therapeutic tactics. This is in marked constrast to orthodox psychoanalytic theory's very limited stipulation of the specifics of practice.

There are marked differences among the major schools in their relative emphasis on the nature and quality of the therapist-patient process. This

FIGURE 4

Structural Dimensions of Schools of Psychotherapy

View of the "Nature of Man":	Biological/Psychological/Sociological
Attention to History:	Focus on Past/Present
Focus of Treatment:	Thought/Affect/Behavior
Role of Therapist:	Active/Passive
Locus of Responsibility:	Therapist/Client
Techniques:	General/Specific Fixed/Flexible
Therapist/Client Relationship:	Crucial/Incidental

relationship is viewed as of vital significance in all psychodynamic formulations of the therapy process, with the concept of transference (and countertransference) occupying a central role. In contrast, the cognitive-behavioral school generally does not give special attention to the dynamics of the therapist-patient relationship beyond care that it meet the general criteria for a good professional-consultative interaction.

In regard to the focus of treatment, the Freudian and Rogersian schools attend closely to thought and emotion, and *relatively* disregard overt behaviors. The cognitive schools emphasize the client's ideational processes as prevalent over or determinative of affective states, and the behaviorists focus on the overt actions of the individual to the *relative* disregard of ideas and emotions.

It is perhaps in this last component—the conceptualizing of the patient's pathology to reside in ways of thinking, or ways of feeling, or ways of acting—that there is a clue to the evolution of different therapy schools, to the efforts at theoretical rapprochement, and to the apparent trend toward eclecticism (Garfield, 1980, 1982; Goldfried, 1982; Kendall, 1982; Messer & Winokur, 1980). The human individual is a cognitive, conative, affective entity—a thinking, acting, feeling organism. As a biological unity, beyond earliest infancy, the individual's acts, thoughts, and emotions are continuously interactive; each affects the others. Disruption of the self, of the *person,* occurs when there is pathology in any of the three dimensions. And pathology in any of the spheres has effects on the other two. For understanding of the individual at the psychological level, this macroanatomy of personhood suffices.

The Evolution of Schools of Therapy

It might be thought that the proliferation of psychotherapy schools (theories and/or tactics) is simply the result of imaginative and innovative therapists finding better (i. e., more effective) ways of conducting therapy. This is a possibility but unlikely, given that most full-time clinicians have neither time nor inclination to experiment in a consistent fashion and make adequate records for validation purposes. Sigmund Freud (1952) and Albert Ellis (1962) are notable exceptions, and they have provided good accounts of their disenchantment with initial experiences and their search for a different and better approach to the treatment of intrapsychic disorders (see also Whitaker, 1972). The following quotation from Freud (1952) is exemplary:

> Increasing experience had also given rise to two grave doubts in my mind as to the use of hypnotism even as a means of catharsis. The first was that even the

most brilliant results were liable to be suddenly wiped away if my personal relation with the patient became disturbed. It was true that they would be re-established if a reconciliation could be effected; but such an occurrence proved that the personal emotional relation between doctor and patient was after all stronger than the whole cathartic process, and it was precisely that factor which escaped every effort at control. . . . I felt that I had now grasped the nature of the mysterious element that was at work behind hypnotism. In order to exclude it, or at all events to isolate it, it was necessary to abandon hypnotism. (p.48–50)

Freud's astute observations anticipated by a half century the research studies of the relative contribution of technique versus relationship (Rogers, 1951; Strupp, Fox, & Lessler, 1969).

It might also be thought that the development of new schools of therapy arose from the work of academicians who had the time and motivation to mount researches of discovery. The literature indicates that the bulk of research, until very recently, slow to start and handicapped by methodological limitations, was directed to testing the efficacy of already existing forms of treatment. Such efforts were not inappropriate, given the strong implication (especially by behaviorally oriented psychologists) that "psycho"-therapy had no convincing evidence of validity (Bergin, 1971; Eysenck, 1952). Increasing amounts of outcome data, with improved research methods, support the conclusion that some patients do achieve significant benefits from some forms of therapy (Brown, 1987; Landman & Dawes, 1982; Shapiro & Shapiro, 1982; Smith & Glass, 1977). We still lack precise guidance as to which kind of therapy is indicated for what kind of problem. The status of the question of effectiveness of therapy results from the fact that many outcome studies have evaluated heterogenous patient samples (i. e., mixed with respect to presenting problem), treated with one or two presumably specific forms of therapy, by therapists with varying levels of experience and expertise, with varying criteria for the appraisal of results (Kazdin, 1985).

An overview of the major systems of psychotherapy strongly suggests that they originated when their founders focused on a particular formulation of the essential nature of the pathology *they perceived in the clients with whom they had their most intensive experiences*. Circumstances of time and place, and the homogenizing effect of having new patients referred by current or former patients, meant that each system builder observed pathology that was similar, at least at the phenomenological level, from patient to patient. From this follows the suggestion that "kinds" of therapy evolved from the recognition of "kinds" of pathology suitable for psychological intervention.

How many reliably and meaningfully differentiable kinds of psychological pathology are there? Certainly not 250! Nor even the dozen or more explicated by some authorities. While appreciative of the particular virtues of the numerous variations, we have to search out the fundamental themes. These are to be found in the basic dimensions of human experience that provide the soil in which the weeds of pathology can be rooted and grow—cognition, conation, and affect—the thinking, striving, and feeling responses of the individual to his or her life situation, with certain response-readiness or sensitivity, and certain coping potentials predetermined genetically, or by very early life experiences.

From this perspective it becomes possible to identify the dimension in which the distressed person's *primary* pathology arises—that is, primary in the sense of providing the core disorder from which dysfunction in the other dimensions may arise as side effects or correlated symptomatology. As noted above, considering the organismic unity of interactive functions that express personhood, there is slim likelihood of a *purely* affective (emotional) illness. But careful assessment will identify the primary locus of disturbance from which there may flow metastatic involvement of the other dimensions.

Thus, the core pathology may be cognitive. Distress may arise from irrational or erroneous ideas held concerning oneself, others, or the world in general. Frank (1985) has provided an explicit description of this type of pathology and its implications for therapy:

> The distinguishing feature of the kinds of distress and disability for which psychotherapy is believed to be the treatment of choice is that they create perturbations in the patient's communications with others. These disturbed communications . . . are linked to distressing subjective states arising from maladaptive features of the patient's "assumptive world"—that is the structure and content of the patient's assumptions about himself, his future, and the world about him. . . . The only features of a patient's psychiatric symptoms that psychotherapy can directly modify, however, are those caused by stress-producing distortions in the patient's assumptive world. (p. 17)

Among therapists who focus on cognitive pathology, there are differences of opinion (theory) as to how much or how little of the "assumptive world" is immediately accessible to and reportable by the patient. The patient may be fully cognizant of his guiding convictions and able readily to express them; or, they may be at least in part hidden from his awareness. In the case of the latter situation, the extent of the "uncovering" that will be necessary determines the work of therapy. Correction and replacement of fallacious ideas is possible only after they are fully acknowledged by the patient.

With delineation of a cognitive form of pathology, it is possible to see that differences among some major schools of therapy are less than what appears at first glance. Thus the psychoanalytic, the client-centered, and the rational-emotive approaches are cognitive therapies. For example, Rogers (1951) did not use the concept of "the unconscious" nor the technique of interpretation in the psychoanalytic sense. However, he wrote: "Successful therapy seems to entail the *bringing into awareness* [emphasis added], in an adequately symbolized way, those experiences and feelings which are currently in contradiction to the client's concept of self."

And Ellis (1962) wrote:

> The main problem of effective living, then, would seem to be not of eradicating people's beliefs, but of changing them so that they become more closely rooted to information and to reason. This can be done . . . by getting people to examine, to question, to think about their beliefs, and thereby to develop a more consistent, fact-based and workable set of constructs than they now may possess. (p. 105)

The techniques of psychoanalysis, client-centered, and rational-emotive therapy are different, but in their theory they are alike in a cognitive focus, in the need to help the patient to awareness of previously denied or unquestioned concepts (assumptions), and in the goal of rational, objective, accurate perceptions of self and others.

The cognitive school of psychotherapy beginning with Freud (interpretation and insight are clearly cognitive processes) has historical preeminence. Psychoanalysis was the only psychotherapy with broad visibility throughout the 1940s. It provided *the* theory of neurosis and the concepts of treatment in medical schools and especially in the residency training of psychiatrists, and it was the guiding rationale in the didactic curricula of schools of social work and graduate programs in clinical psychology (Garfield, 1981).

The first potential challenge to the dominance of psychoanalysis came with Rogers' *Counseling and Psychotherapy* in 1942. While clearly cognitive in orientation, and with attention to the same "uncovering" process and goal of self-understanding (insight) as the Freudian school, it offered a very different formulation of the nature of human beings, and it eschewed interpretation and transference as crucial processes. It had particular appeal and promise for students and counselors who were not associated with medical agencies for training or practice and whose clients were less disturbed than the modal patient of psychiatric facilities. Its appeal was greatly enhanced by its disavowal of diagnosis (an anticipation of the "humanistic" and "existential" movements), by its delineation of a relatively few, apparently simple techniques, and by its emphasis on the corrective influence of the therapist-client relationship for effective intervention (Rogers, 1957). The strong, early appeal of Rogers' client-centered approach, especially to nonmedical therapists, arose also by providing a base for reaction to the "totalitarianism" of Freudian domination prior to the mid-1940s, an "appeal to factors deep within the American culture" (see Harper, 1959, chap. 10). The greatest impact of the Rogersian school, however, came through the application of total verbatim, electronic recording of psychotherapy cases and the beginning of intensive analysis of the therapy process. Rogers and his students established the process of psychotherapy as a phenomenon accessible to scientific scrutiny.

Parenthetically, it should be noted that Rogers' title for his 1942 work highlights a continuing debate, of decreasing interest, about what, if any, are the defining and observable differences between psychotherapy and counseling (Schofield, 1966). Both entail conversation with therapeutic, remedial, or corrective intent. Where does counseling leave off and psychotherapy begin? Those professionals whose training was in graduate programs in counseling psychology or whose job titles identify them as counselors may be content to have their efforts called counseling. Those trained in clinical psychology or psychiatry identify their efforts as psychotherapy, even when their activity is liberally salted with advice, information, and instruction (à la the RET model of Ellis), techniques more commonly associated with counseling. Clinical social workers, who are not explicitly trained to assume the overt role either of psychotherapist or counselor, escape the dilemma by identifying their activity as "case work." Very excellent treatises on case work are clearly primers on psychotherapy, usually with a psychodynamic orientation (e.g., Mackey, 1985). The differentiation of counseling from psychotherapy is afforded less by theory and less by the actual practices entailed than by the nature of the clientele and the problems for which they seek help. The modal client of the counselor brings less deep-seated, less chronic, less intrapsychic and more situational problems than the modal patient of the psychotherapist. The differences are relative, never absolute. Within the course of a particular case, there may be stages that are more of a counseling nature and other stages that are more clearly psychotherapeutic. Thus, early phases may be psychotherapeutic in assisting the patient toward insight as to the origins and nature of previously "covert" conflicts, while later stages may be of a counseling nature, designed to help the client toward exploration of alternative solutions.

As therapy proceeds by working with resistance, the relationship style may need to change to remain therapeutic and consistent with the client's current level of functioning. Therefore, it is conceivable that a therapist might begin therapy with a non-directive style, move to a directive, authoritarian style during the middle phase of treatment, and terminate the relationship by again being non-directive with the client. (Dimond, Havens, & Jones, 1978) (p. 245)

A second clear challenge to the psychodynamic formulation of etiology and focus on "unconscious" mental operations, still within a cognitive framework, came with the work of Albert Ellis. Arising out of his rational critique of psychoanalytic theory and his clinical experience as an analytic practitioner, Ellis began to lay out the formulation of his theory of a cognitively based therapy (Ellis, 1955, 1958). This came to full expression in his 1962 volume, *Reason and Emotion in Psychotherapy*. The title is significant both for its inclusion of cognitive and affective terms and its omission of behavior. The latter term could have been appropriately included because Ellis explicitly recognized the interactive feedback looping of thought-feeling-action. In explicating rational-emotive therapy (RET), Ellis took exception to the earlier cognitive approaches on two counts: (1) He argued that much psychological distress arose from irrational assumptions on the part of the patient that, while possibly arising from early life experiences (indoctrination), especially from family members, teachers, and faulty ego-introjects, were not deeply repressed but could be readily expressed and claimed by the sufferer. (2) He eschewed the passive role of the analytic interpreter or the Rogersian reflector and assigned to the therapist a vigorous role as logician-confronter and counterpropagandist. Because of the emphasis on the focal role played by the client's irrational, unrealistic assumptions or expectations, RET is frequently viewed as a form of cognitive therapy to be contrasted with behavioral therapies. However, the techniques of the RET practitioner frequently include task assignments to provide the client with real-life tests of consequences of more rational actions, and so the RET school is sometimes classified as one of the cognitive-behavioral approaches (Spiegler, 1983).

The first significant challenge to the cognitive hegemony in the treatment of psychological disorders came with the establishment of behavior therapy. While there were earlier roots in the clinical accounts of the treatment of childhood phobias by (re)conditioning techniques, and the "conditioned reflex therapy" of Salter (1950), it was Joseph Wolpe's work *Psychotherapy Through Reciprocal Inhibition* (1958) that provided a rallying point for those clinicians who were philosophically critical of Freudian theory or tempermentally ill disposed toward the long-term "as if" discourses of analytic psychotherapy. No less than the Rogersians, the behaviorists were concerned to establish a scientific respectability for their work. They did this by focusing on *outcome*, specifying very clearly prescribed techniques of intervention, and establishing the effectiveness of their corrective interventions by demonstrating objectively observable changes in overt manifestations of symptomatic behavior. Clear evidence of significant change in neurotic behavior (or inhibition of behavior) within relatively brief periods of treatment made for easy recruitment of homogeneous clinical samples and development of further evidence of the potency of the behavioral approach. Other antecedents to the behavioral school are traceable to the early work of Mary Cover Jones (1924) in the treatment of childhood phobias and to John B. Watson's "behaviorism." (Watson & Rayner, 1920) These, of course, had their scientific foundations in the experiments of Pavlov, Bekterev, and Gantt in establishing and extinguishing experimental neuroses in animals. However, it was the development of the operant conditioning paradigm by B.F. Skinner, demonstrating the shaping and reshaping of behavior by its consequences, and the transfer of controlled experimentation from the animal laboratory to the human clinic and hospital that gave most direct and sustained impetus to the behavioral therapy movement. One of Skinner's students, Ogden Lindsley, is credited with first use of the concept, "behavior therapy" (Lindsley, Skinner, & Solomon, 1953), Lazarus (1958) introduced the term, *behavior therapist*.

Still another contribution to the anticognitive wave within the domain of psychological intervention is credited to the psychologists of the Maudsley Hospital in London, notably Hans J. Eysenck and M. B. Shapiro. Eysenck's challenging review (1952) of the limited and unconvincing evidence of the effectiveness of psychotherapy, notably psychoanalysis, was a prime stimulus for psychologists to stop aping psychiatrists and turn to their own unique tools. Shapiro (1957) developed a program for analysis of the individual case in light of established psychological principles of learning and the application of those same principles to assist the patient toward eradication of maladaptive response patterns and acquisition of new behavioral repertoires.

With the establishment in 1966 of the Association for the Advancement of Behavior Therapy, the scene was set and the actors were in place for a dramatic debate. Resolved: Mental (behavioral-emotional) illness of nonpsychotic nature is a cognitive disorder requiring cognitive correction (or, psychoneuroses and character disorders are symptomatic of underlying cognitive pathology and require cognitive interventions). Or, resolved: Psychological distress, regardless of the form of symptomatic expression, can be treated most effectively, efficiently, and lastingly by a behavioral mode of therapy. The debate was carried on by theoretical and philosophical arguments (polemics) in the learned journals. "The debate between behavior therapists and others has at times reached a level of stridency and acrimony which could only arise from rather absolute convictions of the parties involved regarding their respective positions" (Bergin, 1970). The protagonists were supported in their positions by laboratory analogue studies and by variously controlled clinical studies. In the controversy, both behaviorists and cognitivists scored points, but no objective referee had a clear score by which to declare the match won by either side.

A parenthetical note is in order. The early spate of both laboratory and clinical demonstrations of apparent success by the behaviorists in eradicating symptomatic behavior called for a response (defense) by the cognitivists. A ready argument was at hand, especially by those of psychodynamic persuasion. Partly on the basis of theory and partly on anecdotal evidence, it was held that symptoms were but the surface expression of underlying pathology; removal only of symptoms would leave the pathology undisturbed, and there would be later recurrence of the symptom or of some other form of psychogenic manifestation. The behaviorist reply was to examine the literature for the reported incidence of such revival of previous symptoms or later episodes of symptom substitution. Such searches did not support the psychodynamic formulation and the relative permanency of symptom removal was upheld (Grossberg, 1964; Montgomery & Crowder, 1972; Wolpe, 1961; Yates, 1958). At least two conclusions are suggested by this finding. It may be that the basic psychodynamic formulation regarding the nature of pathology and the pathology-symptom relationship lacks validity. Or, more likely, it may be that the course of behavior therapy has "side effects"—for example, the patients learn something about themselves, or about stress, or about coping techniques, that is, that they "generalize" or "transfer" their training without the intent or awareness of their presumably "pure" behavior therapist! Or, was the behavioral treatment in fact and uncontrollably impure (Kazdin, 1982)?

Other early attacks on behavioral therapy, coming particularly from psychodynamically oriented therapists, criticized the behaviorists as being mechanistic and degrading the therapeutic relationship. These attacks were responded to by psychologists who pointed up the elements of social learning modification and the role of the behavior therapist as a social reinforcer and role model (Wilson & Evans, 1977).

Therapists of psychoanalytic persuasion, influenced by the wave of enthusiasm for the behavioral methods and the increasing evidence of their effectiveness, were concerned to establish points of convergence or integration (Feather & Rhoads, 1972: Rhoads, 1981). In time, the growing streams of theoretical analysis, clinical experience, and the movement toward eclecticism sought a common channel that would accommodate the ardent partisanship of the cognitivists and behaviorists, moving the discourse away from a too simplistic "either/or" and "nothing but" reductionism. The confluence found expression in a new (?) school: cognitive-behavioral therapy (Kendall & Hollon, 1979; Meichenbaum, 1974, 1979; Russell & Brandsma, 1974). The hyphen maneuver did not resolve the controversy but seemed to bring a more penetrating level of discourse.

Points of commonality in the two approaches were noted (Beck, 1970). However, attention was directed to the issue of primacy: Do cognitions have a directive, motive role with respect to behavior, or does behavior, and its consequences, determine thought? Are cognitions a form of behavior and do they respond to the same principles of learning that hold for overt action; or must a new set of theoretical constructs be used to account for acquisition, maintenance, and change in cognitive structures? Is cognition to be viewed as a process or as a product, or both? Thus, the question of the validity of the cognitive-behavioral approach has been examined with respect to the adequacy of its theoretical basis (Schwartz, 1982).

On an empirical level, the merits of the cognitive, behavioral, and cognitive-behavioral schools have been tested against the criterion of results. Neither laboratory analogue experiments nor controlled clinical trials have established that one of the approaches has a clear and significant edge over the other two. Failure to establish differential general effectiveness has been attributed in part to the observation that, claims for theoretical differences aside, the actual practices of practitioners of the three schools are not consistently different (Beidel & Turner, 1986). A separate question is whether the different approaches have different "specific" effects. This issue will be reviewed in chapter 4.

Schwartz (1982), in a penetrating analysis of the cognition versus behavior controversy and the attempted cognitive-behavioral integration, offered the following salient observations:

> Throughout these developments, affect has been and remains the step-child of scientific psychology. In the same way that cognition could not be ignored indefinitely, affect will have to find its place in formal theorizing and clinical practice. . . .
>
> Every aspect of human existence has cognitive, behavioral, and affective aspects that are in some sense non-trivial. Even if this is accepted, the question arises as to whether any of these aspects is primary at the casual and/or intervention level. Can cognition, behavior, or affect be placed at the center of the therapeutic universe? The various contemporary approaches to therapy differ in their choice of the center, but each builds the universe around one. (p. 288)

Figure 5, from Schwartz, is a succinct depiction of the manner in which each of the competing major "schools" conceptualize causal relationships, and on the basis of which they address primary interventive attention to one or another of the primary dimensions. In Schwartz's schema for a "unified-interactive" model, no one of the three elements is awarded centrality, although the relative strengths of the interactive relationships are suggested by the double-headed arrows. Schwartz's position is supported by studies suggesting that, at least in some instances, feeling may precede rather than follow thought, that affect and cognition may be partially independent systems (Zajonc, 1980, 1984).

One researcher and his students have brought the element of affect clearly into consideration. Beck (1963, 1976, 1979) posits that depression, in particular, and other affective disorders arise from pathology in cognitive processing. It follows from his formulation that treatment of the emotional distress entails cognitive modes of attack. It is significant that Beck postulates two sources for an individual's deficits in cognitive processing: a primitive set of structures, possibly genetic in origin, and a set of later developed, experience-based systems for cognitive processing. The distinction between the two can be compared to Freud's differentiation of primary and secondary processes. This conceptualization allows the possibility that defects of primary cognitive structures may render the individual unusually susceptible to depression or other affective disturbance, or that disruptive life experiences may activate the primary structures so that the mature cognitive systems are overridden and the individual lacks recourse to ordinary corrective, cognitive operations. In either case, the emotional manifestations are viewed as symptomatic of a pathology of cognition (Beidel & Turner, 1986). (For a discussion of the implications of this formulation for the role of medication see chap. 5).

Of particular note within the cognitive-behavioral movement and the search for an integrative model is the work of Bandura and his associates in developing a social learning model (Bandura, 1969; 1977a). A particular contribution toward a "unifying theory" came with Bandura's (1977b) explication of the construct of self-efficacy. The individual's expectations (estimations of the likelihood that behavior will be successful) are seen as having a motivational role with respect to whether coping behavior will be initiated, how strongly it will be pursued, and how long it will be maintained. Particular attention is given to the influence of modeling on learning and a role is acknowledged for the therapist in using persuasion and exhortation to influence the learner's appraisal of his or her self-efficacy level. This is of special significance in the treatment of persons who are demoralized and/or immobilized in the face of situations or conflicts that they perceive to be immutable.

FIGURE 5

Models of cognition-affect-behavior relationships in contemporary approaches to psychotherapy.

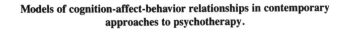

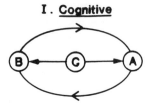

I. Cognitive

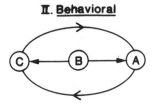

II. Behavioral

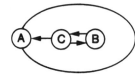

III. Cognitive–Behavioral

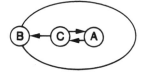

IV. Psychodynamic

V. Unified–Interactive

A = Affect
B = Behavior
C = Cognition

Source: (From Schwartz, R. M., 1982). Cognitive-behavior modification: A conceptual review. *Clinical Psychology Review, 2,* 267–293. Reproduced with permission, American Psychological Association.

In summary, the apparently great diversity in modes of carrying out psychotherapy, the proliferation of techniques, can obfuscate the reality of a small number of forms of basic psychopathology that are amenable to psychological intervention. Theory has sometimes arisen out of very astute clinical observation, reflection, and trial, as exemplified by Freud. It has sometimes followed after successful experimentation with a particular method, as exemplified by Rogers (1942). It has sometimes arisen from laboratory experimentation, witness Wolpe. But theory and technique alike have arisen out of the effort to achieve change in patients and clients who present a particular pathology. The cases from which Freud developed his theoretical structure were clearly different from those on which Rogers arrived at his client-centered therapy. The existential neuroses as diagnosed and treated by Frankl (1959) are different from the phobias treated by Wolpe (1958, 1969).

The validity of psychoanalytic theory and the constructs it encompasses have been subject to criticism on the basis of the very small number of cases from which Freud derived his formulation and their possible erroneous diagnoses (Goshen, 1952). Such criticism ignores the role of clinical observation in the process of discovery, or of hypothesis formation, as distinct from the process of testing. (A single apple [apocryphal?] apparently sufficed for Newton!) Beyond that, it fails to appreciate Freud's special capacity for penetrating reflection and revision (Kanner & Glenn, 1980). Finally, exhaustive reviews of the clinical and analogue literature indicate substantial support for some of the core psychoanalytic concepts (Fischer & Greenberg, 1977; Kline, 1981; Luborsky et al., 1985). The validity status of the theory, however, stands apart from the question of the efficacy and efficiency of psychoanalysis as a therapy. The very limited number of "certified" analysts; the intensity, duration, and cost of orthodox analysis; and the resulting severe limitations on the number of completed analyses; together with a relative reluctance of analytic centers to "open their books" and report data on outcomes, has meant a serious limitation on outcome data (Eagle & Wolitsky, 1985). Such data as exist indicate that psychoanalysis is neither less nor more effective than more "modern" therapies. With respect to efficiency, aside from short-term psychodynamic therapeutic variations, orthodox analysis is clearly deficient in contrast to those methods that emphasize learning theory. Such comparison is not fully appropriate, however, in light of the general criteria for suitable candidates for psychoanalysis, who in terms of socioeconomic status and other demographic variables are very dissimilar from the modal client of nonanalytic therapists (American Psychiatric Association, 1981; Henry, Sims, & Spray, 1971, 1973). Finally, it is notable that despite the very much greater orthodoxy of the training program for psychoanalysts, they are found to be considerably diverse in their later evaluations not only of analytic constructs but of the techniques of therapy as well (Glover, 1955). In the field of group therapy as well, it has been found that group leaders with specific orientations or training backgrounds are not homogeneous in their work practices (Lieberman, Yalom, & Miles, 1973).

The basic forms of psychopathology are limited by primary dimensions of the natural equipment with which the human animal is equipped and that provide the ability to cope, to adapt, to learn—that is, the capacity to think (imagine, compare, and contrast, categorize and conceptualize, recall, recognize, generalize, anticipate, estimate, etc.), to feel (experience euphoria, dysphoria, tension and torpor, etc.), and to act (advance or avoid, walk, talk, create, criticize, choose, explore, risk, etc.). But, doing well or doing poorly, feeling happy or sad, thinking clearly or crookedly, the individual is all of a piece.

Given the organismic unity of the individual, an effective influence on any one of the responding mechanisms will have some effect on the others. This fact undoubtedly accounts in part for the finding that all therapeutic approaches demonstrate some success. It probably also accounts for the fact that success rates with heterogeneous patient samples are essentially equivalent for all therapies. It further suggests that the outcomes of psychotherapeutic endeavors may be considerably determined by factors (influences) that are not specific to a particular set of theory-related procedures or techniques, and that the special potency of a distinctive approach, be it cognitive, behavioral, or other, is diluted when it is applied in comparative group studies to patients who are not homogenous with regard to their presenting pathology (Landman & Dawes, 1982; Luborsky, Singer, & Luborsky, 1975; Shapiro & Shapiro, 1982; Smith & Glass, 1977). These general findings from the research literature have contributed to the increasing number of self-professed "eclectic" therapists. If they practice an essentially casual, therapist-personal albeit nondoctrinaire form of eclecticism that does not vary very much in form or content from case to case, their clients are likely to be subject to as much Procrustean stress as the clients of therapists who hew to the theory and constructs of a particular school.

The Role of Theories

The foregoing has sketched the progress and current status of the major schools of psychotherapy. Psychoanalysis and its related psychodynamic offshoots no longer dominate. There is an active process of competition among the major schools, and there are two only partially related fields in which the competition is expressed. One of these is academic or intellectual and entails appraisal, claims, and counterclaims as to the formal adequacy of each theory qua theory, with attention to the constraints of logic and guided by the philosophy of science. The other field entails the work of investigators who through laboratory analogue experiments seek to test the validity of particular theoretical constructs and to distinguish necessary and sufficient elements from associated or incidental facilitative factors in the prescription of treatment procedures related to a specific theory. For example, research has sought to determine the *specific* influences on outcome of therapies using systematic desensitization or biofeedback techniques, as distinct from the general, deep muscle relaxation of the preparatory phases common to both of these approaches (Levin & Gross, 1985; McGlynn, Mealiea, & Landau, 1981; Silver & Blanchard, 1978). Also in this second field of competition is the work of clinician/ researchers who seek to compare the relative effectiveness (and sometimes the efficiency) of competing therapies. In these ways, theory plays an important heuristic role. As the confirming and disconfirming findings of careful research accumulate, there is a desirable deterrence to adoption of any single, overly simplified conceptualization of the nature of psychopathology, of the nature of corrective psychological processes, or of the *essential techniques* to alleviate psychological distress. The competitive ardor of school adherents is good when it leads to increased rigor in research design and especially when it seeks to parcel out the contribution of specific versus nonspecific sources of therapeutic impact. Given the spirit with which the cognition versus behavior competition has been pursued, there is a need always to be alert to the potential distortions introduced by experimenter bias (Rosenthal, 1966).

For the nonresearcher practitioner, theory has a different role. Basically, at the simplest level, it provides a rationale for what the therapist does and does not do in conducting therapy. Consider the following scenario: After one or two initial sessions, the client addresses the following questions to the therapist: "Tell me, what is your view of what is wrong with me? Why do I have the problems I have outlined? Do you believe you can help me, and why do you think I can be helped? How do you propose to help me? Why do you believe your proposed method is the best?" With more or less ease and immediacy (such queries, perhaps unfortunately, do not occur with high frequency), the therapist would respond, and in answering the client's questions, he or she would be providing a rationale for treatment. The response would entail at least implicit recognition that the client was seeking information as to diagnosis, prognosis, and treatment-of-choice. A silent observer of this brief but important client-therapist exchange would be able to judge that the therapist's rationale was consistent with one or another major theory—psychodynamic, client-centered, rational-emotive, behavioral, cognitive-behavioral—or that it encompassed selective elements from one or several of these. The observer would be able to conclude that the therapist was an orthodox practitioner of a particular school, or an "eclectic" whose formulation of the particular case was more or less reasonable. For the practitioner, the theory or rationale presents a working agenda that includes technique-goal combinations for a series of forward-moving sessions. Without such there may be no continuity of process, and each session may be tied flimsily if at all to those that preceded and those that may follow—if the patient does not become discouraged and terminate the session.

If, regardless of problem and technique, all therapy entails a learning process on the part of the client, the therapist's rationale can be likened to a course plan with each session to be approached with a tentative lesson plan predicated on the therapist's perception of where the client stands in the ongoing learning task. This analogy holds if the guiding rationale is cognitive, behavioral, or some other.

Theory has particular import for the neophyte at the beginning of his or her clinical work. On average this is a younger person who is likely to be immediately confronted by some older clients (example: the 28-year-old, single, recent graduate student assigned to treat an acutely distressed 50-year-old mother of three teenagers). The therapist has not accumulated the experience and sense-of-self maturity that will later bring a comfortable appreciation of preformed rapport in the role of "expert." Supervisors of neophyte therapists recognize the latter's concern with issues both of "what to do" and "why," and with "how" to do it. They are usually relatively less concerned with "why" than with "how." This is because the answers to former questions rest upon a foundation of theory provided in their graduate education. Until they have accumulated experience, their theoretical orientation is likely to be more orthodox than it will become later. Given the importance of theory in enabling the neophyte to *start,* the content of graduate school training is very important; it will be discussed in chapter 8.

There is no unanimity among authorities as to the place and importance of theory.

> There is no need for theory until and unless there are phenomena to explain. Limiting our consideration to psychotherapy, there is no reason for a theory of therapy until there are observable changes which call for explanation. Then a unifying theory is of help in explaining what has happened, and in providing testable hypotheses about future experiences. Thus, in the field of therapy the first requisite is a skill which produces an effective result. Through observation of the process and the result a parsimonious theory may be developed which is

projected into new experiences in order to be tested as to its adequacy. (Rogers, 1951) (p. 15)

In a similar view, London (1972) has observed:

> Whatever value theory may have for dictating laboratory procedures, therapeutic operations have been essentially seat-of-the pants affairs, and still are, because they address immediate practical problems that require solutions in fact, not in principle. . . . good technology always undermines bad theory. (p. 914)

Concerned about the possible meaning of the increased number of therapists who identify themselves as "eclectic," and with the possible weaknesses of atheoretical practice, Norcross (1985) has offered a thoughtful defense of theoretical orientations for clinicians in which certain "popular misconceptions" are addressed: (1) that theories are not related to actual practice; (2) that practitioners who identify with a particular theory are "dogmatic and antiquated"; (3) and that the choice of a theoretical orientation is largely inadvertent and circumstantial rather than deliberate and thoughtful. By contrast, arguing that the therapist's personal characteristics overweigh his or her theoretical orientation, Strupp (1978) has held that the latter is an "over-rated" variable, and Adams (1984) has decried the "pernicious effects" of theoretical allegiances in weakening the therapist's foundation in a scientific discipline. An extensive survey of research on the role of the therapist's orientation and its relation to such variables as actual therapy practices, other therapist attitudes and personality characteristics, and outcomes of therapy has been provided by Sundland (1977). These variables are neither highly nor consistently correlated.

The efforts to achieve a rational accommodation among very different conceptualizations of personality, of psychopathology, and of the therapeutic process will be examined in chapter 7.

The patient is not treated with or by a theory, in the sense of a patient receiving medication, but rather by a set of interventive methods that are derived from the therapist's theoretical orientation. To the degree that the patient is able to perceive the therapist's rationale, or has it explicitly outlined, the patient may derive comfort from the orderliness of the process as well as a means of organizing or reorganizing previously mysterious thoughts, feelings, or actions. Thus, the existence of some rationale for the patient-therapist interaction has been recognized as one of the nonspecific, common factors in all systems of psychotherapy, a factor that may have benefit for the patient independent of the ultimate validity of the particular theory favored by the therapist. More will be said about such common factors in chapter 5.

Potential Sources of Systematic Real Differences

The outline of the major schools of psychotherapy in the next chapter will point up the focal pathology addressed by each and the core process of the therapeutic effort as conceptualized by each. As Figure 6 and the related discussion will indicate, there is a natural overlap between schools, in theory and practice, and the nature of the persons engaged in therapeutic discourse prohibits the existence of hard boundaries between the schools, either in theory or technique. Put otherwise, there is reason to expect that experienced and expert therapists, regardless of their proclaimed allegiances, will behave reasonably and flexibly rather than as programmed technicians.

However, there are *potential* sources of real and systematic differences that could differentiate the therapeutic practices associated with the putatively different schools. As potential differences, these are greater in number than are usually exercised in the actual practices of the variously identified school adherents. In general, only a few are in fact systematically controlled in research studies aimed at comparison of either process or outcome of competing brands of therapy.

Frequency of Sessions

It has become the norm for most therapists, regardless of their orientation, to see clients once a week. This frequency may be increased at the beginning of therapy, as a function of the degree of distress expressed by the patient, and to speed up the early stages of getting the therapeutic process underway. Again, as termination is approached, there may be a gradual increase in the intersession interval. For most therapists and their patients, therapy is conducted on a once-per-week frequency. Only those practitioners who hew to an orthodox psychoanalytic protocol insist on seeing patients more frequently, three or five times per week; even those therapists frequently adapt to the patient's reality situation by establishing and maintaining the "psychoanalytic situation" with less frequent sessions. Thus, frequency of therapy sessions is not a factor that systematically differentiates the practices of the major schools, nor is the provision for posttreatment follow-up or "booster" sessions (Baker & Wilson, 1985).

Length of Sessions

As is the case for frequency of sessions, the duration of each therapy session is not a systematic difference among the schools. The 50-minute hour is the norm for therapists regardless of their theoretical persuasion. This standard appears to have evolved as a natural unit that satisfies the scheduling convenience of the therapist (and, perhaps also, the client) as well as possibly representing the upper limit of the fatigue factor, especially for the therapist (note the similarity to the traditional 45–50-minute classroom session). Again, within a particular therapist-client dyad, at some points in the case particular sessions may be either longer or shorter. It may be appropriate to have initial intake sessions of longer duration to provide adequate time for history taking, contracting, scheduling, and so on. Toward the end of treatment, shorter sessions may suffice for reinforcement, checks on progress, and "booster shots." However, the overwhelming majority of sessions, regardless of the therapist's theoretical orientation, are of 50-minute duration. The length of therapy sessions is a factor that could, but does not, systematically differ among the major orientations.

Duration of Therapy

The length of time over which a course of therapy is conducted is not a variable that contributes to a systematic difference among the major schools. There is an extensive literature on so-called short-term and so-called long-term therapies. There is no generally accepted definition of these terms. In general, the psychoanalytically oriented approaches tend to be long-term, that is, involving at least weekly sessions over a period of several months, and rarely less than a year or more. It is customary to refer to therapy as short-term if fewer than 30–35 treatment sessions are involved. The category of "brief" therapy is reserved generally for treatments of 10 or fewer sessions.

Usually behavior therapy is of shorter duration than that carried on within a psychodynamic framework. However, some clinicians have adapted the psychodynamic perspective to short-term, intensive psychotherapy (Davenloo, 1980; Malan, 1963; Mann, 1973; Sifneos, 1972; Strupp & Binder, 1984). Behavior therapy that achieves the initial goals of therapist and client is occasionally extended to provide attention to other, less behavioral, problem areas that come to light in the course of the initial treatment program.

It is a frequent practice, not consistently associated with any major school, for the initial contract to specify a small number of sessions that are to be exploratory in nature and at the conclusion of which it will be agreed as to whether therapy will be undertaken and as to the format that will be observed (see the discussion of contracting in chapter 6). In the case of psychoanalysis, this "tryout" period can be quite long, a matter of many months. The extent of such a prolonged preparatory phase must be questioned in light of the criteria that have been specified to select candidates for dynamically oriented short-term therapy, that is, the candidate must (1) be of greater than average intelligence; (2) have experienced at least one "meaningful relationship" with another person; (3) be able to appropriately express some emotion during the evaluative interview; (4) be able to communicate a specific, primary complaint; (5) be motivated to change (Sifneos, 1972).

Use of Extratherapy Materials

The major formulations of the therapy process could differ systematically with respect to prescriptions or tasks assigned to the patient for accomplishment between therapy sessions. Some patients are sometimes assigned specific readings. If these consist of a standard or fixed set of materials used by the therapist, this is an adjunctive therapy tool recognized as bibliotherapy (Shrank & Engels, 1981; Stevens & Pfost, 1982). Some therapists occasionally assign a specific reading. However, the use of literature is not a method that systematically differentiates the major schools.

The use of audiotapes has a high frequency but no consistent use by behavior therapists who may provide clients with tapes to be listened to between therapy sessions. In this context, the use of extratherapy "relaxation" tapes is frequent but not universal among behaviorally oriented therapists, especially in the context of desensitization approaches. Some therapists, regardless of their theoretical approach, occasionally tape sessions and request the client to review the tape of the session prior to their next visit. This can be a useful method to help the client to hear himself or herself as heard by others, and can improve the client's communication skills, at least in the context of the therapy session. As a specific technique, this use of audiotapes is not a systematic methodological difference among the major schools.

Use of Extratherapy Information

There are no explicit, systematic differences among the major schools with respect to the collection and use of information apart from that elicited in the therapy sessions. None of the major schools prescribe the use of particular standardized tests, questionnaires, inventories, surveys, or other instruments, either to be completed by the patient or administered by an assistant, as a source of information to be used in clarifying clinical impressions of the patient, extending the therapist's information base, suggesting therapy-of-choice, or checking on therapy progress. While the utilization of such sources of relevant data is more common among psychologists than psychiatrists or social workers, it is not a practice that systematically differentiates the practitioners of one school from those of another. It is notable that the client-centered approach of Carl Rogers explicitly *proscribes* the use of such extratherapy information sources on theoretical grounds (Rogers, 1942).

Given that psychotherapy is a clinical treatment of a clinical problem, given that we now recognize a few major choices among psychological treatment modalities and at least a few major categories of pathology with different rates of response to different interventions (Lazarus, 1958), it is remarkable that psychodiagnostic methods are not used uniformly by most therapists, and that use of such extratherapy information is not a systematic characteristic of any of the major approaches. Apart from the theoretically based exclusion by Rogersian therapists, the general resistance to or neglect of such information sources can hardly be explained by resort to logic or reference to the research literature. It is paradoxical that the use of such psychological data instruments is prominent in the clinical work and research of psychiatrists interested primarily in pharmacological treatments (for example, the use of depression and anxiety scales to evaluate the response to drugs) (Rounsaville, Klerman, & Weissman, 1981; Zuckerman, Prusoff, Weissman, & Padian, 1980).

Other Potential Differences

The above are major, obvious elements on which the major schools could manifest systematic differences. There are a few others. The Freudian school offers the prototype of "rules" for the client, for example, the "fundamental rule" (requirement) that the patient free-associate, and the restriction (expectation) that the patient make no major life changes while in treatment. Other such rules are imaginable, for example, that the client refrain from discussion of the therapy experiences outside of the therapy session, or by contrast, that the client be instructed to share the fact (and content) of therapy with significant persons. By and large the major schools of psychotherapy are not differentiable by the presence of and differences among such explicit rules for the conduct of either therapist or client.

Potential Sources of Nonsystematic Differences

The above section has sketched a number of variables that could, but in general do not, provide bases for systematic differences in the practices of therapists who are, at least by self-report, representatives of the ostensibly different schools of psychotherapy. There are school-to-school and practitioner-to-practitioner differences that are not of a systematic nature and yet that are of great significance in all studies that seek to establish evidence of relative effectiveness. In a word, these nonsystematic differences reside in the personality of the therapist (here it may be helpful to refer to figure 2, in chap. 2). While all elements of the therapist's personality may have some relevance and impact on his or her work, there are some that are of focal import. Among these are the element of experience, encompassing both formal graduate-level instruction, early supervised learning opportunities, and later accumulated case experience. The more senior the therapist, the greater the experience in clinical work, the greater the probability that therapeutic skills have been highly developed and that therapeutic wisdom has been garnered. It is sobering to find that a meta-analysis of the relationship of therapist experience to effectiveness concludes, "In no study to date has therapist experience been shown to be of great significance in determining outcome" (Stein & Lambert, 1984).

For the personality of the therapist to be uniform and consistent within the practice of any school or major approach, for therapist personality to be a stable, nonvariable element in the work of all representatives of a particular school, requires certain preconditions that are unlikely to be satisfied except in very limited degree. Training, both didactic and in supervised clinical experience, would have to be essentially monolithic. Therapists would have to be exposed, indeed immersed, in one and only one theory of pathology and therapy and its associated techniques. The earliest and closest supervised clinical work would have to be supervised exclusively by experienced, expert representatives of the particular school, and therapists would have to be honor bound not to let their later experiences induce them into experimental deviations from the prescribed protocol for conduct of therapy. (Further discussion of training models will be found in chap. 8.) Among the major schools, this degree of uniformity of the therapist's "personality" is sought, and to varying degrees achieved, only by psychoanalysis, as represented by the major training institutes. To a lesser, and less doctrinaire degree, something of the same degree of uniformity of the therapist's personality, at least as a therapist, is inculcated by the Rogersian client-centered school with its emphasis upon the importance of the therapist's congruence, warmth, and accepting attitude. The degree to which therapist attitudes (skills) of empathy, warmth, and genuineness can be trained and the extent to which they account for therapy outcomes has been a subject of extensive and, thus far inconclusive, research (Lambert, DeJulio, & Stein, 1978; Mitchell, Bozarth, & Krauft, 1977; Patterson, 1984).

In general, the personality characteristics of the therapist are a source of nonsystematic differences when the major schools are compared. This is a particular problem for comparative studies of the schools, especially if the important variable of experience is not controlled. Too many of such studies have utilized samples of neophyte school practitioners who have not yet achieved full expertise in the approach they presumably express. This may account in considerable measure for the general finding that all approaches are successful in about the same modest degree.

> While we have more assurance than before that there are efficacious influences present in traditional therapy, the weakness of the average effects implies that only some methods or some therapists are especially effective. It would be a task of high priority, therefore, to assiduously isolate and define those persons and methods that are most effective. Our faith is that whatever is powerful in traditional therapy resides in the work of a minority of its practitioners. It is probable that they account for whatever change is observable, rather than that all therapists cluster around a weak average effect. We assume then that there is little reason to reinforce or reassure the ordinary practitioner of psychotherapy, for we expect future research to show that his labors must be revised toward matching the behavior of a few successful peers who actually obtain most of the therapeutic results. It is also likely that observation of their styles will eventually yield completely new techniques focussed around the actual therapeutic agents that are identified and extracted from their practice. (Bergin, 1971) (p. 263)

Bergin's thesis is supported by the findings of a recent comparative analysis of four outcome studies conducted at four sites with a large complement of therapists and patients (Luborsky, et al., 1986). Treatment modalities included individual psychodynamic therapy, cognitive-behavioral therapy, and group therapy in several combinations for varying treatment periods. The researchers found that therapist-to-therapist success rates varied more than therapy-to-therapy differences, with no indication that therapist success was a function of kind of patient treated.

The problem of nonsystematic differences in variables that may have definite import for the effectiveness of therapy is related to the interest in common factors, dimensions that cannot be easily isolated and measured, let alone excluded, from the therapeutic process. These are discussed in Chapter 4.

References

Adams, H. E. (1984). The pernicious effects of theoretical orientation in clinical psychology. *Clinical Psychologist, 37,* 90–94.

American Psychiatric Association (1981). *Manual of psychiatric peer review: Part 2. Psychoanalytic peer review.* Washington, DC: Author.

Auld, F., Jr., & Murray, E. J. (1955). Content analysis studies of psychotherapy. *Psychological Bulletin, 52,* 377–395.

Baker, A. L., & Wilson, P. H. (1985). Cognitive-behavior therapy for depression: The effects of booster sessions on relapse. *Behavior Therapy, 16,* 335–344.

Bales, R. F. (1950). *Interaction process analysis.* Cambridge: Addison-Wesley.

Bandura, A. (1969). *Principles of behavior modification.* New York: Holt, Rinehart & Winston.

Bandura, A. (1977a). *Social learning theory.* Englewood Cliffs, NJ: Prentice-Hall.

Bandura, A. (1977b). Self-efficacy: Toward a unifying theory of behavior change. *Psychological Review, 84,* 191–213.

Beck, A. T. (1963). Thinking and depression. *Archives of General Psychiatry, 9,* 324–333.

Beck, A. T. (1970). Cognitive therapy: Nature and relation to behavior therapy. *Behavior Therapy, 1,* 184–200.

Beck, A. T. (1976). *Cognitive therapy and the emotional disorders.* New York: International Universities Press.

Beck, A. (1979). *Cognitive therapy of depression.* New York: Guilford Press.

Beidel, D. C., & Turner, S. M. (1986). A critique of the theoretical bases of cognitive-behavioral theories and therapies. *Clinical Psychology Review, 6,* 177–197.

Bergin, A. E. (1970). Cognitive therapy and behavior therapy: Foci for a multidimensional approach to treatment. *Behavior Therapy, 1,* 205–212.

Bergin, A. E. (1971). The evaluation of therapeutic outcomes. In A. E. Bergin & S. L. Garfield (Eds.) *Handbook of psychotherapy and behavior change,* Chapter 7. New York: John Wiley & Sons.

Brown J. (1987) A review of meta-analyses conducted on psychotherapy outcome research. *Clinical Psychology Review, 7,* 1–23.

Chessick, R. D. (1971). *Why psychotherapists fail.* New York: Science House.

Colby, K. M. (1951). *A primer for psychotherapists.* New York: Ronald Press.

Cole, D. R. (1982). *Helping: Origins and development of the major psychotherapies.* Toronto: Butterworths.

Corsini, R. J. (1981). *Handbook of innovative psychotherapies.* New York: John Wiley & Sons.

Davenloo, H. (1980). *Short-term dynamic psychotherapy.* New York: Jason Aronson.

Dimond, R. E., Havens, R. A., & Jones, A. C. (1978). A conceptual framework for the practice of prescriptive eclecticism in psychotherapy. *American Psychologist, 33,* 239–248.

Eagle, M. N. and Wolitsky, D. L. (1985). The current status of psychoanalysis. *Clinical Psychology Review, 5,* 259–269.

Elliott, R., Stiles, W. B., Mahrer, A. R., Hill, C. E., Friedlander, M. L. and Margison, F. R. (1987). Primary therapist response modes: comparison of six rating systems. *Journal of Consulting & Clinical Psychology, 55,* 218–223.

Ellis, A. (1955). New approaches to psychotherapy techniques. Brandon, VT: *Journal of Clinical Psychology.*

Ellis, A. (1958). Rational psychotherapy. *Journal of General Psychology, 59,* 35–49.

Ellis, A. (1962). *Reason and emotion in psychotherapy.* New York: Lyle Stuart.

Eysenck, H. J. (1952). The effects of psychotherapy: An evaluation. *Journal of Consulting Psychology, 16,* 319–324.

Feather, B. W. & Rhoads, J. M. (1972). Psychodynamic behavior therapy: II. Clinical aspects. *Archives of General Psychiatry, 26,* 503–511.

Fiedler, F. (1950a). The concept of an ideal therapeutic relationship. *Journal of Consulting Psychology, 14,* 239–245.

Fiedler, F. (1950b). A comparison of therapeutic relationships in psychoanalytic, non-directive, and Adlerian therapy. *Journal of Consulting Psychology, 14,* 436–445.

Fischer, S., & Greenberg, R. (1977). *The scientific credibility of Freud's theories and therapy.* New York: Basic Books.

Ford, D. H., & Urban, H. B. (1963). *Systems of psychotherapy: A comparative study.* New York: John Wiley & Sons.

Frank, J. D. (1961). *Persuasion and healing: A comparative study of psychotherapy.* Baltimore: The John Hopkins Press.

Frank, J. D. (1985). Further thoughts on the anti-demoralization hypothesis of psychotherapeutic effectiveness. *Integrated Psychiatry, 3,* 17–26.

Frankl, V. E. (1959). *Man's search for meaning: An introduction to logotherapy.* Boston: Beacon Press.

Freud, S. (1952). *An autobiographical study.* (Authorized trans. by J. Strachey). New York: W. W. Norton.

Garfield, S. L. (1980). *Psychotherapy: An eclectic approach.* New York: John Wiley & Sons.

Garfield, S. L. (1981). Psychotherapy: A 40-year appraisal. *American Psychologist, 36,* 174–183.

Garfield, S. L. (1982). Eclecticism and integration in psychotherapy, *Behavior Therapy, 13,* 610–623.

Garfield, S. L. & Kurtz, R. (1974). A survey of clinical psychologists: Characteristics, activities and orientations. *The Clinical Psychologist, 28,* 7–10.

Garfield, S. L. & Kurtz, R. (1977). A study of eclectic views. *Journal of Consulting Psychology, 45,* 78–83.

Glad, D. D. (1959). *Operational values in psychotherapy: A conceptual framework of interpersonality.* New York: Oxford University Press.

Glover, E. (1955). *The technique of psycho-analysis.* New York: International Universities Press.

Goldfried, M. R. (1982). On the history of therapeutic integration. *Behavior Therapy, 13,* 572–593.

Goshen, C. E. (1952). The original case material of psychoanalysis. *American Journal of Psychiatry, 108,* 829–834.

Greenberg, L. S. & Safran, J. D. (1987) *Emotion in psychotherapy: affect, cognition and the process of change.* New York: The Guilford Press.

Grossberg, J. M. (1964). Behavior therapy: A review. *Psychological Bulletin, 62,* 73–88.

Harper, R. A. (1959). *Psychoanalysis and psychotherapy: 36 systems.* Englewood Cliffs, NJ: Prentice-Hall.

Henry, W. E., Sims, J. H., & Spray, S. L. (1971). *The fifth profession*. San Francisco: Jossey-Bass.

Henry, W. E., Sims, J. N., & Spray, S. L. (1973). *Public and private lives of psychotherapists*. San Francisco: Josey-Bass.

Herink, R. (Ed.). (1980). *The psychotherapy handbook: The A to Z guide to more than 250 different therapies in use today*. New York: New American Library.

Howard, K. I., Orlinsky, D. E., & Trattner, J. H. (1970). Therapist orientation and patient experience in psychotherapy. *Journal of Counseling Psychology, 17*, 263–270.

Jones, M. C. (1924). Elimination of children's fears. *Journal of Experimental Psychology, 7*, 382.

Kanner, M., & Glenn, J. (1980). *Freud and his patients*. New York: Jason Aronson.

Kazdin, A. E. (1982). Sympton substitution, generalization, and response covariation: Implications for psychotherapy outcome. *Psychological Bulletin, 91*, 349–365.

Kazdin, A. E. (1985). The role of meta-analysis in the evaluation of psychotherapy. *Clinical Psychology Review, 5*, 49–61.

Kendall, P. C. (1982). Integration: Behavior therapy and other schools of thought. *Behavior Therapy, 13*, 559–571.

Kendall, P. C., & Hollon, S. D. (Eds.). (1979). *Cognitive-behavioral Interventions: Theory, research, and procedures*. New York: Academic Press.

Kline, P. (1981). *Fact and fantasy in Freudian theory* (2nd ed.). London: Methuen.

Lambert, M. J., DeJulio, S. S., & Stein, D. M. (1978). Therapist interpersonal skills: Process, outcome, methodological considerations and recommendations for future research. *Psychological Bulletin, 85*, 467–489.

Landman, J. T., & Dawes, R. M. (1982). Psychotherapy outcome: Smith and Glass' conclusions stand up under scrutiny. *American Psychologist, 37*, 504–516.

Lazarus, A. A. (1958). New methods in psychotherapy: A core study. *South African Medical Journal, 32*, 660–664.

Lazarus, A. A. (1981). *The practice of multimodal psychotherapy*. New York: McGraw-Hill.

Levin, R. B., & Gross, A. M. (1985). The role of relaxation in systematic desensitization. *Behavior Research & Therapy, 23*, 187–196.

Lieberman, M. A., Yalom, I. D., & Miles, M. B. (1973). *Encounter groups: First facts*. New York: Basic Books.

Lindsley, O. R., Skinner, B. F., & Solomon, H. C. (1953). *Studies in behavior therapy*. Waltham, MS: Metropolitan State Hospital, Status Report 1.

London, P. (1964). *The modes and morals of psychotherapy*. New York: Holt, Rinehart & Winston.

London, P. (1972). The end of ideology in behavior modification. *American Psychologist, 27*, 913–920.

Luborsky, L., Crits-Christoph, P., McLellan, P., Woody, G., Piper, W., Liberman, B., Imber, S. & Pilkonis, P. (1986). Do therapists vary much in their success? Findings from four outcome studies. *American Journal of Orthopsychiatry, 56*, 501–512.

Luborsky, L., Mellon, J., van Ravenswaay, P., Childress, A. R., Cohen, K. D., Hole, A. V., Crits-Shristoph, P., Levine, F. J., & Alexander, K. (1985). A verification of Freud's grandest clinical hypothesis: The transference. *Clinical Psychology Review, 5*, 231–246.

Luborsky, L., Singer, B. & Luborsky, L. (1975). Comparative studies of psychotherapists: Is it true that "everyone has won and all must have prizes?" *Archives of General Psychiatry, 32,* 995–1008.

Mackey, R. A. (1985). *Ego psychology and clinical practice.* New York: Gardner Press.

Malan, D. H. (1963). *A study of brief psychotherapy.* Philadelphia: J. B. Lippincott Co.

Mann, J. (1973). *Time-limited psychotherapy.* Cambridge: Harvard University Press.

Marsden, G. (1971). Content-analysis studies of psychotherapy: 1954 through 1968. Chapter 10 in Bergin, A. E. & Garfield, S. L. (eds) *Handbook of psychotherapy and behavior change.* New York: John Wiley & Sons.

McCrary, J. L. (1955). *Six approaches to psychotherapy.* New York: Dryden Press.

McGlynn, F. D., Mealiea, W. L., & Landau, D. L. (1981). The current status of systematic desensitization. *Clinical Psychology Review, 1,* 149–171.

Meichenbaum, D. H. (1974). *Cognitive behavior modification.* Morristown, NJ: General Learning.

Meichenbaum, D. H. (1979). Cognitive-behavior modification: An integrative approach. New York: Plenum Press.

Messer, S. B., & Winokur, M. (1980). Some limits to the integration of psychoanalytic and behavior therapy. *American Psychologist, 35,* 818–827.

Mitchell, K. M., Bozarth, J. D., & Krauft, C. C. (1977). A reappraisal of the therapeutic effectiveness of accurate empathy, nonpossessive warmth and genuineness. In A. S. Gurman, & A. M. Razin (Eds.), *Effective psychotherapy: A handbook of research.* New York: Pergamon Press.

Montgomery, G., & Crowder, J. (1972). The sympton substitution hypothesis and the evidence. *Psychotherapy: Theory, Research and Practice, 9,* 98–102.

Norcross, J. C. (1985). In defense of theoretical orientations for clinicians. *The Clinical Psychologist, 38,* 13–17.

Norcross, J. C., & Prochaska, J. O. (1983). Clinicians' theoretical orientations: Selection, utilization, and efficacy. *Professional Psychology: Research and Practice, 14,* 197–208.

Norcross, J. C., & Wogan, M. (1983). American psychotherapists of diverse persuasions: Characteristics, theories, practices and clients. *Professional Psychology: Research and Practice, 14,* 529–539.

Patterson, C. H. (1984). Empathy, warmth, and genuiness in psychotherapy: A review of reviews. *Psychotherapy, 21,* 431–438.

Porter, E. H., Jr. (1943). The development and evaluation of a measure of counseling interview procedures. *Education and Psychological Measurement, 3,* 215–238.

Rhoads, J. M. (1981). The integration of behavior therapy and psychoanalytic theory. *Journal of Psychiatric Treatment and Evaluation, 3,* 18–21.

Rogers, C. R. (1942). *Counseling and psychotherapy.* Boston: Houghton Mifflin.

Rogers, C. R. (1951). *Client-centered therapy: Its current practice, implications, and theory.* Boston: Houghton Mifflin.

Rogers, C. R. (1957). The necessary and sufficient conditions of therapeutic personality change. *Journal of Consulting Psychology, 21,* 95–103.

Rosenthal, R. (1966). *Experimenter effects in behavioral research.* New York: Appleton, Century.

Rounsaville, B. J., Klerman, G. L., & Weissman, M. M. (1981). Do psychotherapy and pharmacotherapy for depression conflict? *Archives of General Psychiatry, 38*, 24–29.

Russell, P. L., & Brandsma, J. M. (1974). A theoretical and empirical integration of the rational-emotive and classical conditioning theories. *Journal of Consulting and Clinical Psychology, 42*, 389–397.

Russell, R. L. & Stiles, W. B. (1979) Categories for classifying language in psychotherapy. *Psychological Bulletin, 86*, 404–419.

Salter, A. (1950). *Conditioned reflex therapy*. New York: Creative Age Press.

Schofield, W. (1966). Clinical and counseling psychology: Some perspectives. *American Psychologist, 21*, 122–131.

Schwartz, R. M. (1982). Cognitive-behavior modification: A conceptual review. *Clinical Psychology Review, 2*, 267–293.

Shapiro, M. B. (1957). Experimental method in the psychological description of the individual psychiatric patient. *International Journal of Social Psychiatry, 3*, 89–102.

Shapiro, D. A., & Shapiro, D. (1982). Meta-analysis of comparative therapy outcome studies: A replication and refinement. *Psychological Bulletin, 92*, 581–604.

Shrank, F. A., & Engels, D. W. (1981). Bibliotherapy as a counseling adjunct: Research findings. *Personnel & Guidance Journal, 60*, 143–147.

Sifneos, P. (1972). *Short-term psychotherapy and emotional crisis*. Cambridge: Harvard University Press.

Silver, B. V., & Blanchard, E. B. (1978). Biofeedback and relaxation training in the treatment of psychological disorders: Or are the machines really necessary? *Journal of Behavioral Medicine, l*, 217–239.

Smith, M. L., & Glass, G. V. (1977). Meta-analysis of psychotherapy outcome studies. *American Psychologist, 32*, 752–760.

Snyder, W. U. (1945). An investigation of the nature of non-directive psychotherapy. *Journal of General Psychology, 33*, 193–223.

Spiegler, M. D. (1983). *Contemporary behavioral therapy*. Palo Alto, CA: Mayfield Publishing.

Stein, D. M., & Lambert, M. J. (1984). On the relationship between therapist experience and psychotherapy outcome. *Clinical Psychology Review, 4*, 127–142.

Stevens, M. J., & Pfost, K. S. (1982). Bibliotherapy: Medicine for the soul? *Psychology: A Quarterly Journal of Human Behavior, 19*, 21–25.

Strupp, H. H. (1955a). An objective comparison of Rogerian and psychoanalytic techniques. *Journal of Consulting Psychology, 19*, 1–7.

Strupp, H. H. (1955b). Psychotherapeutic techniques, professional affiliation, and experience level. *Journal of Consulting Psychology, 19*, 97–102.

Strupp, H. H. (1960). *Psychotherapists in action*. New York: Grune & Stratton.

Strupp, H. H. (1978). The therapist's theoretical orientation: An overrated variable. *Psychotherapy: Theory, Research and Practice, 15*, 314–317.

Strupp, H. H., & Binder, J. (1984). *Psychotherapy in a new key: A guide to time-limited dynamic psychotherapy*. New York: Basic Books.

Strupp, H. H., Fox, R. E., & Lessler, K. (1969). *Patients view their psychotherapists*. Baltimore: The Johns Hopkins Press.

Sundland, D. M. (1977). Theoretical orientations of psychotherapists. In A. S. Gurman & A. M. Razin (Eds.), *Effective psychotherapy: A handbook of research*. New York: Pergamon Press.

Sundland, D. M., & Barker, E. N. (1962). The orientation of psychotherapists. *Journal of Consulting Psychology, 26,* 201–212.

Thorne, F. C. (1961). *Clinical judgment: A study of clinical errors.* Brandon, VT: Journal of Clinical Psychology.

Watson, J. B., & Rayner, P. (1920). Conditioned emotional reactions. *Journal of Experimental Psychology, 3,* 1.

Whitaker, C. A. (1972). A longitudinal view of therapy styles where N = 1. *Family Process, 11,* 13–15.

Wilson, G. T., & Evans, I. M. (1977). The therapist-client relationship in behavior therapy. In A. S. Gurman & A. M. Razin (Eds.), *Effective psychotherapy: A research handbook.* New York: Pergamon Press.

Wolberg, L. R. (1954). *The technique of psychotherapy.* New York: Grune & Stratton.

Wolpe, J. (1958). *Psychotherapy by reciprocal inhibition.* Stanford, CA: Stanford University Press.

Wolpe, J. (1961). The prognosis in unpsychoanalyzed recovery from neurosis. *American Journal of Psychiatry, 118,* 35–39.

Wolpe, J. (1969). *The practice of behavior therapy.* New York: Pergamon Press.

Yates, A. J. (1958). Symptoms and symptom substitution. *Psychological Review, 65,* 371–374.

Zajonc, R. B. (1980). Feeling and thinking: Preferences need no inferences. *American Psychologist, 35,* 151–175.

Zajonc, R. B. (1984). On the primacy of affect. *American Psychologist, 39,* 117–123.

Zuckerman, D. M., Prusoff, B. A., Weissman, M. M., & Padian, N. S. (1980). Personality as a predictor of psychotherapy and pharmacotherapy outcome for depressed outpatients. *Journal of Consulting and Clinical Psychology, 48,* 730–735.

5

The Therapy-of-Choice

The Meaning of the Concept

For the appropriately trained psychotherapist who has kept informed of the evolution of major therapies and the myriad of reputedly effective techniques, each new case *should* present two primary questions: What is the client's basic problem, and what treatment method is most applicable? These questions do not arise if the therapist is a consistently orthodox practitioner whose treatment of every case is predicated on a single theory of the pathology-symptom-intervention complex. Nor do the questions occur to therapists who practice a catch-as-catch-can therapy, an eclecticism that represents their amalgamation of theory and technique selected from several schools, and salted perhaps with favorite ploys that may have evolved out of particular experiences.

"The paradox of no differential effectiveness despite obvious technical diversity challenges some cherished beliefs of practitioners and underlines our comparative ignorance as to the mechanisms whereby psychotherapies achieve their effects" (Stiles, Shapiro, & Elliott, 1986). Given the plethora of therapeutic approaches described in the literature, and given the *apparently* equal effectiveness of those major approaches that have been placed in contention, a therapist may be forgiven perhaps for not conscientiously pursuing a thoughtfully differentiated program of intervention that addresses the needs of clients with an appropriately individualized therapy program. Therapists who do not practice differential therapies, or who do not screen out applicants inappropriate for their particular approach, may be relying without awareness, and with limited effectiveness, on "placebo" effects to benefit patients.

A demonstration of apparently equal effectiveness (e.g., freedom from symptoms or restored morale upon completion of therapy) does not address the question of efficiency, that is, the amount of time or effort required before a given level of therapeutic benefit is reached. On the latter point, a meta-analysis of 15 studies that reported on the number of psychotherapy patients judged to be improved (self-ratings by patients, ratings by therapist, or ratings by chart review) at various points in the treatment course yielded pertinent findings (Howard, Kopta, Krause, Orlinsky, 1986). Across all studies, an average of slightly more than half of all patients were "improved" after as few as 8 sessions; this figure increased to nearly three-fourths of patients at 26 sessions. For patients continuing in treatment for another 26 sessions, there was a gain of less than 10% in the number judged improved. For patients who were treated for over 100 sessions, there was still an average of 10% considered to be unimproved. Over the 15 studies surveyed, the upper limit on the number of therapy sessions per patients ranged from a low of 20 to a high of 200. These 15 studies involved therapists whose "orientations were generally psychodynamic or interpersonal." It is of particular interest to note that different rates of response were found for patients grouped by major diagnostic categories. Chart-based ratings of improvement showed that at the 26–session point, 86% of "anxiety" patients were improved; 73% of "depressives," and only 38% of "borderline-psychotic" patients.

Other surveys have suggested a generally positive relationship between the amount of therapy received and the amount of benefit experienced by the patients, the greater the number of treatment sessions the greater the patient's improvement (Orlinsky & Howard, 1978). Such a relationship conforms to expectation; if an intervention is therapeutically potent, the more a client receives, the greater should be the response. However, such findings must be accepted with considerable reservation; the longer a treatment continues, the greater the investment that both therapist and patient have in it and the more loath each will be to acknowledge there has been little if any "surplus" benefit. Also, efficiency and effectiveness must be considered in the light of a possible "trade-off" balance. Degree of improvement at termination, or number of patients improved at the end of therapy, tells a partial story. Ellis (1980) maintains that efficient therapy is concerned with the maintenance of therapeutic gains and attends to prevention of future problems. Long-term follow-up is required to determine if therapeutic gains are maintained. Depending on the nature of the client's problem, efficient short-term therapy may suffice. With some problems, less "efficient" therapy may lead to better long-term stability of client changes. An analysis of follow-up studies indicates that patients who show positive changes upon completion of treatment tend generally to maintain their gains (Nicholson & Berman, 1983).

For the therapist who is neither a "purist" nor an "eclectic" (and neither stance is supported by current knowledge), each new client requires a decision as to the "therapy-of-choice." Therapy-of-choice is a concept that arose in medicine and has two possible meanings: (1) For a given condition, there is one and only one procedure with established evidence of likely effectiveness. Or (2), for a given condition, there may be several interventions that are appropriate, but they differ in potency, in cost, in number and significance of potential side effects, and other factors. When the latter condition holds, the accumulated medical literature may communicate a consensus as to either the treatment-of-choice or the order in which alternative methods should be tried. With recently discovered pathologies, or with several relatively new treatments, the practitioner has to make a judgment. In some instances, the physician recognizes that the treatment is not a cure or correction of the underlying pathology but rather an important medium of palliation. It is his or her responsibility to see to it that the patient's expectations of the prescription are informed and realistic.

As in medicine, psychotherapy must begin with a careful assessment. The client's presenting problem (symptoms or complaints) are only part of this. A thorough evaluation will include history of the disturbance, including any previous episodes and treatment; overview of the client's present life situation with respect to family, other personal relationships, work or school; and a personal history of greater or lesser specificity depending on the nature of the current problem. The therapist should determine whether the client's distress is of acute or chronic nature and what social resources are present. Much if not all of this basic information can be obtained in the initial, "intake" interview. The therapist may confirm (or disconfirm) initial, clinical impressions by one or more psychological tests.

With all of this information at hand, the therapist is enabled to make a decision as to whether to accept the client for treatment and, if so, which therapeutic approach to use. This decision will sometimes be directed by the client's need for immediate symptomatic relief; for example, the radio broadcaster with an acute, hysterical aphonia is not a candidate for long-term, psychodynamic therapy. In other cases, with a clear history of long-standing overuse of repression and denial, the therapist may deliberately choose to relatively ignore the client's presenting complaints of tension headaches (recognizing nevertheless that the symptoms would probably respond quickly to relaxation training, with or without biofeedback) and focus on the client's chronic pattern of inadequate or inappropriate coping methods.

Selection of a Focal Therapy

When a true crisis situation is not present and when the patient's complaints do not demand immediate relief, the therapist has the opportunity and the responsibility to select a mode of intervention that addresses the nature of the pathology that is causing the client's distress.

Figure 6 outlines the major modes of psychotherapy as represented by schools that have evolved out of clinical experience with patients who present different core pathologies and reflects the evolution of schools as discussed in chapter 4. The "common designations" will be familiar to most therapists. The "core processes" are identified by special terms that are oversimplifications but serve as useful mnemonics in maintaining an awareness of essential differences in the conduct of therapy. The brackets imply overlap between adjacent approaches and suggest the nonexistence of "pure" treatments. The chart provides a very general guide to the "treatment-of-choice." Thus, interpretation is not the treatment-of-choice for specific phobias or other disorders in which behavior is the primary pathology to be addressed. Instigation (*Webster's:* "to goad; to urge forward; to set on; provoke; incite") is not the appropriate treatment method for individuals' whose overt behavior is adaptive but who suffer internal conflict.

The interpretive process is integral in all of those therapies that are basically psychodynamic, that emphasize "uncovering," and whose goal is the patient's achievement of "insight." Characteristically these are intensive treatments as defined both by the frequency of treatment sessions and the duration of therapy over time. The dynamics of the transference neurosis and its resolution may or may not be a necessary part of such therapy when it is successful. However, the intensity of the therapist-client relationship is crucial and may dictate the amount of time required for clients to be fully trusting of the therapist and, in such trust, able perhaps for the first time to move toward an undistorted view of themselves and of their relationship with others.

FIGURE 6

Major Modes of Psychotherapeutic Intervention and their Associated Pathologies

Common Designation	Core Process	Core Pathology
Psychodynamic	Interpretation	Ideational
Counseling	Instruction	Behavioral
Behavior Therapy	Instigation	Situational
Supportive	Inspiration	

The duration of orthodox psychoanalytic therapy (psychoanalysis) is not critical to the active utilization of certain psychodynamic concepts. Beginning with the innovations presented by Alexander and French (1946) and augmented by the contributions of Davenloo (1980), Malan (1963), Mann (1973), Sifneos (1972), and others, it has been demonstrated that the essential processes of psychodynamic therapy can be utilized in short-term and time-limited therapy.

The term *ideational* is used to emphasize that the core problem is the patient's long-standing acceptance of a relatively fixed set of fallacious ideas. Many severely psychologically incapacitated or handicapped persons persist in basically delusional thoughts (fixed, false ideas that are contrary to fact and resistant to evidence and argument); these usually include very negative self-concepts. Their fallacious ideas about their unworthiness, unattractiveness, inability (or all of these) results from accumulated experiences for which the sensitizing initiation may have arisen in the parent-child relationship, fostering the primary, implicit premise: "My mother (father, parents) apparently did not love me; ergo, there is something basically wrong with me."

The core process of instruction is applicable when the symptoms and discomfort of the client rest in sizable measure not upon dynamically determined introjects but rather upon erroneous conceptions of self and others that stem from limited experience or overgeneralization from specific experiences, restricted educational opportunities in the broad sense, lack of specific, objective information about abilities and aptitudes or correctible deficiencies, and uncertainty about what is "normal." Instructional therapies (education about self) relate to the need for more accurate self-understanding along dimensions other than insight into dynamics. When the client's deficiencies of knowledge of self and knowledge of others is accompanied, as it frequently is, by pervasive insecurity and lack of confidence, the process entails more than the techniques of educational and vocational counseling. It is personal counseling in a much broader sense and its differentiation from psychotherapy is frequently ambiguous, as noted in chapter 4.

The term *instigation* is useful to denote the active role of the therapist in influencing the patient's level of motivation and overt patterns of undesirable behavior or inhibition of action.[1] The therapist is active in designing specific learning (relearning) situations for the patient. He or she functions as coach and critic, model and manipulator. Processes of deconditioning and/or reconditioning are designed and monitored. The therapist's effectiveness as an instigator requires a knowledge of techniques and procedures, and a background of scientific information very different from those entailed in the therapies of interpretation or instruction.

The therapy of inspiration is indicated when the client's distress, and especially demoralization, arises from situational stressors. Perhaps the client is required to live in circumstances that cannot be altered. It may be that there are immutable reality factors in the client's situation, or that there are value commitments that prohibit escape from a demoralizing life situation. Therapy cannot manipulate the environmental conditions that provide a crucial situational matrix for the client's suffering, nor does it attempt to change his or her value structure. Rather, the therapist provides an opportunity for catharsis and for a search for those aspects of self and situation from which some satisfaction or comfort may be derived. Chronic physical illness or disability in the patient, or the need to sacrifice personal desires in the interest of the welfare of others for whom the patient accepts responsibility, may not permit of anything more than a degree of amelioration afforded by the therapist's empathic understanding and encouragement to go on. These processes of therapy are usually labeled "supportive" and commonly denigrated as not being "real" therapy. Amelioration of the distress of the situationally pressured or deprived individual is important, not simply in the interests of humaneness, but with a view to prevention of total demoralization and severe personality disruption. It is an important part of the total domain of psychotherapy, and its most effective application requires skills, training, and knowledge just as do the so-called deeper approaches (Werman, 1984). It is a reflection, at least in part, of attitudinal biases of professionals that inspiration, although recognized as a normal and not uncommon human experience, has received very little study as to its psychological dimensions and potency as a long-range influence on human behavior. While inspiration is generally an unexpected, spontaneous experience, as a human event it has psychological dimensions that should be specifiable. With its clear impact on motivation, knowledge of how to elicit inspiration in the demoralized patient has an obvious place in psychotherapy. Neglect of inspiration as a research topic undoubtedly reflects its common connotation as relating vaguely to "religion." This is unfortunate (Schofield, 1979).

The Therapist as General Practitioner

The concept of therapies "of choice," as outlined above, and their functional relationship to differential pathologies, carries implications for the therapist who wishes to practice as a generalist and does not wish to limit his or her caseload by specializing in one mode of therapy, thus serving primarily one type of patient (i.e., one form of psychopathology). The general psychotherapist, who may limit practice only in terms of major age groupings (e.g., children, adolescents, or adults), must be familiar with theory of at least three major approaches and have developed skill in the consistent application of the basic techniques and tactics associated with the respective theoretical formulations of psychopathology. To practice differential psychotherapy effectively, the general therapist must be a capable diagnostician, not in the sense of applying the nomenclature of the official diagnostic manual, but rather in discerning, case by case, the nature of the core pathology. It is relevant to note that *core* as used here with respect to pathology connotes centrality, primacy, and causality—not unitary purity in the sense that the other dimensions of personality are unaffected. (See the discussion of the thought-action-affect complex in chap. 3) This view of the meaning of a general practice in psychotherapy carries special implications for the structure and content of the graduate education of the psychotherapist; these will be discussed in chapter 8. The advantages to the therapist who is a one-school specialist is not without risks. "Therapists who rely on one technique will be unable to treat many patients; some may be hurt because of inappropriate treatment . . . and specific indications for a therapeutic procedure will be obfuscated" (Shapiro, 1971) (p. 463). The therapist who elects to specialize is not freed of the need to be skilled in differential diagnosis along the dimensions sketched in figure 6, for he or she will be required to recognize those cases to be referred to a generalist or to therapists with other foci of specialization. The psychodynamicist needs to recognize the relevance of a behavioral approach to some cases just as the behaviorist has to recognize the relevance of counseling or psychotherapy in cases without a focal behavioral disorder.

Basic Cautions

The present knowledge about the effectiveness of psychotherapy and the suggested shift of many therapists toward "eclectic" practice has serious implications. If it is accepted as true that all modes of therapy have essentially the same and modest degree of effectiveness, there is encouragement to the therapist to be more casual, or at least less critical, of his or her work than is in the best interest of the client. If it is thought that psychotherapy has only an average limited potential to accomplish good results, it may be believed that it is unlikely to cause any harm. In other words, there may be a general notion that the *worst* outcome will be that the patient achieves no benefit and is *unchanged*. However, research findings suggest that some individuals are worse after treatment, that is, that the process of treatment exacerbates their problem (Bergin, 1963, 1966; Lambert, Bergin, & Collins, 1977; Franks & Mays, 1980; Grunebaum, 1986; Mays & Franks 1985; Strupp, Hadley, & Gomes-Schwartz,

1977). Such findings can provide paradoxical support for the belief that psychotherapy is more than an innocuous ritual, but it imposes a necessity that the therapist take care that the therapeutic endeavor is not itself pathogenic. *Primum non nocere* is a cardinal rule for all the healing arts—above all, cause no harm.

The possibility for the psychotherapist to cause injury arises in several ways (Zilbergeld, 1986). Obviously, a faulty assessment of pathology can result in use of a treatment method that is inappropriate. This will mean that the client derives no benefit, or responds much more slowly than should be the case and is delayed in receiving more efficient treatment. Furthermore, failure to achieve change may cause further demoralization as the client interprets it to mean that his or her condition is hopeless. There is injury also if therapy is pursued in the absence of pathology; one study suggests that as many as 10% of therapy clients seen in private practice are evaluated as "relatively healthy" (Henry, Sims & Spray, 1973).

Perhaps the most frequent source of potential harm to the patient is overtreatment. Holding a patient in treatment beyond the point of optimal and likely benefit can be the result of one or more of several factors:

1. *Overpathologizing.* Mental health professionals, perhaps as a result of much clinical training, often develop a chronic "professional paranoia," that is, the mind-set that there is always "more than meets the eye," that the client is really "sicker" than is suggested by the presenting picture and that the client will require more rather than less treatment. This source of overtreatment is more likely if the assessment process focuses almost exclusively on the patient's symptoms and deficits and fails to similarly appraise his or her strengths and assets. This can result in failure to observe the general rule that conservative approaches should always be tried before resorting to more complex and costly procedures.

2. *Conversion of pathology.* This is related to overpathologizing. It occurs when the therapist refuses to accept the patient's complaint and desire for relief but insists on treating "what is really wrong." Sometimes this is a valid clinical judgement, but it can be a failure to respect the patient's accurate self-appraisal because it does not fit the therapist's preferred mode of treatment (see the discussion in chapter 3, and chapter 4).

3. *Furor therapeuticus.* This is the uncritical, frequently naive enthusiasm, especially of the less experienced therapist, who believes that "everyone can be helped" and who is unaware or unaccepting of the poor response of certain psychological disorders to psychotherapy. The experienced therapist is not immune to the arousal of augmented therapeutic

fervor when working with a YAVIS client—one who is young, attractive, verbal, intelligent and successful (Schofield, 1986).

4. *Ambiguity of goals.* Unnecessarily prolonged treatment can result when there is no clear understanding, early on, about what the client wishes therapy to accomplish. This is not a problem when the client is explicit about desired changes in patterns of behavior. It is a serious problem when the therapist accepts vague complaints of "lack of confidence," "tension," "anxiety," etc. Without explicit, nonambiguous goals, neither therapist nor client can or will measure whether therapy is affecting a change.

5. *Neglect of situational factors.* If the therapist is not attentive to the acute versus chronic status of the patient's distress, and does not differentiate reactive from endogenous responses, there will be failure to allow for self-limiting (recovery) "spontaneous" potentials, and therapy may be unduly prolonged.

6. *Neglect of social resources.* Some individuals with serious psychological distress are lacking, circumstantially or by a pattern of severe self-determined isolation, the social resources by which the work of therapy can be extended and amplified. However, the isolation is frequently a result of the client's deliberate withdrawal, self-containment, or "self-encapsulation." Failure of the therapist to attend to the client's social resources and to encourage utilization of them to generalize from the relationship of therapy can unnecessarily prolong the course of treatment. The therapist should be alert also to the treatment-potentiating benefits of the client's referral for group therapy or to an appropriate "self-help" group (Hurvitz, 1970).

7. *Failure to use adjunctive therapies.* Among applicants for psychotherapy, those with predominant presenting symptomatology of anxiety or depression are prime candidates for psychological intervention. However, in some cases, at initial contact, the severity of symptoms may be such as to preclude, or at least significantly delay, effective utilization of therapeutic discourse. This is particularly likely to be the case with endogenous (i.e., nonneurotic or nonreactive) depressions or excitement. It is a serious professional error for the psychotherapist to fail to promptly assist the patient toward consultation with a physician so that the immobilizing distress can be relieved sufficiently with appropriate medication, and so that the patient can become enabled to participate meaningfully in the work of psychotherapy. The therapist needs to have at least basic knowledge of the major psychotropic drugs so as to provide a suitable consultative referral to the patient's physician or to a psychiatrist with whom the psychotherapist has an established professional relationship (Byrne & Stern, 1981). Pointing out that Freud was optimistic about future possibili-

ties for pharmacotherapy, Karasu (1982) outlined six sources of resistance to the development of guidelines for simultaneous, intermittent, or sequential use of drugs with psychotherapy. Uhlenhuth, Lysman, & Covi (1963) proposed four models for the possible interactive effects of drugs with psychotherapy (addition, potentiation, inhibition, and reciprocation) and concluded that whether and how to combine psychotherapy and drugs is best determined by the factors of diagnosis, severity, duration, and change of treatment. "It would be negligent, if not criminal for a therapist to withhold lithium and offer nothing but a warm, supportive, and empathic relationship when consulted by someone with a manic-depressive illness" (Lazarus, 1980).

Depression has been a particular focus for research on the comparative effectiveness of psychotherapy, drug therapy, and combined therapies. (Holder, 1986) From a review of these studies, Beckham and Leber (1985) concluded: "The evidence thus far suggests that neither psychotherapy nor pharmacotherapy has any clear superiority in treating outpatient depression. There are indications that medications may be a necessary component of treatment for melancholic depressions, and that patients receiving psychotherapy tend to have better social adjustment." (p 336) (For a review of biochemical theories of depression in relation to the action of antidepressants, see McNeal & Cimbolic, 1986). The notion that chemotherapy and psychotherapy are antagonistic and that combined treatments reduce the potential effectiveness of each mode alone is not supported. (Beck, Hollon, Young, Bedrosian, & Budenz, 1981; Beitman & Klerman, 1984; Conte, Plutenik, Wildtkarazu, 1986; Rounsaville, Klerman & Weissman, 1981)

Schizophrenia has been less frequently examined as to relative response to psychotherapy versus drug treatment. Psychotherapy has not been accepted generally as a primary treatment modality for this psychosis. However, one study has concluded that schizophrenics receiving intensive psychotherapy (an average of 70 sessions) responded better on a number of criteria than those patients treated with medication (Karon & Van denBos, 1981). This finding is clearly at odds with the often-cited research of May (1968) and May, Tuma, and Dixon (1981).

For the nonmedical psychotherapist to undertake sole treatment of a patient with major (i.e., psychotic) affective or cognitive disorder (i.e., other than neurotic distortions) is counterindicated. Adequate professional responsibility for such patients requires that the psychotherapist refer them to a psychiatrist for diagnostic consultation and consideration of possible adjunctive medication and/or hospitalization.

The question of adjunctive medication needs to be considered in light of the finding that, across a wide variety of health complaints, female patients more frequently receive drug prescriptions from physicians than do males with comparable health problems (Verbrugge & Steiner, 1985). The difference is particularly notable for patients with diagnoses of "neurosis." This finding has complex psychosocial implications and does not tell us whether the difference relects a greater readiness of female patients to elicit and accept prescriptions, a greater physician readiness to prescribe for the female patient, or, as is likely, an interactive phenomenon. It does suggest, however the possibility that a significant number of appropriate candidates for psychotherapy who consult physicians may be casually medicated rather than referred to a psychotherapist. The ready access of the general physician to "drug company education" increases the probability of this shortstopping action.

8. *"You doctor—me patient."* In the beginning of therapy, it is not unusual for the patient to assume the modal doctor-patient set and expect the therapist to be directive and prescriptive. Even when this has been confronted and corrected, a degree of subtle dependency may persist, with the patient waiting for the therapist to say when the "cure" is complete. The therapist must not casually assume that when the patient continues to request and keep appointments, an active process of therapy is underway with additional benefits being derived. The therapist has to share responsibility for determining that therapy, in the proper sense, has in fact terminated.

9. *Therapy addiction.* It is generally recognized that some patients become overly invested in the "fringe benefits" and status of being "in therapy", and that they can become emotionally attached to their therapists. Such attachment is not simply a matter of patient transference or failure of the therapist to assist in the resolution of the transference neurosis. Rather, especially in the context of a long-term, intensive uncovering type of therapy, the therapist has become a "significant other." It is less generally recognized, or admitted, that the therapist can develop an "attachment" to some patients, who become, albeit in a properly limited way, "significant others" for the therapist. When the essential work of therapy has been accomplished, a meaningful relationship is in place, and there may be mutual reluctance to say goodby. This is especially likely when the patient is a YAVIS-type (Schofield, 1986). It is clearly a responsibility of the therapist to initiate termination. This does not preclude provision for follow-up contacts in the interest of normalizing a human experience.

A constant concern for medical care givers—physicians, nurses, and hospital personnel—is the prevention of *nosocomial infections,* that is the contraction by the patient of an infection that he or she did not have upon entering the hospital. This is a special focus of the class of ailments (distresses) called iatrogenic, that is, caused by the physician. Psychotherapists are similarly at risk, especially through inadvertence, to cause harm. The therapist is at greatest risk to "infect" those clients who are healthiest at the time of initial consultation. The greater the degree and extent of the person's psychological distress the less likely that the assessment will overestimate the extent of disturbance. By contrast, because the relatively healthy applicant gives promise of success for the therapeutic endeavor, the therapist is encouraged to work harder and may prolong treatment unduly, with the consequence that an extended treatment period may infect clients with the idea that they are really "sick."

The personal and social costs of overtreatment can be avoided by careful attention to (1) the initial assessment of the applicant; (2) use of problem-specific technique when research has established that there is such, e. g., graded in vivo exposure experiences for patients with phobias (Lazarus, 1984); and (3) regular monitoring of the *progress* of therapy in light of the specific treatment goals. At assessment, if it is determined that the candidate has a history of mature adaptation and is responding with a reactive anxiety state or depression to a recent or current situational stress, explicit contracting for brief therapy will prevent overtreatment. Furthermore, it affords some opportunity for the patient to have the prophylactic experience of learning something about the self-limiting character of reactive emotional states.

If the therapist, at appropriate intervals, initiates with the client an *audit* of the course of therapy, this provides an estimate of the work accomplished/work remaining ratio and can indicate the desirability of beginning a tapering-off process. Such an audit is an opportunity to clarify that "complete cure" is not the goal, but rather that the patient will have achieved sufficient learning of new perspectives and new coping skills to be able to move ahead independently to accomplish further changes.

The Role of Common Factors

As early as 1936, Saul Rosenzweig in a paper entitled "Some Implicit Common Factors in Diverse Methods of Psychotherapy," offered a keenly perceptive analysis of non-theory-specific, non-method-specific influences that might account for both a significant portion of the positive impact of psychotherapy and the lack of significant evidence of superiority of one school or approach over others. Rosenzweig's analysis anticipated some of the more recent efforts to explain equality of outcomes across schools as well as to encourage rapprochements of divergent, frequently passionate, viewpoints.

A *common factor* is a variable, dimension, influence, or process that is present in *all* psychotherapeutic transactions. Furthermore, it is a factor of such a nature that it would be difficult, if not impossible, to control, let alone eliminate, from the dyadic discourse of therapy. An overly simplistic example of such a common factor is the specification as one of the "necessary and sufficient conditions" for psychotherapeutic effect that two persons be in psychological contact (Rogers, 1957). More significantly, Rogers and "client-centered" therapists have argued that all successful therapy rests primarily upon the quality of the therapist-client relationship as fostered by the therapist's provision of accurate empathy, warmth, and genuineness. Research support for the centricity of therapist-engendered "facilitative conditions" is ambiguous (Lambert, DeJulio & Stein, 1978; Patterson, 1984; Truax & Mitchell, 1971).

A common factor may be also understood as one that is not deliberately manipulated or utilized by the therapist, or one of which the therapist is unaware or to which he or she is inattentive. Some literature refers to nonspecific factors as synonymous with common factors; in this meaning the common factors are not specified, but not necessarily without specific effect.

Common factors in the psychotherapy process are not psychologically inert and, therefore, not appropriately thought of as placebo. However, in some controlled studies, especially of drug effects, some form and degree of psychotherapy has been presented as a check against placebo effect. (For a thorough analysis of the issue of placebo effect in psychotherapy, see Shapiro, 1971.) Common factors can be viewed as giving rise to a placebo effect to the extent that their *specific* effect, that is, their specifiable contribution to the variance in outcome measures, is unknown. Also, they could be viewed as contributing to a placebo effect in comparative studies of different modes of therapy if it could be assumed that they were all present equally and in similar degree in all the therapies being compared (Frances, Sweeney, & Clarkin 1985; O'Connell, 1983; Patterson, 1985; Strupp & Hadley, 1979; Wilkins, 1984, 1986a, b).

Rosenzweig's original listing has since been extended by some experts and shortened by others. The common factors that have been delineated include descriptions of process, descriptions of the therapy relationship, qualities or states of the therapist, and qualities or states of the patient.

Theoretical Formulation

In delineating possible common factors, it is appropriate to begin with the suggestion that a "theory" is present *in some form* and *some degree* in all psychotherapy. The exact nature of the theory or the degree to which it is explicitly shared with the client is not critical. The common aspect or ubiquity of the theory factor resides in two elements: (1) The therapist has a formulation of the case, that is, a set of ideas as to the probably significant etiological factors, the manner in which they have been experienced by the client and their relationship to the latter's present problems; and a choice as to the appropriate mode of intervention—all of these may or may not derive from a formal, theoretical "school" to which the therapist subscribes. (2) This "theory of the case" is communicated directly or indirectly to the client. Thus, there is some theoretical structure underlying all therapy work. In the words of Rosenzweig (1936), "psychological events are so complex and many sided in nature that they may be *alternatively formulated* with considerable justification for each alternative"; it follows that any interpretation is likely to capture some truth. As a potential source of benefit, this "theory," as perceived by the client, serves to bring order where there has been confusion, to provide reassurance, and to influence the client's motivation to work. There is reassurance in that the client's perception of the "theory" means that his or her problems are not rare or unique, rather that they are understandable and understood by the therapist. The communication of a "theory"-related process to be pursued can contribute to the client's hope of being helped and in turn to his or her motivation.

The notion of theory as a significant common factor has implications. If it were possible to conduct a truly atheoretical course of therapy, it might be that either efficiency or effectiveness would be reduced to the degree that the patient was without the benefit of the enhancing or synergistic contribution of theory. Furthermore, it is likely that efficiency and effectiveness of therapy would be lessened if the therapist were without a guiding theme, and as a consequence, there were no session-to-session continuity in the pursuit of therapeutic goals. Also, there is the implication that if "theory" contributes a common, *active* ingredient to the process, it behooves the therapist to explicitly and clearly communicate the rationale of the treatment method, to the patient. It follows, also, that even an inappropriate or incomplete formulation may contribute to patient gains though possibly only initially and for a limited period.

Status Differential

Every professionally guided therapeutic relationship has an unavoidable status hierarchy. The therapist has authority, prestige, and power of expertise, or at least is so perceived by the patient. The patient is a supplicant and views himself or herself, especially at the outset, as dependent upon the therapist. This status differential, which cannot be completely eliminated from the therapy relationship, has the potential to contribute either positively or negatively to the therapy process. The therapist may either deliberately or unwittingly behave in ways that not only maintain the status discrepancy but increase it so that the dependency of the patient, which may be a part of the pathology, is increased. There are those features of orthodox psychoanalytic practice, notably the use of the couch and the "invisibility" of the analyst, that would seem to fuel the dependency elements of the status differential. Freud was concerned with the problem of "interminable" therapies and provided an exhaustive exploration of whether psychoanalysis could be expected to yield total "cures" or result in permanent prophylaxis, but he did not speak directly to the question of prolonged dependency. Clearly, he accepted the status differential as a necessary part of the therapy relationship: ". . . He [the analyst] must be in a superior position in some sense if he is to serve as a model for his patient in certain analytic situations, and, in others, to act as his teacher" (Freud, 1937).

There has been a general sweep of social movements toward less authoritarian institutions and, in particular, recognition that the psycho-therapy relationship is particularly vulnerable to abuse. Some leaders, especially within the humanistic movement, seek elimination of elements of the therapist-client relationship that suggest or support the status differential (Hamachek, 1982). From this viewpoint, the therapist, from the outset, should seek to explicitly establish a relationship in which the therapist and client are peers, equal partners in the task of finding solutions (Vardy & Kay, 1982). This is consistent with the desirability of establishing a "therapeutic alliance," a concept that is widely applied to denote an optimal mutuality of roles in all clinical endeavors. It may be desirable to diminish cues or practices that unnecessarily signal the status differential (e. g., the display of diplomas and certificates, seating arrangements that favor the comfort of the therapist, insistence on being addressed formally, etc.). It is possible that other practices (e. g., insisting on mutual use of first names, creating a nonoffice environment, etc.) may discomfit if not seriously put off the client who seeks expert assistance and not comforta-ble comaraderie with a self-disclosing professional (Curtis, 1981). Despite motives and efforts to democratize the therapy relationship, it is unlikely that a proper professional exchange can be totally freed of the status differential as a common factor. Furthermore, it is doubtful whether achievement of such an equality of roles would enhance or impair the progress of therapy, especially since the status hierarchy is closely related to other potentially helpful qualities of the therapy relationship.

A Controlled Relationship

All interpersonal relationships have boundaries, controls, limits, and contractual obligations that are frequently implicit or vague, perhaps too frequently so. The boundaries and expectations of personal relationships evolve, expand, shift, and decay, often without preparation or control by the individual. It is common to all schools of psychotherapy that the relationship is a controlled one that offers a stability on which the patient can rely. The therapist spells out the limits that will be observed and what will be required of the client. The therapist provides reliability of access, constancy of attention, and stability of attitude. In these ways the relationship of psychotherapist and patient is very special and very different from the other personal relationships of everyday life. When properly in place and consistently observed, the controlled aspects of the relationship may significantly undergird the effectiveness of special therapeutic techniques. If poorly observed, they may account in part for reduced effectiveness of therapy. Managed well or ineffectively, the controlled elements of the relationship are a common factor in all therapies, regardless of the focus of therapy theory or method.

An Accepting Relationship

As obvious as the "controlled and limited" aspects of all psychotherapy relationships, but of greater potential contribution to therapeutic impact, is that quality of the relationship represented by the therapist's "acceptance" of the client, that is, the therapist's communication of his or her respect for the client as a human being of worth. It is a tenet of all therapists, regardless of school allegiances, that they do not pass judgments or "goodness" or "badness" on the client as a person; they do not respond to the client from a critical or judgmental stance; they do not make moral evaluations; they do not challenge client values that are simply deviant from their own. (For discussion of possible difficulties arising from therapist-client discrepancies in value structure, see chap. 1.) In brief, while not all therapists agree to the Rogersian goal of offering "unconditional positive regard" (Rogers, 1957), they do strive to create an atmosphere of acceptance. To paraphrase St. Augustine, thus, a common factor across schools of therapy is the therapist's acceptance of an injunction to "love the person but hate the pathology." As a common factor, this attitudinal, "atmospheric" contribution may well be a highly significant determinant of the client's capacity to respond to the specifics of therapy and to change.

Transference

The elements of a status hierarchy, and a controlled, accepting relationship, as common to all psychotherapy dyads, contribute to the potential for the process of transference to be another common factor. In contrast to everyday nonhierchical relationships, in psychotherapy there is a distinctly enhanced probability for the occurrence of transference. This means a special opportunity for the therapist to perceive that the patient is unconsciously projecting into the therapy and onto the therapist fears, sensitivities, resentments, and other reactions that represent the activation of attitudes generated in the patient's earlier relationships to significant others. The process of transference provides the therapist with the opportunity, either via interpretation or by nonreinforcement of the patient's expectations of a reproduction of earlier role stresses, to assist the patient toward both insight and attitudinal changes.

Parenthetically it may be noted that many therapists, especially those who are beginners and who have not had a basic grounding in psychodynamic concepts, use the term *transference* (or *countertransference*) in referring to any and all interactions in which there is an apparent affective reaction, positive or negative, on the part of the patient (or therapist). This is a careless and unhelpful perversion of an important concept for therapeutic understanding and impact. Therapists need to understand that they can arouse strong reactions of resentment or rejection by patients as a direct response to gaffes or insensitivity on their parts. ''The time is past when one could conveniently blame the patient for lack of therapeutic progress. . . . The term 'negative therapeutic reaction' has frequently been used as an umbrella to shift responsibility from the therapist to the client, and to exonerate the former from responsibility for possible negative outcomes'' (Strupp et al., 1977, p. 128). Unthinking assignment of *all* such patient responses to ''resistances'' arising from transference prevents the therapist from recognizing therapeutic errors and from correcting them in a forthright manner that can contribute to therapeutic progress through the realities of the here-now relationship.

In brief, the therapeutic process of transference and its resolution is a potential common factor of varying probability in all psychotherapy relationships. It has a greater probability of activation in all cognitive therapies, especially those of a psychodynamic structure, and a lesser probability in the more behaviorally oriented therapies. Waterhouse and Strupp (1984) have provided a comprehensive overview of the role of the patient-therapist relationship as a determinant of therapy outcome.

Complementarity of Expectations

Both the therapist and the client begin the therapy relationship with certain expectations. The therapist who has made a proper, thorough assessment of the candidate for treatment and his or her presenting problems, and has agreed to accept the client for therapy, has certain expectations; basic among these is the expectation of being helpful. In turn, the client, who may have some precontact assumptions about the expertise of the potential therapist, and who has experienced the thoughtful study and appraisal of the therapist, followed by acceptance as a patient, has the expectation of being helped. There need not be explicit communication of these two expectations, although such direct communication may be an important facilitation of the early work of therapy. Ideally, this complementarity of expectations of therapist and client fosters the activation of the process of positive suggestion, transmitted by the therapist and received by the client (Goldstein, 1962). While there is only weak evidence that positive therapeutic expectancies contribute significantly to therapeutic progress (Wilkins, 1978), the mutuality of therapist and client expectations is a likely common factor, contributing positively, at least in early stages, to the success achieved by all therapy approaches. The thesis that modification of expectancies is a *specific* element of psychotherapy (Kirsch, 1985) has been closely examined and found unproved (Wilkins, 1986b). It is likely that negative expectancies of either therapist or patient may impede, if not totally vitiate, the process of therapy.

Catharsis

Included in Rosenzweig's sketch of "implicit" common factors in all methods of psychotherapy was the concept of catharsis. Historically, this process is rooted in the early work of Joseph Breuer whom Freud credits with founding the "cathartic procedure", originally based on hypnotic recovery of repressed memories (Freud, 1916). In its original. technical reference to method (free association, dream analysis, and interpretation) and result (purging, release of previously dammed up affect) it has continued to play a role, albeit peripheral, in psychodynamic therapies (Glover, 1955). Catharsis has come to have a more general meaning as a phenomenon recognized by most therapists and common to early stages of therapy where it is often a source of significant relief experienced by the patient. In this more general context it is recognized that the patient's discharge of strong emotion need not necessarily relate to repressed or unconscious material.

"Confession," "talking things out" and "getting things off one's chest," in relation to a friend or a professional person, like a physician, minister, or teacher, are common methods of relieving emotional tension. Beneficial effects are due to the release of pent-up feelings and emotions and the subjection of inner painful elements to objective reappraisal. The mere verbalization of aspects of the self of which the individual is ashamed or fearful helps him to develop a more constructive attitude toward them. (Wolberg, 1954) (p. 28)

It is improbable that any method of psychotherapy can totally eliminate some degree of the action and benefits of catharsis. The skilled therapist will not simply tolerate the patient's early emotional release, but will encourage it, and then move toward ventilation, encouraging the patient toward exploration, clarification, and assimilation of the now less emotionally charged experience (Nichols & Efran, 1985).

There are additional factors common to all psychotherapy. Of these, as noted in chapter 1, the condition of *confidentiality* is not only general across all schools or approaches but is likely to play an important role in catalyzing the processes of therapy. Also, there is a *common mode of communication;* this means not only that therapist and client speak the same language, but that to a considerable degree they have access to the same cultural analogies and metaphors in facilitating the crucial goal of communication, that is, mutual understanding.

Finally, a common factor of central import to all psychotherapy is the process of *learning;* however conceptualized by the therapist and however experienced by the client, when therapy is successful, the client is changed by virtue of a process of acquisition, extinction, or reformulation of attitudes, habits, skills, self-concepts, aspirations, and expectations of self and others. In brief, the client has demonstrated the capacity to be a good student in a supportive learning environment in which the therapist has been an effective guide, model, or preceptor.

Some authorities on psychotherapy have suggested conditions that they believe are sine qua non for effective psychotherapy. To the extent that their specifications are valid they may be considered factors common to all effective treatment regardless of the therapeutic theory presumably represented. Rogers (1957) indicated "necessary and sufficient conditions," Strupp (1973) specified "basic ingredients," and Frank (1982) has noted "therapeutic components shared by all psychotherapies." Rogers identified the nature of the client as "incongruent" and "vulnerable"; he stipulates that the effective therapist must have an empathic understanding of the client's internal frame of reference and an "unconditional positive regard" for the client, both of which are communicated. Strupp stated that the effective therapist creates and maintains a helping relationship "characterized by respect, interest, understanding, tact, maturity, and a firm belief in his ability to help.'' He further noted that the client must have capacity and willingness to profit from experience, that is, to learn. Frank, building on the central core of his demoralization hypothesis, has denoted "ritual" as one of four components common to all psychotherapies; among the functions of ritual he sees a particular role for the therapist in establishing and in "inspiring and maintaining the patient's expectation of help." Frank concludes, "The effectiveness of any psychotherapy with a specific patient depends on the morale-building features it shares with all other psychotherapies as well as its specific rationale and procedures" (1982, p. 33). It is significant that these three scholars who have conducted extensive research on the phenomena of psychotherapy, one from a phenomenological/humanistic orientation, one from a predominantly psychodynamic orientation, and one from a social-situational emphasis, arrive at a similar emphasis on the quality of the therapist-client relationship and the personal attributes of the therapist as common ingredients.

The concept of factors that are common to all therapeutic approaches (and not susceptible to total, controlled elimination) may be viewed in two ways. It may be inferred that the positive outcomes of all kinds of psychological intervention are produced primarily by the impact of these common factors, and, in turn, that the apparent equivalence of results produced by different therapies arises from the operation of the common factors. Also, the concept may be viewed to imply that, despite obvious differences in apparent goals and procedures, different modes of therapy do not have *specific* effects. The argument that different therapies may not have specific effects, or that their impact is overshadowed by the potency of the common factors, has particular significance for proponents of a particular model (theory) of therapy, and for the training of therapists. Uncertainty about the question of specific effects has been laid in part to the use of *general* criteria of patient improvement in comparative studies of therapeutic approaches instead of applying criteria for the measurement of *specific* effects (Frances et al., 1985; O'Connell, 1983; Patterson, 1985; Strupp & Hadley, 1979).

Given the rationale for the probable positive, albeit somewhat general, therapeutic potency of the common factors, it behooves all therapists, regardless of their theoretical allegiances and preferred therapy modes, to be attentive to the potential contribution of these factors and to see that their therapeutic potential is realized in an optimal fashion. It is important also that the therapist be alert to, and acknowledge the impact of, extratherapy life events in markedly effecting the patient's apparent "therapeutic" progress (Lazarus, 1980).

The Question of Specificity

The history of both physiologic and psychologic treatment is largely the history of the placebo effect: Those who forget it are destined to repeat it.

Shapiro, 1971 (p. 463)

The ferment in psychotherapy and the vigorous debate among the adherents of the major schools hinges on the question of specificity. Do the therapeutic gains achieved by patients treated with the methods and techniques of practitioners of a particular approach result from those *specific* procedures and are those therapeutic gains a meaningful *increment* over and beyond such salutary changes as may result from the impact of those *common factors* that operate in all good therapist-client relationships? (Orne, 1977)

To establish the fact and extent of specific effects of a particular psychological intervention would seem to require only the standard research design that has been productive in medical research: comparison of carefully matched samples of patients, one sample of which receives the experimental treatment and the other of which serves as a "placebo" control. In drug research this is easy; an active medication is administered to the experimental group and a physiologically *inert* substance—the placebo—to the control group. The problem in study of psychological interventions is that there are no standardized "psychological placebos," that is, treatments for the control group that are psychologically *inert* (Parloff, 1986a). In fact, the finding of *limited* specific gains for an experimentally treated group over changes in a "control" sample are sometimes explained as due to the fact that the so-called placebo group indeed received an alternative therapy process (Parloff, 1986b).

Those detractors from the general thesis that psychotherapy *is* effective who argue that positive gains are *nothing but* placebo effect fail to recognize that the uncontrollable, *ubiquitous* "common factors" in therapy are not inert but rather psychologically potent. In fact, those proponents who argue that it is the therapist-patient relationship that powers positive change in patients see the apparently equal and not insignificant effectiveness of presumably different psychotherapies as resting upon the beneficial force of the elements common to all human interactions with therapeutic intent. Kazdin (1985) has provided an excellent analysis of methodological problems in comparative studies of psychotherapy outcomes, that is, studies in which one therapy modality is presumably placed in fair competition with one or more other. He points out the accretions of knowledge and understanding that result from such studies at the same time that he recognizes their serious and perhaps insurmountable limitations. As an example of the relevance of the characteristics of the therapy deliverers, he notes the finding from the often-cited study of Sloane, Staples, Cristol, Yorkston, and Whipple (1975) that both behavior therapists and psychotherapists were observed to manifest warmth toward, and positive regard for, the patients they were presumably treating differently!

Parloff (1986b), after noting the impossibility of meaningful placebo controls in psychotherapy research, recommends that comparative studies should concentrate on designs in which alternate treatment forms, each based on different hypothetical constructs and utilizing different techniques, are put in direct competition, so that "each would serve as a natural placebo control for the other" (p. 85). Given the importance of therapist personality, would such comparative studies not require that the same therapists be the providers of both forms of treatment? This has been done in some studies, but presents the problem of therapist bias. "Therapists do not have the same attitudes toward all treatments, placebos, or clients. As a consequence, there may be unintentional differences in the confidence and enthusiasm with which treatments and placebo are administered to clients" (Wilkens, 1986a).

Strupp (1986), who is not hopeful that there can be a parsing out of the specific and the nonspecific elements in psychotherapy, notes that the "therapist's personal and technical skills are inextricably woven into every aspect of the structure and process of his or her relationship with the patient."

In attempting to provide a framework that encompasses the dimensions of specificity and nonspecificity in psychotherapy, Karasu (1986) worked from circumscribed procedural techniques toward a schema of universal processes. He located the very large number of specific techniques generated by, or associated with, therapy schools under three categories of nonspecific change agents: (1) affective experiencing; (2) cognitive mastery; and (3) behavioral regulation. These general processes would encompass the common factors noted above and provide a structural organization of techniques under each of the core therapeutic processes suggested in Chapter 4. Karasu did not address the issue of specific *effects*, but his schema offers a useful heuristic for cross-school comparisons with regard to overlap of techniques.

Do the specific elements of psychotherapuetic procedure dictated by the major schools really account for most of the positive gains experienced and changes manifested by patients? Or, do the techniques of intervention simply provide a socially acceptable rationale to justify the coming together of therapist and client so that the latter can benefit from the facilitating influence of a positive, supportive, accepting human relationship? Given the extreme difficulty of achieving the critical control of variables required to answer these questions, it is unlikely that research will resolve the issue. Comparative studies will continue to enhance our knowledge of therapists, clients, and the ways in which they can interact to both the advantage and detriment of each. "As long as the field of psychotherapy continues to spawn systems, schools, and other nonspecific and all embracing orientations, there is little hope of achieving far-reaching scientific respectability. The need for greater specificity cannot be overstated" (*Lazarus*, 1984, p.47).

The responsibility of the therapist is clear: to be informed on the most current findings of the effectiveness of specific procedures for specific problems, and to be ever aware of the therapy enhancing influence of the factors common to all therapist-client relationships.

Note

1. For the historical record it may be noted that the writer associated the "instigation" process with behavioral therapy in lecturing on pragmatic psychotherapy beginning in the early 1960s. It is pertinent to note that in their 1966 paper on behavior therapy, Kanfer and Phillips wrote of "instigation therapy" as one of four *(paradigms)* for the conceptualization of behavior therapy.

References

Alexander, F. & French, M. (1946) *Psychoanalytic therapy*. New York: The Ronald Press Co.

Beck, A. T., Hollon, S. D., Young, J. E., Bedrosian, R. C., & Budenz, D. (1985) Treatment of depression with cognitive therapy and amitriptylin. *Archives of General Psychiatry*, 42, 142–148.

Beckham, E. E. & Leber, W. R. (1985) The comparative efficacy of psychotherapy and pharmacotherapy for depression. In Beckham, E. E. & Leber, W. R. (Eds) Handbook of depression: *Treatment, assessment, and research*. Homewood, IL: Dorsey Press.

Beitman, B. D. & Klerman, G. L. (Eds.) (1984) *Combining psychotherapy and drug therapy in clinical practice*. Jamaica, NY: Spectrum

Bergin, A. E. (1963) The effects of psychotherapy: negative effects revisited. *Journal of Counseling Psychology, 10*, 244–250.

Bergin, A. E. (1966) Some implications of psychotherapy research for therapeutic practice. *Journal of Abnormal Psychology, 71*, 235–246.

Byrne, K. & Stern, S. L. (1981) Antidepressant medication in the outpatient treatment of depression: Guide for nonmedical psychotherapists. *Professional Psychology, 12*, 302–308.

Conte, H. R., Plutenik, R., Wild, K. V. & Karazu, T. B. (1986). Combined psychotherapy and pharmacotherapy for depression: A systematic analysis of the evidence. *Archives of General Psychiatry, 43*, 471–479.

Curtis, J. M. (1981) Indications and contraindications in the use of the therapist's self-disclosure. *Psychological Reports, 49,* 499–507.

Davenloo, H. (Ed) (1980) *Short-term dynamic psychotherapy.* New York: Jason Aronson.

Ellis, A. (1980) The value of efficiency in psychotherapy. *Psychotherapy: Theory, Practice & Research, 17,* 414–419.

Frances, A., Sweeney, J. & Clarkin, J. (1985) Do psychotherapies have specific effects? *American Journal of Psychotherapy, 39,* 159–174.

Frank, J. D. (1982) Therapeutic components shared by all psychotherapies. In Harvey, J. H. & Parks, M. M. (Eds) Psychotherapy research and behavior change (The Master Lecture Series, Vol. 1) Washington, DC: American Psychological Association.

Franks, C. M. & Mays D. T. (1980) Negative effects revisited: A rejoinder. *Professional Psychology, 11,* 101–105.

Freud S. (1916) *The history of the psychoanalytic movement.* Nervous and mental disease monograph series, No. 25. New York: Nervous and Mental Disease Publishing Co.

Freud, S. (1937) Analysis terminable and interminable. (Trans. Joan Reviere) *International Journal of Psychoanalysis, 18,* 373–405.

Glover, E. (1955) *The technique of psycho-analysis.* New York: International Universities Press.

Goldstein, A. P. (1962) *Therapist-patient expectancies in psychotherapy.* New York: MacMillan.

Grunebaum, H. (1986) Harmful psychotherapy experience. *American Journal of Psychotherapy, 50,* 165–176.

Hamachek, D. E. (1982) Humanistic psychology: Theoretical-philosophical overview and principles. *Journal of Humanistic Psychology, 21,* 2–8.

Henry, W. E., Sims, J. H., & Spray, S. L. (1973) *Public and private lives of psychotherapists.* San Francisco: Jossey-Bass.

Holden, C. (1986) Depression research advances, treatment lags. *Science, 233,* 723–726.

Howard, K. I., Kopta, S. M., Krause, M. S., & Orlinsky, D. (1986) The dose-effect relationship in psychotherapy. *American Psychologist, 41,* 159–164.

Hurvitz, N. (1970) Peer self-help psychotherapy groups and their implications for psychotherapy. *Psychotherapy: Theory, Research and Practice, 7,* 41–49.

Kanfer, F. H. & Phillips, J. S. (1966) Behavior therapy: A panacea for all ills or a passing fancy. *Archives of General Psychiatry, 15,* 114–128.

Karasu, T. B. (1982) Psychotherapy and pharmacotherapy: Toward an integrative model. *American Journal of Psychiatry, 139,* 1102–1113.

Karasu, T. B. (1986) The specificity versus nonspecificity dilemma: Toward identifying therapeutic change agents. *American Journal of Psychiatry, 143,* 687–695.

Karon, B. P. & Van denBos, G. R. (1981) *Psychotherapy of schizophrenia: The treatment of choice.* New York: Jason Aronson.

Kazdin, A. E. (1986) Comparative outcome studies of psychotherapy: Methodological issues and strategies. *Journal of Consulting and Clinical Psychology, 54,* 95–105.

Kirsch, I. (1985) Response expectancy as a determinant of experience and behavior. *American Psychologist, 40,* 1189–1202.

Lambert, M. J. Bergin, A. E. & Collins, J. L. (1977) Therapist-induced deterioration in psychotherapy. In A. S. Gurman & A. M. Razin (Eds) *Effective psychotherapy: A handbook of research*. New York: Pergamon Press.

Lambert, M. J., Dejulio, S. S., & Stein, D. M. (1978) Therapist interpersonal skills: Process, outcome, methodological considerations and recommendations for future research. *Psychological Bulletin, 85,* 467–489.

Lazarus, A. A. (1980) Toward delineating some causes of change in psychotherapy. *Professional Psychology Research and Practice, 11,* 863–870.

Lazarus, A. A. (1984) The specificity factor in psychotherapy. *Psychotherapy in Private Practice, 2,* 43–48.

Malan, D. H. (1963) *A study of brief psychotherapy*. Philadelphia: J. B. Lippincott Co.

Mann, J. (1973) *Time-limited psychotherapy*. Cambridge: Harvard University Press.

May, P. R. A. (1968) *Treatment of schizophrenia*. New York: Science House.

May, P. R. A., Tuma, A. H., & Dixon, W. J. (1981) Schizophrenia: A follow-up study of the results of five forms of treatment. *Archives of General Psychiatry, 38,* 776–784.

Mays, D. T. & Franks, C. M. (Eds) (1985) *Negative outcome in psychotherapy and what to do about it*. New York: Springer Publishing.

McNeal, E. T. & Cimbolic, P. (1986) Antidepressants and biochemical theories of depression. *Psychological Bulletin, 99,* 361–364.

Nichols, M. P. & Efran, J. S. (1985) Catharsis in psychotherapy: A new perspective. *Psychotherapy Theory, Research, and Practice, 22,* 46–58.

Nicholson, R. A. & Berman, J. S. (1983) Is follow-up necessary in evaluating psychotherapy? *Psychological Bulletin, 93,* 261–278.

O'Connell, S. (1983) The placebo effect and psychotherapy. *Psychotherapy: Theory, Research and Practice, 20,* 337–345.

Orlinsky, D. E. & Howard, K. I. (1978) The relation of process to outcome in psychotherapy. In Garfield, S. L. & Bergin, A. E. (eds) *Handbook of psychotherapy and behavior change* (2nd ed) New York: Wiley.

Orne, M. T. (1977) The search for specific treatments in psychiatry. In Brady, J. P., Mendels, J., Orne, M. T., & Rieger, W. (Eds.) Psychiatry: Areas of promise and advancement. New York: Spectrum.

Parloff, M. B. (1986a) Frank's "common elements" in psychotherapy: nonspecific factors and placebos. *American Journal of Orthopsychiatry, 56,* 521–530

Parloff, M. B. (1986b) Placebo control in psychotherapy research: A sine qua non or a placebo for research problems? *Journal of Consulting and Clinical Psychology, 54,* 79–87.

Patterson, C. H. (1984) Empathy, warmth, and genuineness in psychotherapy: A review of reviews: *Psychotherapy Theory, Research, and Practice, 21,* 431–438.

Patterson, C. H. (1985) What is the placebo in psychotherapy? *Psychotherapy, 22,* 163–169.

Rogers, C. R. (1957) The necessary and sufficient conditions of therapeutic personality change. *Journal of Consulting Psychology, 21,* 95–103.

Rosenzweig, S. (1936) Some implicit common factors in diverse methods of psychotherapy. *American Journal of Orthopsychiatry, 6,* 412–415.

Rounsaville, B. J., Klerman, G. L. & Weissman, M. M. (1981) Do psychotherapy and pharmacotherapy of depression conflict? Empirical evidence from a clinical trial. *Archives of General Psychiatry, 38,* 24–29.

Schofield, W. (1979) Psychology, inspiration, and faith. *Journal of Religion and Health, 18,* 197–202.

Schofield, W. (1986) *Psychotherapy: The purchase of friendship*. New Brunswick, N J: Transaction.

Shapiro, A. K. (1971) Placebo effects in medicine, psychotherapy, and psychoanalysis. In Bergin, A. E. & Garfield, S. L. (eds) *Handbook of Psychotherapy and Behavior Change: An Empirical Analysis*. John Wiley & Sons.

Sifneos, P. (1972) *Short-term psychotherapy and emotional crisis*. Cambridge: Harvard University Press.

Sloane, R. B., Staples, F. R., Cristol, A. H., Yorkston, N. J., & Whipple, K. (1975). Psychotherapy versus behavior therapy. Cambridge: University Press.

Stiles, W. B., Shapiro, D. A. & Elliott, R. (1986) "Are all psychotherapies equivalent?" *American Psychologist, 41,* 165–180.

Strupp, H. H. (1973) On the basic ingredients of psychotherapy. *Journal of Consulting and Clinical Psychology, 41,* 1–8.

Strupp, H. H. (1986) The nonspecific hypothesis of therapeutic effectiveness: A current assessment. *American Journal of Orthopsychiatry, 56,* 513–520.

Strupp, H. H. & Hadley, S. W. (1979) Specific vs. non-specific factors in psychotherapy: A controlled study of outcome. *Archives of General Psychiatry, 36,* 1125–1136.

Strupp, H. H., Hadley, S. W. & Gomes-Schwartz, B. (1977) *Psychotherapy for better or worse; The problem of negative effects*. New York: Jason Aronson.

Truax, C. B. & Mitchell, K. M. (1971) Research on certain therapist inter-personal skills in relation to process and outcome. In Bergin, A. E. & Garfield, S. L. (Eds) *Handbook of psychotherapy and behavior change*. New York: Wiley.

Uhlenhuth, E. H., Lysman, R., & Covi, L. (1963) Combined pharmacotherapy and psychotherapy. *Journal of Nervous & Mental Diseases, 148,* 52–64.

Vardy, M. M. & Kay, S. R. (1982) The therapeutic value of psychotherapists' values and therapy orientations. *Psychiatry, 45,* 226–233.

Verbrugge, L. M. & Steiner, R. P. (1985) Prescribing drugs to men and women. *Health Psychology, 4,* 79–98.

Waterhouse, G. J. & Strupp, H. H. (1984) The patient-therapist relationship: Research from the psychodynamic perspective. *Clinical Psychology Review, 4,* 77–92.

Werman, D. S. (1984) *The practice of supportive psychotherapy*. New York: Brunner/Mazel.

Wilkins, W. (1978) Expectancies in applied settings, In Gurman, A. S. & Razin, A. M. (Eds) *Effective psychotherapy: A handbook of research*. New York: Pergamon Press.

Wilkins, W. (1984) Psychotherapy: the powerful placebo. *Journal of Counseling and Clinical Psychology, 52,* 570–573.

Wilkins, W. (1986a) Placebo problems in psychotherapy research: Social-psychological alternatives to chemotherapy concepts. *American psychologist, 41,* 551–556.

Wilkins, W. (1986b) Therapy-therapist confounds in psychotherapy research. *Cognitive Therapy and Research, 10,* 3–11.

Wilkins, W. (1986c) Invalid evidence for expectancies as causes: Comment on Kirsch. *American Psychologist, 41,* 1387–1388.

Wolberg, L. R. (1954) *The technique of psychotherapy*. New York: Grune & Stratton.

Zilbergeld, B. (1986) Psychabuse. *Science 86, 7,* 48–52.

6

The Conduct of Psychotherapy

As stated in the Introduction, this book is not an instructional manual on "how to do" psychotherapy. It does not address in any detail the intervention techniques associated with any one or several of the major approaches to psychological intervention. Rather, it is intended to stimulate an appreciation of the particular role and limitations of psychotherapy in our culture at the present time. It seeks to provide the reader with a guide to "how to think about" psychotherapy in all its rich complexities. Although not explicating specific techniques, there are certain issues bearing on the conduct of therapy that are of a general nature, with relevance to all modes or schools. For the beginning professional therapist or the therapist-in-training, an excellent discussion of basic procedural issues is provided by Zaro, Barach, Nedelman, and Dreiblatt (1977). For the student or practitioner seeking detailed directions on specific therapy techniques, there is a large library of appropriate texts. (See the Selected General References at the end of this book.)

Assessment

Across all major schools of psychotherapy, with the exception of the Rogersian client-centered approach, there is agreement that there should be some amount and form of assessment of the applicant. However conducted, the assessment addresses the basic question, "Is this applicant a suitable candidate for psychotherapy?" Ideally, the question should be extended to ". . . for the type of therapy I prefer to practice and with which I am most experienced?" The latter part of the question is especially applicable when the therapist is not a generalist (or a self-identified "eclectic") but rather is a specialist in one therapeutic modality (e.g., psychodynamic or behavioral) and prefers to work with clients suitable for his or her approach. It is essential that the therapist assess the candidate's motives, expectations, and the source and nature of any ambivalence about entering upon a course of therapy (Halgin & Weaver, 1986).

Appraisal of the suitability of the candidate rests upon information obtained in the initial one or two contacts; if the assessment is conducted efficiently, its goal is generally reached within one session and will rarely require more than two contacts. In the interests of efficiency, it is frequently desirable to allow more than the usual hour for the initial meeting so that the task of assessment can be completed then.

Therapists will differ, in part as a function of their theoretical orientation, as to how they conduct the appraisal of the candidate. Basically, good assessment requires highly developed interviewing and observational skills that overlap with those utilized in the conduct of therapy. Certain general rules for good interviewing are applicable: (1) Allow the client time to become comfortable and "warm up," that is, do not start with highly specific questions in sensitive areas. (2) Avoid "district attorney—cross-examiner"-type probes initially. (3) Use open-ended, nonleading questions that do *not* encourage brief, yes or no, or evasive responses. (4) Do not rush the interviewee, but rather allow time for extended responses. (5) Use gentle, persistent probes (e.g., "Please tell me more about that," or, "I'm not sure I understand") to encourage more extended responses. (6) Listen attentively for attitudes and affects as well as content. (7) Hold in mind a structure (topical outline) for the assessment so that no relevant areas are inadvertently omitted.

The more in-depth focus on certain areas will be related in part to the therapist's theoretical orientation. The dynamically inclined practitioner will give relatively more attention to information about the family of origin and early life experiences; the behaviorist will attend relatively more to the client's current situation. Apart from such variations in emphasis, all experienced therapists, regardless of their orientation, will cover certain basic areas of information about the candidate: (1) presenting complaint, that is, the nature, in detail, of the symptoms, distress, conflicts, and confusions being experienced; their history, evolution, and current level of severity; and the history of any prior experiences of treatment; (2) the personal history of the individual with attention to family background, educational and vocational history and attention to particular "high" and "low" points; social history, including psychosexual development and marital history; (3) any significant medical history; and (4) current life situations, with special attention to work or study, current primary relationships, and general social resources.

The taking of a functional history need not (should not) be by rote or formula. Depending on the presenting problems, certain areas may be only briefly surveyed. If encouraged by appropriately general probes, the potential client likely will expand on those areas of most relevance to those problems for which help is sought. However, it is necessary for the therapist to have a broad historical "scanner" in mind so as to be aware, if therapy later ensues, of those areas of the client's life experience of which the therapist is without knowledge.

Appropriate and thorough conduct of the "intake" interview will provide the clinician with data and observations relevant to many of the general categories of the traditional "mental status examination": (1) *general appearance* (notable physical features, dress, etc), *attitude* (responsiveness, vigilance, reserve, etc), and *behavior* (immobility, nervous mannerisms); (2) *thought* (primary content, special trends, e.g., suspiciousness, vagueness, etc); (3) *stream of speech* (e.g., terseness vs. verbosity, blocking, circumstantiality, mannerisms); (4) *mood and affect* (predominant emotional tone (e.g., apathy, anxiety, depression), constancy vs. variability over the session, appropriateness of emotion to content being discussed; (5) *sensorium and intellect* (orientation for time, person and place (i.e., reality contact) and apparent level of intellectual function (reflected primarily in vocabulary and grammer); and (6) *insight* (degree of apparent acceptance that his or her troubles have a psychological component). While most applicable to evaluation of the patient with serious psychiatric disorder and possible need for hospitalization and medical intervention, as a record of basic observations the mental status examination provides one base line for assessing therapeutic progress.

A word is in order here about *note taking*. There are arguments pro and con the desirability of the therapist recording notes during a *therapy* session, versus recording after a session. This issue will be addressed later. However, in regard to the assessment interview and history taking, it is obvious that both accuracy of detail and of coverage require that the interviewer take notes. The skilled interviewer/recorder can do this in a manner that is nonobtrusive and noninterruptive. The end product is a basic document to which there can be ready reference when the therapist needs to check the file for certain facts of history. The great majority of persons seeking psychotherapy will have had prior experience with other professionals, notably physicians, and will expect both to have their history reviewed and notes to be made. The process can contribute to the early phases of rapport building and convey that the potential therapist is professionally competent. For the therapist to be superficial about this aspect of assessment may arouse some reservations on the part of the client. Those therapists who are inclined to be indifferent or casual about this aspect of the "intake" process might benefit from a bit of prospective imagery: Imagine being on the witness stand as a defendant in some type of suit—after appropriate prior questioning, the attorney for the plaintiff (or the court) remarks, "Do you mean to say, Doctor, that you undertook to threat Mr. Jones without ever inquiring about . . . ?"

A word about *computer-based interviews*. Computer technology has developed programs whereby comprehensive interviews, such as a general history, psychiatric history, or other circumscribed questionnaires (e.g., symptom inventories) can be administered and responded to by a client sitting at a computer console (Reynolds, McNamara, Marion, & Tobin, 1985). This method of eliciting information has certain clear advantages. The question inputs are standardized, the response format for the interviewee is standardized, the standardized format provides objectivity, replicability, and ready printout of a permanent, standard record. The average person can be prepared for a computer interview with brief, simple instructions. The advantages of standardization and objectivity are obvious. Experience suggests that most candidates respond positively to computer inquiry if it is followed after a *brief* interval by an appropriate *personal* follow-up. The efficiency of collection of important intake information about potential therapy clients can be considerably facilitated. Experience suggests that at least some interviewees are initially more forthcoming and frank in responses to the computer than to a personal interviewer. However, the computer format places very stringent limits on the ability of respondents to qualify or explicate their responses, and it provides no information (cues) as to the feeling or affective components of their responses. If computer interviews are to be used efficiently, they should precede the initial personal interview with a professional and provide a guide to critical areas for more penetrating examination.

To use or not use *psychological tests* as part of intake assessment is a topic on which therapists are of diverse opinion, partly in relation to theoretical stance (orthodox client-centered therapists eschew the use of such instruments), perhaps more in relation to basic training and experience. It is readily understandable that psychologist/therapists are more likely to use tests or inventories, while psychiatrists and social workers do so less frequently. Three patterns of use are discernable: (1) routine; (2) occasional and selective; (3) never. That psychological instruments are rarely used by psychiatrists, social workers, and other mental health professionals results directly from the fact that their graduate training rarely includes basic instruction in psychometric theory, or on the nature, applicability, and limits of psychological tests, or, perhaps most critically, *on the extensive sources of error and the limited reliability of unaided clinical observation and judgment.* Since these very elements of substantive knowledge are part of the core graduate instruction of psychologists, it is remarkable that many psychologist/therapists make no use of appropriate instruments in assessing candidates for psychotherapy (Wade &

Baker, 1977). A common rationale for this neglect is, "In the course of therapy, sooner or later, I will find out everything I need to know." Is it in the best interests of anyone, patient or therapist, for the latter to find out *later* that the former is prone to prevaricate, is prone to abuse drugs, has a significant conflict regarding sex role identity, etc.? It is ironical that many psychiatrists who would not think of mounting a research study to evaluate a new drug without including objective measures of the patient's psychological status pre- and post-treatment, are prone to treat clinical, nonresearch patients without making use of such measures. It is especially appropriate that beginning therapists augment their limited experience in assessing candidates for therapy by extending their knowledge of the applicant with the broad base of information about others that is built into properly constructed and validated psychological tests.

Assessment is not synonymous with diagnosis in the formal sense. In relation to decisions as to whether psychotherapy is indicated, the goal of assessment is not simply to arrive at one or more suitable diagnoses based on the criteria of the official diagnostic manual (American Psychiatric Association, 1980). Cumulative experience indicates that individuals who do conform to certain diagnoses, for example, borderline personality, are poor risks, that is, unlikely to respond positively to psychotherapy. But, the goal of assessment is directed less to the itemized clinical elements of official diagnoses and more to a comprehensive assay of those aspects of the candidate's personality that are directly relevant to his or her capacity to respond to treatment (motivation, capacity to relate to the therapist, capacity to learn). On the question of possible sources of therapeutic failures (patients who do not change or who become worse with therapy), a significant number of experienced therapists relate such failures to deficiencies of assessment (Strupp, Hadley, & Gomes-Schwartz, 1977).

Upon completion of the assessment process, the therapist is prepared for either of two possible communications to the applicant. It is easy to tell candidates that they are suitable for treatment, that the therapist is willing to work with them and, at least by implication, that the therapist expects to be helpful. It is difficult to tell a candidate that he or she is not acceptable for treatment, at least by the particular therapist; this can be a painful piece of information and may be readily overinterpreted by the candidate to mean that he or she is hopeless. It is reprehensible for the therapist, especially after the time and expense of the assessment process, to lie and use the lame extrication of, "I'm sorry but I don't have time for you now on my schedule." It is acceptable to turn down the candidate who does not fit the therapist's mode of practice; when this occurs, the therapist has an ethical responsibility to help the candidate with suitable referral to a *specific* other therapist. Such a nonfit is one of the most common reasons why full-time practitioners make referrals to other therapists (Tryon, 1983). When the therapist has doubts, not certainty, about the suitability of the candidate, in terms either of general personality variables, past history, or current level of motivation, it is appropriate to suggest a trial period of a few sessions. There is rarely any justification for allowing such a trial to exceed more than six sessions. Keeping a clear focus on the "try-out" nature of the early sessions is helped by stipulating a definite number, that is three, four, etc., with the understanding that at the end of the last specified session there will be a decision either to continue or terminate. It has been suggested that the trial period may be used effectively to test both the motivation and the therapy "aptitude" by setting specific tasks for the client to achieve between sessions (writing a portion of an autobiography; keeping a log of certain behaviors, etc.). Ideally these should be assignments that are consistent with the therapeutic modality that the therapist plans to use (O'Connell, 1984; Omer, 1985).

It may be that upon conclusion of the trial period the client is disinclined to continue with therapy. At this point the therapist may be subject to several possible errors. If the therapist has "overpathologized" (see chapter 5) he or she may, without adequate review of the trial period and reappraisal, more or less automatically treat the client's decision as "resistance" and importune the client to continue. This error is likely if the therapist is prone, especially by theoretical stance, to discount the possibility that a client can make significant and sufficient gains within a very few sessions. (This is akin to the general practice in research studies of recording "dropouts" and "premature terminators" as therapeutic failures.) While this practice supports conservatism in evaluating the impact of therapies, it involves assumptions that are of doubtful validity, i.e., that the "lost cases" are composed entirely of patients who derived no or very little benefit [Schofield, 1966; Silverman & Beech, 1979]).

The opposite error is also possible, that is, that the therapist may passively accept the client's decision not to continue when a thoughtful appraisal (instead of a reaction formation against being authoritative or directive) would indicate that the patient should be encouraged to continue in therapy.

Clearly the probability of error on the part of the therapist is greater if his or her response to the client's decision not to go ahead with therapy is a habitual, automatic one, that is, either *always* to encourage continuation or *always* to passively accept the client's withdrawal. The situation is one in which the clinician should exercise a case-specific judgment. Although all such judgments are subject to error, the probability of a serious mistake, in either direction, can be reduced if the therapist encourages time for further reflection by both participants. Thus, rather than either challenging or passively accepting the client's intent to discontinue, it can be helpful to suggest a "recess" of a few weeks before a "final" session in which to review the accomplishments of the trial period, to check the status of therapy goals, and to reinforce those learnings and new responses that may have occurred (Seligman, 1984). It is appropriate for the therapist to indicate his or her accessibility and interest should the patient wish to return for further work at a future time.

A different issue is presented when clients at any point in therapy "drop out," that is, fail to appear for or cancel an appointment, and do not seek to arrange further appointments (Reder & Tyson, 1980). Again, two errors by the therapist are possible, that is, to pursue the clients or to "neglect" them. The "disappearing" case is a particular concern for therapist-in-training who may take such a "loss" of the client as evidence of a tactical gaffe or general inadequacy on their part, or anticipate such judgment on the part of supervisors. The tyro therapist, unless counseled, is likely to feel strongly impelled to telephone the missing client. Such a telephone call has the virtue of immediacy and efficiency. However, such pursuit of the client entails an invasion of the latter's privacy. Beyond that, it creates a degree of pressure on the client to give a socially acceptable (normative) response to agree to a further appointment—which may or may not be kept! It is preferable to allow a sufficient period of time to pass (e.g., the equivalent of two regular intersession intervals), during which the client may renew contact, and then to send a brief note indicating the therapist's continuing interest and desire to have the client's intentions clarified. Such a written communication provides "closure" for the case file, is responsive to the patient who may be testing the degree of the therapist's interest and concern, and provides protection against any subsequent claim of "abandonment" by the therapist.

Contracting

Once the assessment stage has been completed, the candidate has agreed to enter treatment, and the therapist has accepted the candidate for treatment, there are in place, at least implicitly, the elements of a contract. All that may be explicit, at least initially, are agreements as to the times, frequencies, and duration of appointments and the fees that will be charged. Other elements of a contractual nature may evolve as the therapy proceeds. These will include what come to be mutually agreed upon as responsibilities of the patient and therapist respectively. It may be tacitly agreed, for example, that the patient will appear on time for each appointment and will be responsible for initiating the therapeutic discourse. It may be tacitly agreed, and a matter of simple good manners, that each participant will notify the other whenever it becomes necessary to alter the schedule of meetings or to break an appointment. Sometimes a temporary termination speeds the process of therapy (Seligman, 1984). It may be understood that the patient's communications will be held in strictest confidence—subject to those limitations imposed by the "duty to warn" (of imminent danger to the patient or others, i.e., "threats" of suicide, homicide, etc. as stipulated by law). When does the therapist impart this limitation on confidentiality? If done at the outset, (which the law may specify) unless done in a carefully pro forma and "legal" manner, it may be "read" by the client as meaning that he or she is perceived by the therapist as potentially "dangerous." If done only at the point at which the client has made a threat, it is likely to be perceived as contractual deviation and a "breaking of faith" on the part of the therapist. The 1976 precedent-setting Tarasoff decision in California, and its parallels in other jurisdictions have created knotty ethical dilemmas for therapist (Beck, 1982; Knapp & VandeCreek, 1982; Myers, 1986; Quinn, 1984; Southard & Gross, 1982; Stone, 1986).

While it is possible for therapy to be started and pursued with a largely tacit understanding about the mutual responsibilities of the participants, such an approach is likely at best to give rise to eventual misunderstandings or conflict or at worst to disappointment and discouragement if not premature termination. There will almost certainly be some inefficiency of process, especially in the early stages.

There is one element of the therapy contract that demands explicit verbalization and mutual agreement of therapist and patient—namely, the question of what the *goal* is. There must be clear understanding of what it is that the patient seeks to change—feelings, thoughts, behavior, relationships, or situation. Absent an understanding as to an explicit goal(s) it is not possible for the therapist to choose an optimal therapeutic approach nor for either patient or therapist to meaningfully monitor the progress of therapy or absence thereof. Because of the focus on target behaviors by behavior therapists, they have been notably expressive about this element of the therapy contract while also explicit about other desirable elements of a contract (Kirschenbaum & Flanery, 1984; 1985). Public concern for the rapidly rising costs of health service and the increased provision of coverage of mental health services in comprehensive health insurance policies have brought new focus on the importance of contracts (Motta, 1981).

Although oriented to guidance of the client consumer, the following list suggests contractual elements for which the therapist shares responsibilities:[1] The client should be informed as to:

- professional competence, training, and experience of the therapist and any other professional or personal information relevant to the services to be provided;
- the general method of therapy to be used and an estimate of the probable number of treatment sessions required to achieve the goals of therapy;
- whether and in what manner any relatives or significant others may be involved in the therapy;
- proposed fees, methods of payment, possible insurance coverage, form and frequency of billing, and any related matters;
- policies, practices, and limitations on the privacy of any information provided to the therapist.

In addition to these "good sense" expectations, some states *require* the therapist to inform potential clients of such legal rights as:[2]

- the right to have direct access to the therapist's clinical records;
- the right to have any technical information (e.g., from tests) clearly explained;
- the right to be properly informed as to where and how to direct any complaint or grievance about the therapist or about the services provided, and the right to express such grievances without interference, coercion, or discrimination;
- the right not to be terminated or referred by the therapist without adequate explanation and in the instance of either termination or referral to be actively aided by the therapist in seeking other sources or forms of help.

In some jurisdictions, the statutes specify that the therapist *must* provide the above information at the outset to the prospective client, and the therapist who fails to do so, in any part, is subject to disciplinary action for breaking the law. On the other hand, much of the required communication (e.g., re breaking of confidentiality in the instance of perceived risk of "violence") relates to potential behavior having a very low base rate and is negatively suggestive in a way that can, as noted previously, have a detrimental effect on the establishment of initial rapport. Beginning therapists had best hold to the letter of the law. The experienced therapist will exercise judgment, based upon assessment of the client, as to the appropriate degree of pro forma communication of rights. Laws as drafted are frequently the best possible compromise of means-ends considerations as viewed by a particular legislature at a certain time. They are subject to revision as their applicability is tested in the courts. Historically, this has meant that some professionals, risking contempt of court charges, have held to their ethical principles; improved laws have sometimes resulted.[3]

Setting

It has been commonly observed that peoples' table manners are better when eating in public than when eating in the privacy of their homes. Our behaviors are governed in part by the expectations cued by the situation in which we find ourselves. It is relatively much easier to attend to work in a work situation (e.g., our office) than in a nonwork situation (e.g., our den at home). Effective psychotherapy requires *work* by both patient and therapist; that work is facilitated if the setting is clearly professional. This does not require a drab, impersonal, "institutional" setting for therapeutic conversation. On the other hand, soft lights, overstuffed chairs, incense, and background music are counterindicated. The patient should be provided a reasonable degree of physical comfort but not a setting of such comfort that relaxation is stimulated more then reflection. While the therapist spends many more long hours in the therapy room than does the patient, the physical arrangements should not grossly favor the former.

There are differences of opinion among therapists as to the degree to which decor should be impersonal versus revealing something of the tastes and interests of the therapist. Conduct of a polygraph examination might be facilitated by a windowless, pictureless room; the conduct of psychotherapy is a different matter. There is growing evidence and consensus that therapeutic effectiveness is enhanced when the therapist is "real" (see chapter 4). A discrete and limited selection of a few personal effects, such as pictures, photos, mementos, and so on, can convey something of the therapist as a normal human being. Because of their potentially biasing communications of presumed value orientations, plaques or certificates attesting to membership in the Knights of Columbus, the American Legion, a political party or similar "special interest" organizations are much less appropriate than diplomas attesting to professional affiliations.

Apart from fixed macroaspects of the physical setting, it is very important that the therapist be able to give full, undivided, and continuous attention to the patient. This means putting well aside any unfinished business (correspondence, memos, messages, open books, or journals) that might draw the therapist's even fleeting attention or might convey to the patient that he or she has "interrupted" the therapist, albeit appearing for a scheduled appointment. This reduction or elimination of potentially distracting stimuli is helped if the therapist has a work table apart from the "therapy" desk or table. It is obviously facilitated in the orthodox analytic situation of the couch and out-of-sight therapist. Obviously the therapist should arrange not to be interrupted by telephone calls, or even by a ringing but unanswered phone.

Therapist Behavior

No fashion designer (yet!) has proposed a professional uniform for the psychotherapist. Just as the physical setting can have facilitating or off-putting impact on the client, the therapist's garb can subtly enhance or detract from the work of therapy. For the physician therapist (notably the psychiatrist) the traditional clinical white coat of the medical discipline may not be inappropriate. However, it does contribute silently to the potentially negative "you doctor—me patient" attitude of the client (see chap. 5), and encourage an expectation of prescription rather than preceptorship. Some psychologists, especially those who are hospital based, have the privilege of wearing "staff" white coats. Beginning therapists, particularly in their need to have the security and prestige of "doctor" status, may adopt this dress without awareness of its potentially negative impact on their therapeutic endeavors. (In many psychiatric in-patient wards, nursing personnel have adopted street clothes in place of the traditional nurses' whites. There is an appropriate rationale for this change. Whether the assumed therapeutic benefits via the concept of therapeutic "milieu" outweigh possible losses has not been systematically studied.) In the matter of uniform versus nonuniform, where the former is a possibility, the general principle of *flexibility* should be observed. With some patients at some times the white coat (or the loosened necktie) may hold therapeutic agency.

The candidate for therapy expects and deserves to be received with dignity and respect by a professional person. The therapist's mode of dress indirectly conveys the dignity and respect with which the client is received. There are cultural and subcultural differences in client expectations that would make it unrealistic to *prescribe* suit and tie for the male therapist or to proscribe shorts and halter for the female therapist. It can only be cautioned that the therapist's mode of professional dress should not be determined exclusively by considerations of his or her comfort or personal style.

More important than dress in the conduct of therapy are certain elements of *general* behavior, as distinct from specific techniques of treatment. The matter of smoking is a case in point. It may be appropriate to post a "No Smoking" notice in the outer office or waiting room; in some states such areas may be defined by law as "public" and require such posting. In the privacy of the therapist's office, does the therapist permit smoking by clients? Or, consistent with the therapist's value system (commitment to preventive health practices) does he or she prohibit smoking? Or, utilizing the principle of *flexibility*, does the therapist sometimes (at particular points in the course of treatment, i.e., during a particular session,) request the patient to forgo the usual cigarette or pipe?

The issue is perhaps more critical, and less frequently thought out, by the therapist who is a smoker. It may be natural (i.e., comfortable) for the therapist to smoke with the client who does, and to refrain with the client who does not. This would appear to express a degree of flexibility that is desirable. But smoking and eating are personal patterns of consumption that are not a part of professional treatment situations. Quite apart from the current antismoking public stance, and long before the notable decline in use of tobacco by physicians, any physician who smoked while conducting a physical examination would offend the patient, smoker or not, and be subject to criticism by colleagues for nonprofessional behavior. For the psychotherapist to smoke during sessions seems equally nonprofessional; it detracts from the *work* focus as it conveys that the therapist is "taking care of self" while presumably attending the patient.

Similarly, the *routine* offering of coffee, soft drinks, or condiments, while serving all the motives of observing social amenities, contributes to the perception of the exchange as like many others and detracts from the desirable focus, by both therapist and client, on the therapy hour as a special piece of *work*.

The use of names by the therapist is yet another specific behavior that can be automatic, nondeliberate, and a routine practice based on questionable *assumptions* of the therapist as to what fosters rapport and a therapeutic alliance. Thus, the therapist may regularly, after early sessions, address the patient by his or her first name. Does this encourage intimacy, a sense of acceptance, and companionable pursuit of mutual goals? Or, does such practice represent a form of ingratiation, or a demeaning loss of dignity, an infantilizing of the patient? Does the impact of the practice depend upon the particular patient? The same questions pertain to the therapist's encouragement (or discouragement) of being addressed by first name by the patient. Any *routine* practice in this matter is of doubtful validity. Again, selectivity and flexibility should determine the therapist's behavior. Thus, over the course of treatment with a particular client, the therapist may choose to address the client at one time formally with last name, and at another time deliberately by first name, depending upon the specific nature and intent of the communication the therapist is making at the time.

Note Taking

The professionally responsible therapist will maintain a file of clinical notes covering the salient points of each session with each client. Efficiency in the recording of useful clinical notes is a skill that develops over time. The format of such notes is sometimes dictated by an agency of which the therapist is a staff member. Within such a format the clinician can develop his or her own system of notation provided it is not so idiosyncratic as to be noncommunicative to any other professional who may subsequently have authorized responsibility for review.

The tyro therapist may initially be frustrated in the effort to record, in court-reporter style, everything that transpired in a session, especially if there is an expectation that such recording will be required by a supervisor. The experienced therapist records sufficient case notes to provide a useful record to which reference can be made to refresh his or her memory as needed and, importantly, to provide a basis for appraising the client's progress. (For a suggested outline for recording therapy session notes, see Appendix A.)

Whether notes are recorded during or after a therapy session is a matter of decision by the therapist, provided that scheduling allows time for posttherapy recording. Given the fallibility of memory, the postsession interval before notes are recorded should be as short as possible.

The therapist's recording of notes during a session need not impede the flow of discourse. Mental notes can be stored briefly and recorded during a "quiet" period. If the therapist is judicious about timing and extent of writing, the note taking will not be disruptive and may help to maintain the professional, consultative context of the relationship.

However accomplished, the establishment of clinical records is a professional responsibility of the therapist and must conform to the minimal requirements imposed by any federal, state, or agency regulations that are relevant (Sheldon-Widgen, 1982).

Choice of Language

Individual psychotherapy may be defined, as to its basic nature, as conversation with therapeutic intent. However, it is not simply the intent of the conversation that distinguishes it from all the other conversations of daily life. True, it has a focus and occurs in a context of confidentiality that differentiates it. As conducted skillfully by the expert therapist, it has other qualities that set it apart from casual, nonprofessional conversations.

The therapist is thoughtful and deliberate about what he or she says and how it is said, and about when and why silence is maintained. The effectiveness of a therapeutic session is in significant measure a function of the precision with which the therapist's thoughts are expressed and the skill with which the therapist facilitates the communication, and, hence, the understanding of the patient (Wachtel, 1980). Given a particular thought, hypothesis, or query that occurs to the therapist, there are a variety of ways in which it can be expressed. The art, or skill, of therapy consists in part in the ability of the therapist to select rapidly from a large number of possibilities a careful phrasing and to offer his or her comment in a manner likely to have the greatest therapeutic impact, that is, to be consistent with the therapeutic intent of the conversation. Is the intent to challenge? to clarify? to comfort? or deliberately, as is sometimes appropriate, to confuse the client? The skilled therapist is never careless, casual, or sloppy about grammar and vocabulary. This does not mean reliance upon a technical lexicon, which may overwhelm the client, or preciosity and high-flown language, which may inhibit the client. The structure and content of basic English (or other national language) is adequate for the purposes of therapy when used incisively by the therapist.

Words are critical elements in the therapeutic communication. Used with perceptive selectivity, they can serve as hammers or needles, as balms or bombs, as solvents or as glue. With some patients, no amount of repetition makes a point as clearly and lastingly as a well-chosen, well-planned metaphor or analogy.

Professionals who supervise beginning therapists have frequent opportunity to observe the tendency of the inexperienced therapist to carry the habits of casual, everyday conversation into the therapy room. When required to tape their sessions and subsequently replay them, trainees are frequently able to note (and are sometimes appalled) that what they *said* to the client was not what they meant. Similarly they can be sensitized to an awareness that the casual insertion of "I think," "perhaps," and "maybe" can sometimes vitiate or reduce the impact of an otherwise salient observation. There are appropriate times and places for such qualifying reservations; they should not be used habitually or casually.

Observing the "Rules"

Except for specific aspects of behavior modification or behavior therapy, the conduct of psychotherapy is not a technology. There are no rule books that direct the therapist as to when and how to apply prescribed interventions: "If condition A, use technique B," or "When X occurs, stop Q and switch to Z." Recently, in the interests of research projects to study the relative impact of different treatment modalities, manuals have been developed to guide the therapist in the conduct of a specific mode of psychotherapy for the treatment of depresstion (Waskow, 1984). Such manuals do not stand alone; they require an extensive period of specialized training for the therapists who are to pursue the particular approach (Elkin, Parloff, Hadley, & Autry, 1985). Such manuals are essential if there is to be a reasonable degree of standardization of therapeutic practice. However, the therapist is not a computer who serves simply as a processor to assure a fixed transformation from "stimulus in" to "response out." Eventually we will have data on the degree to which such manuals in fact increase the consistency of therapist-to-therapist behaviors with reasonably comparable patients.

In the meantime, such manuals provide a degree of technical direction (and reduction of anxiety) for the neophyte therapist. Even with further development and proliferation, given the complexity of the dynamically interacting variables (refer to chapter 2, figure 2), it is doubtful that such manuals will serve to reduce psychotherapy to a scientifically based technology.

With the growth of psychotherapy, general "rules" to guide all psychotherapists, regardless of their individual theoretical persuasions or favored techniques of intervention, have evolved. These are generally presented with the prescriptive terms "never" or "always." They have an obvious rationale and they are chiefly concerned with the best interests of the patient and the general goals of therapy. They are usually offered as nearly absolute imperatives, that is "the therapist must always," "the therapist must never." Are they, should they, be inviolable?

Confidentiality

To start with an easy and *relatively* noncontroversial one, there is the rule of confidentiality. The therapist (and especially the trainee) learns early and explicitly never to violate the confidences of the patient, and that the *privilege* of confidential communication rests with the patient, not with the therapist. Court actions (most notably the Tarasoff decision) and the requirements of "third-party" insurers for diagnostic and therapy information have generated active debate among authorities as to whether the principle of confidentiality should be observed absolutely and in all cases (Applebaum, 1985; Jagim, Wittman & Noll, 1978; Knapp & VandeCreek, 1982; Myers, 1986; Shah, 1970; Siegel, 1979). Everstine et al (1980) provide an excellent review of the relevant issues and a suggested outline of the client's "rights" as they relate to issues of confidentiality. Apart from those legal statutes defining the circumstances under which the therapist is required to violate confidentiality, it is extremely unlikely that the therapist who observed the rule absolutely would ever be subject to significant professional criticism. (For a review of state-by-state laws governing privileged *communications and confidentiality,* see DeKraai & Sales, 1984.) To break the rule always exposes the therapist to some risk, if not of actual legal suit, at least of possible dissolution of the therapeutic alliance. Obviously the risk to the therapist is greater if he or she breaks this element of the contract without forewarning to the client. Neither clients nor the general public are well-informed about the limits on confidentiality; when queried, they are nealy unanimous in expressing a wish to be informed about confidentiality at the outset of a professional consultation (Miller & Thelen, 1986). Should the therapist observe the rule without exception, even though clinical judgment indicates that it would not be in the best interest of the client? The court decisions that have reduced the absolute guarantee of confidentiality are a reminder to the therapist that while primarily a servant of the client, he or she is always in some degree an agent of the society of which both client and therapist are members (see chap. 2).

Reassurance

Less thorny but subject to equally mindless incorporation, especially by the beginning therapists, is the injunction that one should *never reassure.* It is usually transmitted as an absolute; it would be less troublesome if the prescription were never to carelessly (casually) reassure the patient. Tyro therapists are particularly gun-shy about reassuring statements. Their tendency to rigidly withhold any such expression seems to be based on two elements: (1) a recognition that reassurance implies a guarantee of therapeutic efficacy about which they are in fact quite uncertain; and (2) the related recognition of an implied prediction any subsequent falsification of which would be an embarrassment. There may be reasonable concern that reassurance (or, is it too much reassurance given too soon?) will reduce the client's motivation to *work* in therapy and/or create the expectation that the "expert" will do the work. On the other hand, how will strict withholding of any reassurance affect the patient's expectations and readiness to invest in therapy? When the patient asks, "Can you help me?," there are a variety of possible answers: "I don't know," or "Perhaps," or "Maybe," or "We shall have to see," or even, "I don't think so." The therapist who has a habitual, routine (by formula) response to all requests for reassurance, however indirect, is failing to apply astute, clinical, individualized judgment to use or not to use a powerful psychological force.

Advice

Another general rule especially subject to overincorporation by beginning therapists is the rule that the therapist should never advise a patient. In its basic rationale it is a good rule because its aim is to prevent the therapist from taking over, however inadvertently, the decision-making responsibilities of the patient. Put bluntly, the rule means that the therapist should not direct the client as to how to live his or her life. The rule implies that if the therapist is directive and gives advice, he or she becomes "responsible" for the client. Is the possibility for clear communication and understanding of the separation between the therapist's advisory role and the client's decision-making responsibility so remote or unlikely that the formal contract must include the disclaimer: "I, Dr._____, will not be held to any responsibility for any decisions made by _____during or immediately following the period of (his/her) therapy."?

Closely related to the prohibition against giving direction or advice on major areas of conflict is the injunction against offering opinions. The therapist is viewed usually (perhaps necessarily) as a person of professional knowledge, expertise, and accumulated wisdom. It is likely that if the therapist offers an informed opinion about the likely outcome of certain courses of action by the client, the latter will be guided at least in part by the therapist's opinion. Is that bad? Is that to be avoided under all circumstances? Or, is the informed opinion of the therapist part of what the client can reasonably believe is being paid for with the professional fees? Is it possibly a violation of ethics or of professional responsibility when the therapist categorically refuses to offer an opinion? It can be said, almost categorically, that the therapist who seeks to avoid the sharing of an opinion by claiming that he or she does not have any (a psychological improbability) is deliberately lying; all but the most naive of clients will probably detect the falsity, with subsequent erosion of the trust that is crucial to effective therapy. It can be conducive to the therapeutic alliance for the therapist to communicate that no opinion will be offered on an action or decision of the client *after* it has been taken!

There are other "rules" for the conduct of psychotherapy that, while less prominent than the above, have become part of accepted lore. For example, the therapist-in-training is enjoined never to argue with a patient and never to use sarcasm or ridicule. These are good rules and their rationale is obvious; the inexperienced therapist is well-advised to observe them. However, unyielding observance can, in some circumstances, deny the therapist (and the patient) of the therapeutic impact of special forms of communication. Can effective cognitive therapy be pursued without at least the formal elements of argument and counterargument? Are sarcasm and ridicule (at least helping the patient to see the ridiculousness of his or her stance or behavior?) not effective modes for *instigation* of the patient who is inadequately motivated? The desirable impact of subtle sarcasm or ridicule is sometimes achievable through the judicious use of *labels*. The "rule" is not to apply labels that denigrate or needlessly affront the patient. It is a good rule. But consider the opportunity for the therapist to describe the patient's behavior as "immature" or "irresponsible" or to describe his or her behavior as "like" that of an "alley cat." Which has greater likelihood of satisfying the therapist's therapeutic intent?

Finally, there are certain rules, injunctions, and prohibitions that have been, from the time of the ancients, a part, at least implicitly, of the ethical code of therapists. The Oath of Hippocrates, for example, enjoined physicians from sexual intimacy with their patients or members of their patient's household. In recent years, violations of the obvious ethical prohibition against physical intimacy between therapists and their clients have become such a common source of malpractice suits that injunctions concerning them have been formally incorporated not only into professional codes of ethics but into statutory law governing the practice of licensed professionals. It is perhaps not surprising in light of the great increase in the number of practicing therapists (of varying backgrounds, education, training, and supervision) and the corresponding increase in the number of persons in treatment, that there has been an increasing incidence of sexual intimacies in therapy. It is only slightly more surprising that such behavior should be rationalized by a few therapists as "part of the therapy." Such rationalization is the crassest form of justification for selfishness. Studies have shown that effective therapy and concurrent physical intimacy between therapist and patient cannot be sustained; in the majority of such instances the client breaks off therapy. Beyond that the exploited client is likely to experience exacerbated psychological disturbance and difficulty in initiating treatment with another therapist (Bouhoutsos, Holroyd, Lerman, Forer, & Greenberg, 1983; Gartrell, Herman, Olarta, Feldstein, & Localio, 1986; Geldman-Summers & Jones, 1984; Holroyd & Bouhoutsos, 1985). The interdiction against physical *intimacy* should not inhibit the therapist from recognizing the healing power of touch and using the grasp of the arm or the pat on the back or shoulder as a judiciously timed reinforcer of the general therapeutic message of acceptance and support (Edwards, 1981).

Freud stipulated that therapists should avoid even extratherapy *social* or business relations with patients. It has been recognized that apart from the possible contamination of the transference relationship, any extratherapy interactions between therapist and client involve the likelihood of conflict of interest and a corresponding impairment of the therapist's necessary objectivity.

These two rules, even if not codified, relate to therapist behavior with clear and likely injurious impact on clients; they are properly viewed as absolutes never to be violated, and with severe consequences for both therapist and client when they are contravened.

The therapist must be continuously mindful of all the general rules and understand their rationale; he or she must know that violation of any of them entails risks. The expertise of therapy, in a small part, entails knowledge of these ground rules and the relation of their observance to effective therapy. The skill of experienced therapists consists, also in a small part, of knowing when, why, and how to violate those rules that are not absolute. Effective and efficient therapy requires more than adherence to formula—it requires continuous *judgment* and *flexibility*.

Notes

1. Adapted in part from "A Guide for Consumers of Psychological Services," prepared by The Minnesota Psychological Association, 1986.
2. Adapted in part from "A Guide for Consumers of Psychological Services," prepared by The Minnesota Psychological Association, 1986.
3. Many years ago a Minnesota clergyman was found in contempt for refusing to testify in court on the content of counseling sessions he had conducted with certain parishioners. Upon appeal the clergyman's conviction was reversed and the precedent of this case established privileged communication for the counselees of Minnesota clergy.

References

American Psychiatric Association. (1980). *Diagnostic and statistical manual of mental disorders* (3rd ed.). Washington, DC: Author.

Applebaum, P. S. (1985). Tarasoff and the clinician: Problems in fulfilling the duty to protect. *American Journal of Psychiatry, 142,* 425–429.

Beck, J. C. (1982). When the patient threatens violence: An empirical study of clinical practice after Tarasoff. *Bulletin of the American Academy of Psychiatry and Law, 10,* 189–201.

Bouhoutsos, J., Holroyd, J., Lerman, H., Forer, B. R., & Greenberg, M. (1983). Sexual intimacy between psychotherapists and patients. *Professional Psychology: Research & Practice, 14,* 185–196.

DeKraai, M. B., & Sales, B. D. (1984). Confidential communications of psychotherapists. *Psychotherapy Theory, Research, and Practice, 21,* 293–315.

Edwards, D. J. (1981). The role of touch in interpersonal relations: Implications for psychotherapy. *South African Journal of Psychology,* 11, 29–37.

Elkin, I., Parloff, M. B., Hadley, S. W. & Autry, J. M. (1985) NIMH treatment of depression collaborative study: Background and research plan. *Archives of General Psychiatry, 42,* 305–316.

Everstine, L., Everstine, D. S., Heyman, G. M., True, R. H., Frey, D. H., Johnson, H. G., & Seiden, R. H. (1980) Privacy and confidentiality in psychotherapy. *American Psychologist, 35,* 828–840.

Gartrell, N., Herman, J., Olarte, S., Feldstein, M., & Localio, R. (1986) Psychiatrist-patient sexual contact: Results of a national survey, I: Prevalence. *American Journal of Psychiatry, 143,* 1126–1131.

Geldman-Summers, S., and Jones, G. (1984) Psychological impacts of sexual contacts between therapists or other health care providers and their clients. *Journal of Consulting and Clinical Psychology, 52,* 1054–1061.

Halgin, R. P. & Weaver, D. D. (1986) Salient beliefs about obtaining psychotherapy, *Psychotherapy in Private Practice, 4,* 23–31.

Holroyd, J. & Bouhoutsos, J. C. (1985). Biased reporting of therapist-patient sexual intimacy. *Professional Psychology: Research & Practice, 16,* 701–709.

Jagim, R. D., Wittman, W. D. & Noll, J. O. (1978) Mental health professionals' attitudes toward confidentiality, privilege, and third-party disclosure. *Professional Psychology: Research and Practice, 9,* 458–466.

Kirschenbaum, D. S., & Flanery, R. C. (1984). Toward a psychology of behavioral contracting. *Clinical Psychology Review, 4,* 597–618.

Kirschenbaum, D. S., & Flanery, R. C. (1985). Behavioral contracts: Outcome and elements. In M. Herzen, R. Eisler, & P. M. Miller (Eds.), *Progress in behavior modification.* New York: Academic Press.

Knapp, S., & VandeCreek, L. (1982). Tarasoff: Five years later. *Professional Psychology: Research and Practice, 13,* 511–516.

Miller, D. J., & Thelen, M. H. (1986). Knowledge and beliefs about confidentiality in psychotherapy. *Professional Psychology: Research & Practice, 17,* 15–19.

Motta, R. W. (1981). Use of contracts in psychotherapy. *Psychological Reports, 49,* 319–325.

Myers, C. J., (1986). The legal perils of psychotherapeutic practice: The farther reaches of the "duty to warn." In L. Everstine (Ed.), *Psychotherapy and the law.* New York: Grune & Stratton.

O'Connell, S. (1984). Promise-of-treatment as an opening strategy for psychotherapy. *Psychotherapy: Theory, Research and Practice, 21,* 473–478.

Omer, H. (1985). Fulfillment of therapeutic tasks as a precondition for acceptance in therapy. *American Journal of Psychotherapy, 39,* 175–186.

Quinn, K. M. (1984). The impact of Tarasoff on clinical practice. *Behavior Sciences & The Law, 2,* 319–329.

Reder, P. & Tyson, R. L. (1980). Patient drop out from individual psychotherapy: A review and discussion. *Bulletin of the Menninger Clinic, 44,* 229–252.

Reynolds, R. V. C., McNamara, J. R., Marion, R. V., & Tobin, D. L. (1985). Computerized service delivery in clinical psychology. *Professional Psychology: Research and Practice, 16,* 339–353.

Schofield, W. (1966). In sickness and in health. *Community Mental Health Journal, 2,* 244–251.

Seligman, L. (1984). Temporary termination. *Journal of Counseling and Development, 63,* 43–44.

Shah, S. T. (1969). Privileged communications, confidentiality, and privacy: Privileged communications. *Professional Psychology: Research and Practice, 1,* 56–69.

Shah, S. T. (1970). Privileged communications, confidentiality, and privacy: Confidentiality. *Professional Psychology: Research and Practice, 1,* 159–166.

Sheldon-Widgen, J. (1982). Avoiding legal liability: The rights and responsibilities of therapists. *Behavior Therapist, 5,* 165–169.

Siegel, M. (1979). Privacy, ethics, and confidentiality. *Professional Psychology: Research and Practice, 10,* 249–258.

Silverman, W. H., & Beech, R. P. (1979) Are dropouts, dropouts? *Journal of Community Psychology, 7,* 236–242.

Southard, M. J. & Gross, B. H. (1982). Making clinical decisions after Tarasoff. *New Directions for Mental Health Services, 16,* 93–101.

Strupp, H. H., Hadley, S. W. & Gomes-Schwartz, B. (1977). *Psychotherapy for better or worse: The problem of negative effects.* New York: Jason Aronson.

Tryon, G. S. (1983). Why full-time private practitioners refer patients to other professionals. *Psychotherapy in Private Practice, 1,* 81–83.

Wachtel, P. L. (1980). What should we say to our patients? On the wording of therapists' comments. *Psychotherapy: Theory, Research & Practice, 17,* 183-188.

Wade, T. C. & Baker, T. B. (1977) Opinions and use of psychological tests: A survey of clinical psychologists. *American Psychologist, 32,* 874–882.

Waskow, I. E. (1984) Specification of the technique variable in the NIMH treatment of depression collaborative research program. In J.B.W. Williams & R.S. Spitzer (Eds.) *Psychotherapy research: Where are we and where should we go?* New York: Guilford.

Zaro, J. S., Barach, R., Nedelman, D. J. & Dreiblatt, I. S. (1977). *A guide for beginning psychotherapists.* Cambridge: Cambridge University Press.

7

Theory vs. Theory—
Technique vs. Technique

In the realm of human thought directed to the understanding of complex phenomena, there are sequential stages that can be observed to operate in all fields of inquiry. In brief, there are successive phases in the sociology of science: (1) The invention of theory to account for the interrelationships of laboratory and field observations and to provide lawful, testable predictions; (2) attacks upon inadequacies of the theory, supported by research leading to new or improved observations and eventually to a new theoretical formulation; (3) a period of active partisan support for competing theoretical formulations; (4) a period of "overview" during which some workers are motivated to search for rapprochement or integration, to argue that some of the "truths" of one theoretical formulation are not antithetical to some of the "truths" of a competing theory, and to demonstrate that constructs (hypotheses and/or methods) must be drawn from each in order to afford a fuller comprehension of the target phenomena.

These stages of inquiry, theorization, and debate have marked the history of psychotherapy. The fourth stage, marked by efforts to rationalize a unification of apparent divergences of viewpoints and practices, might appear to be of recent onset if judged by the frequency of calls for rapprochement. Goldfried (1982) has provided a history of such efforts in which he points out that as early as 1932, Thomas M. French (1933) sought to correlate the Freudian concept of repression with the Pavlovian concepts of inhibition and extinction. This was one of the earliest efforts to draw together fundamental pieces of psychodynamic and behavioral psychology, an effort that has persisted (Wachtel, 1977). A highlight in the psychoanalytic-behavioral integration literature was Dollard and Miller's (1950), *Personality and Psychotherapy*. Commenting on that classic work, Feather and Rhoads (1972) noted that "no distinctive therapy technique has evolved from it." Goldfried (1980) remarked on the initial rejection of

Breger and McGaugh's (1965) criticism of behavior therapy as overly dependent on Pavlovian and Skinnerian learning theory, but saw that critique as a significant stimulus to the development of "cognitive behavior therapy."

While focusing on the efforts to integrate psychodynamic and behavioral concepts, Goldfried (1982) acknowledged the contribution toward unification provided by Rosenzweig (1936), Frank (1961) and others in their exposition of common factors (see chapter 5). Overlooked are those debates and moves toward rapprochement arising from the nonpsychodynamic cognitive schools of therapy, for example, Ellis (1962), Beck (1970), and others versus the behaviorists, and leading to cognitive-behavioral integrations (Meichenbaum, 1979).

It is difficult to assess the impact of the efforts to date to provide an all-encompassing structure for the theoretical constructs and associated techniques of psychotherapy. The major schools continue to be visible and vigorous in training, in research, in clinical work, and in scholarly writing. For the practitioner who adheres to a particular school, there are advantages: a sense of security and confidence (possibly misplaced) about what he or she does, and the correlated benefit to the client who responds in part to the therapist's confidence; the opportunity to become progressively experienced and efficient in the application of a set of specific, theory-based techniques; the support of a *professional network* (Goldfried, 1982) of societies, journals, and so on, and a common technical language for communication within that network; the esprit de corps and excitement of being a combatant against the limitations, excesses, and "errors" of other camps. The primary disadvantage for the "purist" therapist is that he or she will not recognize those therapeutic failures resulting when a client does not fit his or her particular approach.

Although the major psychotherapy schools show no signs of involutional decay and they are unlikely to become, like the vacuum tube radio, phenomena of only historical interest in the near future, there are indications that each school has a somewhat waning influence on the actual day-to-day practice of psychotherapy. There are two observations that bear on this impression. One rests in the evidence, experimental and anecdotal, that therapists who may profess very differently actually practice very similarly (Fiedler, 1950a, 1950b; Klein, Dittman, Parloff & Gill, 1969; Larson, 1980; Strupp, 1955a, 1960). The other comes from surveys of therapists, especially psychologists, that indicate that a growing number of therapists self-identify as "eclectic" in their orientation rather than as Freudians, Rogerians, or adherents of other schools (Garfield & Kurtz, 1974, 1975). Also, we have witnessed the appearance of eclectic texts (Beutler, 1983; Garfield, 1980; Lazarus, 1981) a *Handbook of Eclectic*

Psychotherapy (Norcross, 1986) and even a *Journal of Eclectic Psychotherapy.* In the introductory chapter of the *Handbook,* Norcross (1986) observed, "Only within the last 15 years . . . eclecticism has developed into a clearly delimited area of interest. And this has occurred less as an orderly scientific advance than as a developing climate of opinion." (p. 4) In an often-quoted depiction, Eysenck (1970) wrote of "broad spectrum" eclecticism (Lazarus, 1970) as a "mish-mash of theories, a hugger mugger of procedures, a gallimaufry of therapies and a charivaria of activities having no proper rationale, and incapable of being tested or evaluated." (p. 145) Norcross (1986) offered six reasons for the growth of eclecticism: (1) the rapid proliferation of therapies; (2) the apparent limitations of each extant therapy; (3) the absence of convincing evidence of the differential effectiveness of the different therapies; (4) the gradual acceptance of the idea that client characteristics and the therapist-patient relationships are the most potent elements; (5) the search for common elements; and (6) "sociopolitical contingencies." Included in the last category would be the weakening attractions of guild membership.

The trend to eclecticism, however that term is to be understood, probably reflects the joint influence of the theoretical literature on integrated therapy and the growing experience of clinicians who find in their day-to-day work that "one shoe will not fit all."

Rapprochement

In reading that part of the voluminous literature on psychotherapy that is concerned with the perplexities arising from the multiplicity of theory and the diversity of techniques, two themes or purposes are discernable. One of these is the appeal for rapprochement and the other is the effort at integration. The two overlap considerably.

Rapprochement—(Webster's Ninth New Collegiate Dictionary, 1985)— "Establishment of or state of having cordial relations." The definition implies two or more parties to a dispute of some kind whose relations have been less than mutually accepting and warm. With respect to psychotherapy, the efforts at rapprochement have been philosophical and theory oriented. At one level the efforts represent an intellectual search for *unifying principles* and rests on the premise that natural phenomena, in the final analysis, rest upon one rather than several sets of "laws." At another level, proposals for rapprochement express the desire to meliorate the early stridency of "school" claims and counterclaims, acknowledging that each theory (school) has a piece of the truth. In this context, while not always explicitly issuing a call for rapprochement, those scholars who have searched out and identified "common factors" have contributed to this endeavor (Prochaska, 1984; Prochaska & DiClemente, 1984).

Where theory is at issue it is possible for debate to arise and discourse to persist only if the competing protagonists have securely established and adequately delineated structures of concepts and axioms and a respectable amount of accumulated observational (evidentiary) support for their respective stances. This is why the earliest and most ardent thrusts and parries, and the later efforts at rapprochement, have involved the psychodynamicists (psychoanalytically oriented) and the behaviorists (psychologically oriented).

Rapprochement is chiefly an intellectual endeavor at the level of theoretical constructs, formulations, hypothesized variables, and more or less formalized axioms. It is not an exercise for the laboratory or the clinic, although data from those settings can be and have been used to fortify particular theorized entities. It is in the clinic and laboratory that one may see substantive *integration* of theory-based practices. If rapprochement of the psychoanalytic and behavioral camps were to attract the interest of nonpartisan, unaffiliated scientist/logicians,its possibilities might receive a fair shake and some actual collapsing, fusing, or coordinating of concepts (or, at least, a glossary of semantic equivalents) might result. Thus far, the primary seekers for unitary truth between the two camps have had strong school identifications. This makes for vigorous debate and some clarifications, but there seems little likelihood that present signatories to an *entente cordiale* will move toward a sovereign unified state under one flag. The movement toward rapprochement has had sufficient impetus to generate a Society for the Exploration of Psychotherapy Integration (note the term), SEPI. Editors of an early number of SEPI's newsletter observed that in the last 50 years, rapprochement had been the topic of 125 articles, 27 chapters, and 36 books. (Goldfried & Wachtel, 1984). The title of a recent edited book on the subject includes the question: "Is Integration Possible?" (Arkowitz & Messer, 1984). The best answer would seem to be: possible but unlikely.

Messer and Winokur (1980) explored the possibility of moving these two camps toward a common ground, observing that some psychoanalysts emphasized suggestion and abreaction and that some behaviorists were attentive to the thoughts and feelings of clients. They cited Wachtel's (1977) encouragement to analysts to attend more to the patient's present than to the past and to give more attention to the interpersonal than the intrapsychic, while urging behavior therapists to apply dynamic concepts to understanding clients' problems and to be more attentive to the client-therapist interactions in sessions. Although generally hopeful for the possibility that these "corrections" could move the two camps toward a common center, Messer and Winokur raised the possibility that a genuine rapprochement might be prevented or significantly inhibited by the existence of a profound difference in the way in which analysts and behaviorists view "reality." Referring to Schafer's (1976) characterization of the psychoanalytic view of the world, Messer and Winokur described disparate perspectives on reality: the psychodynamic therapist expressing idealism, subjectivism, and introspection, while the behaviorist's perspective is one of realism, objectivism, and "extrospection."

There are some studies that bear on the issue of cognitive predilections. Using a structured questionnaire to measure epistomological preferences, Schacht and Black (1984) compared samples of behavioral and psychoanalytic therapists. They found the analysts to be relatively homogenous in their preference for metaphorism, rationalism, and empiricism, in that order. By contrast, the behavior therapists were heterogeneous and expressed no predominant epistomological style. Schacht and Black concluded "Basic visions of reality, operationalized as epistemic styles, are *possible* barriers to therapeutic integration." (p. 321)

On the basis of a model proposed by Brickman et al. (1982), McGovern, Newman, and Kopta (1986) hypothesized that therapists of different theoretical orientation would differ in their attributional styles. They measured the degree of assignment of "responsibility for problems" and "responsibility for change" either to the patient or to the therapist by small samples of psychodynamic, cognitive-behavioral, eclectic, and family therapists respectively. Contrary to their hypothesis, the psychoanalytically oriented therapists assigned low responsibility to patients both for their problems and for change. By contrast, the other therapist samples were similar in attributing to patients high responsibility both for their problems and for necessary changes.

In another study of attributional bias (response readiness), Plous and Zimbardo (1986) compared samples of psychoanalysts, behavior therapists, and nontherapists. They used clinical vignettes to measure the tendency of the therapists to attribute causality for problems to dispositional (personality) versus situational (environmental) factors. They found that the analytic therapists made a significantly greater number of dispositional attributions than did the behaviorists, while the latter showed a distinctive reverse finding. Also, the psychoanalysts "demonstrated a clear attributional bias by perceiving the problems of others as primarily psychological in origin and perceiving their own problems as primarily physical in origin." (!) (p. 569) This finding raises a question as to the validity and adequacy of that part of the training of analysts that requires that they undergo a personal analysis.

To the extent that these "cognitive perspectives" or perceptual biases are stable characteristics of the therapist's personality (and responsible in part for his or her attraction toward one theory rather than another), they could reduce the therapist's openness to a position of rapprochement. This would be consistent with Lazarus's (1967) observations: "Faced with this complex, contradictory and often confusing array of psychological theories and systems, most practitioners seek refuge in those notions which best satisfy their own subjective needs." (p. 415) It is also consistent with the findings of Schacht and Black (1985) that psychoanalysts have a distinctive "epistemic style" that is different from that of behaviorists.

Integration

According to Webster, the verb *integrate*, means "to form, coordinate, or blend into a functioning or unified whole." In psychotherapy, efforts at integration have focused on the proposal that specific techniques of treatment can be drawn from a variety of schools or theories, provided that the techniques have been demonstrated to be effective. The therapist who is not theory-bound need not be technique-bound. The assumption is that specific modes of intervention with established validity can be effectively applied in a course of treatment that is not consistently modeled on any single theory with which some of the basic techniques are primarily associated. Thus, in the course of a particular treatment case, the "integrationist" therapist might make use of Rogersian reflection of affect, Ellisian counterpropagandistic rationalism, Freudian interpretation of manifest content, Wolpeian desensitization, Pavlovian in vivo extinction, Franklian paradoxical intention, and so on. To do so, the therapist would not be guided by an integration of theories but rather by a selective integration of techniques, a judicious chronology of those techniques in accordance with his or her "theory of the case." The therapist would not be applying a "therapy-of-choice" but rather a systematic sequence of "techniques-of-choice." If selection of appropriate technique is best determined by the problem being treated, it is obvious that "integrated therapy" is appropriate when the client presents a variety of problems, not necessarily interconnected, and does not have a single pathology that is expressed exclusively in cognitive or affective or behavioral symptoms.

Intermediate to the efforts at rapprochement of theories and the integration of techniques is the suggestion of Goldfried (1980) that consensus might be found "at a level of abstraction somewhere between theory and technique." this is the level of "clinical strategies," and Goldfried suggested two such strategies that may be common to all schools of therapy: (1) "providing the patient/client with new, corrective experiences, and (b) offering the patient/client direct feedback." Without specifying the specific techniques related to each of these two strategies, the latter could be viewed as belonging in the compendium of "common factors" noted previously (chap. 5).

The most prominent exposition of an approach to treatment based upon a conceptualization of clinical strategies is Lazarus's *Multimodal Therapy* (1981). Lazarus's integration begins with a structural analysis of personality into the following elements: behaviors, affective responses, sensations, images, cognitions, interpersonal relations, and biological functions. The first letters of each element provide the mnemonic acronym BASIC-IB. Substituting "D" (drugs) for the biological element, provides "the more compelling acronym BASIC-ID," a conversion that Lazarus rationalizes by suggesting that "D" be understood to comprise not only drugs but also "nutrition, hygiene, exercise, and the panoply of medical diagnoses and interventions that affect personality" and adjustment or maladjustment. With this formulation, in contrast to most other schools of therapy, Lazarus has proposed an approach to therapy that corrects for the dominant dualism of other systems that ignore the vital potentials of "adjunctive" therapies.

Multimodal therapy begins with a careful assessment of the patient to determine the nature and extent of problems, if any, in each of the seven components of BASIC-ID. In this assessment attention is paid to the patient's characteristic "firing order," that is, in which of the components does the patient's pathological response usually begin and how does that response relate to activation of disturbance in other components? This analysis determines the therapist's priority of attention to problems and the techniques of intervention to be used for initial emphasis. Lazarus acknowledges that not all clients manifest significant disturbance in all seven components and recognizes that successful intervention in some cases can result from focus on those techniques appropriate to only one or two areas of distress.

A recent contribution to integrated therapy at the level of clinical strategy is offered by Howard, Nance and Myers (1986) in their proposal of Adaptive Counseling and Therapy (ACT). They cite Beutler (1983) and Brammer and Shostrom (1977) as examples of earlier efforts at integration arising from the counseling context. In contrast to their formulations, which draw from contesting theory-technique complexes found in the psychotherapy literature, Howard, Nance, and Myers (1986) propose an integration of strategies that rests on a model of organizational behavior, namely, the Situational Leadership Theory of Hersey and Blanchard (1977). The essence of ACT derives from the interplay of two basic therapist dimensions with the client's level of "maturity." Therapist style is an expression of locus along two dimensions: directive behavior and supportive behavior. These generate the possibility of four relatively distinct and presumably characteristic "styles" of therapist behavior, for example, high directiveness with high supportiveness, high directiveness with low supportiveness, and so on. Client maturity is an expression of "readiness" to change, with degree of readiness, as construed by Hersey and Blanchard, determined by "willingness, ability, and self-confidence." The ACT model postulates four levels of client readiness that are correlated with the four optimal therapist styles generated by the high-low categories on the supportive-directive dimensions. The assessment task for the therapist is to determine the level of client readiness and then to provide the particular mix of direction-support considered appropriate to that level. It is expected that the client's readiness (maturity) will shift positively in response to effective intervention. When this happens, it behooves the therapist to alter the support-direction mix. However, in positing a predominant therapist "style," Howard et al. imply the possibility of poor client-therapist pairing and the importance of referral. This internal "static" of the ACT model can be eliminated if the support-direction combinations are conceptualzed as *strategies* rather than styles, with emphasis on the importance of therapist flexibility. The authors of ACT have provided a set of clinical vignettes and possible responses that afford therapists an opportunity to determine their predominant style and also obtain an index of their relative flexibility.

Multimodal therapy and ACT represent very different efforts at integration at the level of clinical strategy. They are not concerned with rapprochement of conflicting theories. The multimodal therapy of Lazarus, with its rich exposition of specific techniques addressed to specific disturbances, will have a natural appeal to the behaviorally oriented (preferential style?) therapist. The ACT model, at its present stage of development, is without prescription of specific techniques but with its implicit emphasis on attitudinal factors will appeal to the therapist who views (preferential style?) the client-therapist relationship as the heart of the therapeutic process.

Eclecticism

Those scholars who have explored the possibilities for rapprochement among ostensibly different theories of psychological disorder (its etiology and correlated indications of intervention modalities) and those who have exposited the rationale for an integrated application of diverse techniques of therapy have contributed toward a prominent movement in psychotherapy—namely, the adoption of an *eclectic* stance by practitioners.

In a 40-year appraisal, Garfield (1981) noted the dominance of psychoanalytic theory and psychodynamic process in the decades of the 1940s and 1950s. The challenge to the hegemony of classical psychoanalytic treatment offered by Alexander and French (1946), with their presentation of technical innovations to make treatment more flexible and of shorter duration, was a forerunner to the brief dynamic therapies proposed with greater impact much later by Davenloo (1980), Malan (1963), Mann (1973), and others, but it did not significantly detract from the preeminent position of psychoanalysis.

Psychoanalysis faced its first real and lasting challenge with the appearance of new "schools" of therapy, notably the Rogersian "client-centered" approach and the rediscovery of behavioral therapy (see chap. 4 for an overview of the evolution of competing schools of psychotherapy).

The advent of several prominent schools with their competing theoretical formulations of pathology and treatment offered practitioners the possibility, if not the necessity, of choice as to how they would conceptualize and practice. When the earliest comparative studies of effectiveness appeared, they did not provide a basis for clear preference—as suggested in one survey, "everyone has won and all must have prizes" (Luborsky, Singer, & Luborsky, 1975).

Both the dialectic literature on contrasting theories and the research literature on comparative effectivensss probably have affected the way therapists respond when asked to profess their school allegiances. As early as 1974, one survey (Garfield & Kurtz) of clinical-psychologist-therapists found over half of them claiming an "eclectic" orientation when offered the opportunity to identify themselves as aligned with one or another position, including Adlerian, behavioral, cognitive, existential, Gestalt, humanistic, psychoanalytic, Rogersian, and so on. In later surveys of similar samples of therapists (Garfield & Kurtz, 1975; Prochaska & Norcross, 1983; Sundland, 1977), the percentage of self-identified "eclectics" has varied between one third and one half, in each instance representing the most popular choice, followed by "psychodynamic" as second-most-frequent orientation. In summarizing the findings of several surveys of psychologist therapists, Norcross and Wogan (1983b) concluded, "A retrospective analysis of these surveys indicates changes over time toward a growing percentage of eclectics and behaviorists and a corresponding decrease in orthodox psychoanalysts." (p. 537) Unfortunately, most such surveys have not offered the respondents a definition of *eclectic,* and the meaning of such identity is ambiguous.

Eclectic, "1: Selecting what appears to be best in various doctrines, methods, or styles; 2: Composed of elements drawn from various sources" *(Webster's Ninth New Collegiate Dictionary, 1985).* It is of note that the first definition suggests an element of quality (validity?) in the choice of what is adopted from various sources; the second does not. Neither definition suggests any necessary process of *integration* of what is selected. Do the self-identified eclectic therapists express primarily a negative stance, that is a rejection of allegiance to any one established doctrine? Or, do they, with proper understanding of the first definition, assert postively that they select the best from several sources? The survey results do not answer these questions.

In a follow-up study of psychologist therapists who were identified as eclectic in an earlier survey, Garfield and Kurtz (1977) determined that nearly one half had previously adhered to a particular theoretical orientation; of these, the "overwhelming majority" indicated that their previous theoretical allegiance had been psychoanalytic. When asked to identify the two most *positive* orientations contributing to their eclecticism, the most frequently chosen combination was "learning theory" and "psychoanalytic." Garfield and Kurtz concluded that "the designation eclectic covers a wide range of views, some of which are apparently quite the opposite of others." (p. 79)

In their survey of psychologist therapists Prochaska and Norcross (1983) invited their sample of self-identified eclectic therapists to further indicate their orientation by chosing one of three types of eclecticism: *atheoretical, synthetic*—"integrating a diversity of contemporary theories," and *technical*—"use of a variety of techniques within a preferred theory." Only 4% indicated an atheoretical orientation; one third identified with technical eclecticism. The overwhelming majority (65%) chose synthetic eclecticism, as identified above. Prochaska and Norcross concluded that "the real challenge for synthetic eclectic therapists and theorists alike is to construct models of systematic [sic] eclecticism that have both empirical validity and clinical utility." (p. 168)

Attempts at providing a theoretical rationale for eclecticism are not intellectually impressive. There is much spading of old ground from which the treasures have been long exhumed and distributed. There is no pressing need for metatheory or eclecticism of eclecticism. What is needed is persistent research addressed to the crucial question first posed by Paul in 1967, "What treatment, by whom, is most effective for this individual with that specific problem, and under what set of circumstances?" (p. 111)

At the level of therapeutic practice, eclecticism may be expressed in the therapist's *consistent,* case-to-case idiosyncratic amalgamation of theoretical constructs and specific techniques. Asked to define the eclectic orientation, one of Garfield and Kurtz's (1977) respondents replied, "It is a mixture of psychoanalytic, neo-analytic, Rogersian, existential theories, plus a heavy reliance on learning theory, particularly as applied to behavior modification techniques.'' (p. 82) Presumably all the clients of such a therapist would be treated with the same amalgam.

By contrast, another respondent defined eclectic to mean "use whatever theory or method seems best for the client. Select procedures according to the client and his problem." By inference from their respective definitions, one would expect the former eclectic to behave more consistently from case to case while the latter would display greater case-to-case variability.

With growing evidence of a move toward therapeutic eclecticism, Lazarus (1967) offered an argument for "technical eclecticism." Agreeing with London's (1964) observation that patients are treated with techniques and not with theories, Lazarus was skeptical of the possibility for eclecticism at the level of theory. He observed, "the eclectic theorist who borrows bits and pieces from divergent theories in the hope of building a composite system must inevitably embrace contradictory notions and thus is likely to find himself in a state of confusion more confounded." (p. 416) This argument for technical eclecticism is consistent with Lazarus's view that there are treatments of choice for specific disorders (Lazarus, 1980, 1984) and with his development of multimodal therapy. While focusing on specific intervention techniques, Lazarus systematized his approach with at least an anatomy of personality if not a theory.

While most of the development of eclecticism in psychotherapy has occurred in psychology, psychiatry has attended to some of the related issues. Simon (1974) noted that in psychiatry the earliest meaning of eclectic was "anti-Freudian." Yager (1977) proposed that eclecticism was the natural result of the properties of our perceptual-cognitive apparatus, of "how we organize reality," noting, for example, that American psychiatrists observe and record a larger number of symptoms than do British psychiatrists.

Despite the advantages to the practitioner of having a firm theoretical or school identification, as noted earlier, and Goldfried's (1980) observation that "to be an eclectic is to have a marginal professional identity," eclecticism is a significant movement in contemporary psychotherapy. It appears to represent the openness of therapists to continue to learn beyond their formal graduate training. Survey data (Norcross & Prochaska, 1983) for psychologist/therapists indicate clinical experience as the most significant determinant of theoretical orientation, while dependence on theory to direct therapy decreases with experience (Sundland, 1977).

At least for psychologists, if not for other mental health professionals, there is a natural discomfort about practicing an atheoretical or purely clinico-empiric procedure. Accordingly, there have been proposals to introduce system into eclectic therapy. Dimond, Havens, and Jones (1978) have offered a "conceptual framework" for "prescriptive eclecticism." Their framework is organized, like Lazarus' around the structure of personality, with attention to the biophysical, intrapsychic, phenomeno-logical, and behavioral levels of adaptation as these relate to the psycho-analytic stages and structures of development. Assessment and goal setting precede intervention. The techniques of intervention are to be selected with particular attention to problems of resistance, relationship style, and the use of interpretation, and each intervention is to be followed by an evaluation of its effectiveness.

Held (1984) built on the metatheory of Dimond et al., and proposed a formulation of "strategic eclecticism" in which the following questions are addressed: What is the client's problem? What is the client's goal? What ineffective coping methods has the client used? What is maintaining the symptomatic behavior? Held's particular contribution is not in such conceptualization of the eclectic process but in the sketching of specific techniques for reducing client resistance (e.g., taking a "one-down" position by therapist, discussing the dangers of client improvement, and various applications of paradoxical intention).

Figure 7 is a schematic outline of three ways in which the therapist's training (and experience) may be related to the form of practice. The monolithic model is self-evident; more will be said about it when training is discussed in chapter 8. It suffices here to note that all clients of the monolithic therapist are treated (and conceptualized) similarly.

The eclectic schema suggests that the therapist has been schooled to some degree in several theories of psychotherapy and that she or he has arrived at a personally consistent amalgamation of concepts and interven-tions from the several approaches. Again, each of the eclectic therapist's clients will be treated in an essentially similar manner. The eclectic therapist will show more case-to-case variability in treatment behavior than the monolithic (unimodal) therapist but the greater variability is of small degree.

Pragmatism

The *pragmatic* orientation suggested in figure 7 indicates that the thera-pist has been well trained in several major schools and their associated techniques of intervention and uses them differentially according to the specific problems and needs of individual patients. The pragmatic therapist can be thought of as practicing *selective* as contrasted with *generalized* eclecticism. To use qualifying adjectives such as *technical, prescriptive,* and *strategic* to focus or restrict the implied meaning of eclecticism as applied to psychotherapy has at least two disadvantages. It leaves the

FIGURE 7

Models of Training in Psychotherapy and Related Practice Patterns

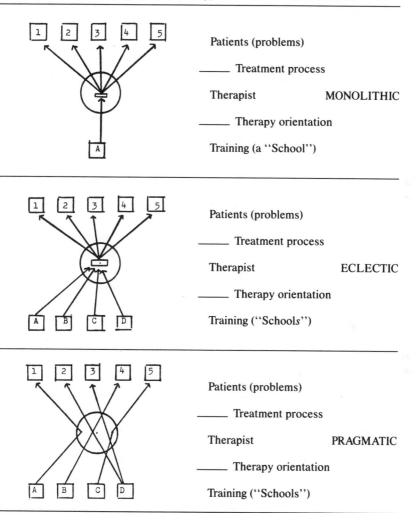

Patients (problems)

_____ Treatment process

Therapist   MONOLITHIC

_____ Therapy orientation

Training (a "School")

Patients (problems)

_____ Treatment process

Therapist   ECLECTIC

_____ Therapy orientation

Training ("Schools")

Patients (problems)

_____ Treatment process

Therapist   PRAGMATIC

_____ Therapy orientation

Training ("Schools")

mildly pejorative connotation of "catch-as-catch-can" and "trial-and-error" approaches to therapy. Also, it encourages the notion that all cases are best treated by some combination of techniques that are diverse as to their theoretical basis. The concepts of pragmatic therapy, or a pragmatic orientation, is preferable.[1] Pragmatism is not antithetical to eclecticism; an eclectic approach to a particular case can be incorporated by a therapist who operates within a pragmatic framework; similarly, when appropriate, the pragmatic therapist will conduct intervention within a single conceptual framework.

Originating in the philosophical contributions of C.S. Pierce, William James, and John Dewey, pragmatism argues that "the meaning of conceptions is to be found in their practical bearings, that the function of thought is as a guide to action, and that the truth is preeminently to be tested by the practical consequences of belief." (*Webster's International Dictionary,* 2nd ed.) Pragmatic means practical. Applied to psychotherapy, the pragmatic approach means the selection of a mode of treatment that, based on experience and research, has the greatest likelihood of being both *effective* and *efficient* with a particular disorder or distress. The mode of therapy should be determined by the core nature of the problem presented and the goals expressed by the client. The pragmatic psychotherapist is akin to the family physician, capable of providing appropriate treatment and management to a range of illnesses, while recognizing the need for timely referral of some cases to specialists. The pragmatic orientation is consistent with recognition of the appropriateness that some therapists self-select to become specialists (e.g., as psychodynamicists, or behavior therapists) and to recognize those cases requiring referral to experts with advanced experience. Knowledge alone of some 40 or more *techniques* (Lazarus, 1981) will not suffice as a basis for a truly pragmatic practice.

Traditional training programs for the primary mental health professionals may suffice for the preparation of the therapist who will practice monolithic, single theory-single technique form of treatment. It is doubtful that their time constraints and limited supervised experience (practica and internships) can provide an adequate foundation for an eclectic practice. It is very clear that the established training programs at best can only prepare the student for the further post-graduate study and supervised practice required if he/she is to have sound foundation in the major theories and techniques necessary for the conduct of pragmatic psychotherapy. Chapter 8 discusses training implications in detail.

Note

1. For the historical record, the terms *pragmatic* and *pragmatism* have occurred *en passant* in the literature on psychotherapy, with a suggestion of increasing

frequency in recent time. They have sometimes been suggested as synonyms for *eclectic* and *eclecticism* in surveys of therapeutic orientation (Garfield & Kurtz, 1977), and some individual respondents to surveys have used it in spelling out their eclectic orientation. There is a recent book entitled, *Pragmatic Psychotherapy* (Driscoll, 1984). The present author has developed the concept of pragmatic therapy, as presented in this volume, over the past 20 years and gave graduate seminars on "Pragmatic Psychotherapy" as early as 1960.

References

Alexander, F., & French, T. M. (1946). *Psychoanalytic therapy*. New York: Ronald Press.

Arkowitz, H., & Messer, S. B. (Eds.). (1984). *Psychoanalytic therapy and behavior therapy: Is integration possible?* New York: Plenum Press.

Beck, A. T. (1970). Cognitive therapy: Nature and relation to behavior therapy. *Behavior Therapy, 1*, 184–200.

Beutler, L. E. (1983). *Eclectic psychotherapy: A systematic approach*. New York: Pergamon Press.

Brammer, L. M., & Shostrom, E. L. (1977). *Therapeutic psychology* (3rd ed.). Englewood Cliffs, NJ: Prentice-Hall.

Breger, L., & McGaugh, J. L. (1965). Critique and reformation of "learning theory" approaches to psychotherapy and neurosis. *Psychological Bulletin, 63*, 338–358.

Brickman, P., Rabinowitz, V. C., Karuza, J., Coates, D., Cohen, E., & Kidder, L. (1982). Models of helping and coping. *American Psychologist, 37*, 368–384.

Davenloo, H. (Ed.) (1980). *Short-term Dynamic Psychotherapy*. New York: Jason Aronson.

Dimond, R. E., Havens, R. A. & Jones, A. C. (1978). A conceptual framework for the practice of prescriptive eclecticism in psychotherapy. *American Psychologist, 33*, 239–248.

Dollard, J. & Miller, N. E. (1950). *Personality and Psychotherapy: An Analysis in Terms of Learning, Thinking, and Culture*. New York: McGraw-Hill Book Company.

Driscoll, R. (1984). *Pragmatic psychotherapy*. New York: VanNostrand Reinhold.

Ellis, A. (1962). *Reason and emotion in psychotherapy*. New York: Lyle Stuart.

Eysenck, H. J. (1970). A mish-mash of theories. *International Journal of Psychiatry, 9*, 140–146.

Feather, B. W. & Rhoads, J. M. (1972). Psychodynamic behavior therapy: I. Theory and rationale. *Archives of General Psychiatry, 26*, 496–502.

Fiedler, F. (1950a). The concept of an ideal therapeutic relationship. *Journal of Consulting Psychology, 14*, 239–245.

Fiedler, F. (1950b). A comparison of therapeutic relationships in psychoanalytic, non-directive, and Adlerian therapy. *Journal of Consulting Psychology, 14*, 436–445.

Frank, J. D. (1961). *Persuasion and healing: A comparative study of psychotherapy*. Baltimore: The Johns Hopkins Press.

French, T. M. (1933). Interrelations between psychoanalysis and the experimental work of Pavlov. *American Journal of Psychiatry, 89*, 1165–1203.

Garfield, S. L. (1977). Research on the training of professional psychotherapists. In A. S. Gurman & A. M. Razin (Eds.), *Effective psychotherapy: A handbook of research*. New York: Pergamon Press.

Garfield, S. L. (1980). *Psychotherapy: An eclectic approach.* New York: John Wiley & Sons.

Garfield, S. L. (1981). Psychotherapy: A 40-year appraisal. *American Psychologist, 36,* 174–183.

Garfield, S. L., & Kurtz, R. (1974). A survey of clinical psychologists: Characteristics, activities and orientations. *Clinical Psychologist, 28,* 7–10.

Garfield, S. L., & Kurtz, R. (1975). Clinical psychologists: A survey of selected attitudes and views. *Clinical Psychologist, 28,* 4–7.

Garfield, S. L., & Kurtz, R. (1977). Clinical Psychologists: A survey of selected attitudes and views. *Clinical Psychologist, 28,* 7–10.

Garfield, S. L., & Kurtz, R. (1977). A study of eclectic views. *Journal of Consulting and Clinical Psychology, 45,* 78–83.

Goldfried, M. R. (1980). Toward the delineation of therapeutic change principles. *American Psychologist, 35,* 991–999.

Goldfried, M. R. (1982). On the history of therapeutic integration. *Behavior Therapy, 13,* 572–593.

Goldfried, M. R., & Wachtel, P. L. (Eds.). (1984). *Newsletter of the Society for the Exploration of Psychotherapy Integration, 2,* (1).

Held, B. S. (1984). Toward a strategic eclecticism: A proposal. *Psychotherapy: Theory, Research and Practice, 21,* 232–241.

Hersey, P., & Blanchard, K. H. (1977). *Management of Organizational Behavior: Utilizing Human Resources* (3rd ed.). Englewood Cliffs, NJ: Prentice-Hall.

Howard, G. S., Nance, D. W., & Myers, P. (1986). Adaptive counseling and psychotherapy: An integrative, eclectic model. *The Counseling Psychologist, 14,* 363–442.

Klein, M., Dittman, A. T., Parloff, M. B., & Gill, M. M. (1969). Behavior therapy: Observations and reflections. *Journal of Consulting & Clinical Psychology, 33,* 259–266.

Larson, D. (1980). Therapeutic schools, styles, and schoolism. *Journal of Humanistic Psychology, 20,* 3–20.

Lazarus, A. A. (1967). In support of technical eclecticism. *Psychological Reports, 21,* 415–416.

Lazarus, A. A. (1980). Toward delineating some causes of change in psychotherapy. *Professional Psychology: Research and Practice, 11,* 863–870.

Lazarus, A. A. (1981). *The practice of multimodal therapy.* New York: McGraw-Hill.

Lazarus, A. A. (1984). The specificity factor in psychotherapy. *Psychotherapy in Private Practice, 2.* 43–48.

London, P. (1964). The modes and morals of psychotherapy. New York: Holt, Rinehart & Winston.

Luborsky, L., Singer, B., & Luborsky, L. (1975). Comparative studies of psychotherapies: Is it true that "everyone has won and all must have prizes?" *Archives of General psychiatry, 32,* 995–1008.

Malan, D. H. (1963). *A study of brief psychotherapy.* Philadelphia: J. B. Lippincott.

Mann, J. (1973). *Time-limited psychotherapy.* Cambridge: Harvard University Press.

McGovern, M. P., Newman, F. L., & Kopta, S. M. (1986). Metatheoretical assumptions and psychotherapy orientation: Clinician attributions of patients' problem causality and responsibility for treatment outcome. *Journal of Consulting and Clinical Psychology, 54,* 476–481.

Meichenbaum, D. H. (1979). *Cognitive-behavior modification: An integrative approach.* New York: Plenum Press.

Messer, S. B., & Winokur, M. (1980). Some limits to the integration of psychoanalytic and behavior therapy. *American Psychologist, 35,* 818–827.

Norcross, J. C. (Ed.). (1986). *Handbook of eclectic psychotherapy.* New York: Brunner/Mazel.

Norcross, J. C., & Prochaska, J. O. (1983). Clincians' theoretical orientations: Selection, utilization, and efficacy. *Professional Psychology: Research and Practice, 14,* 197–208.

Norcross, J. C., & Wogan, M. (1983). American psychotherapists of diverse persuasions: Characteristics, theories, practices, and clients. *Professional Psychology: Research and Practice, 14,* 529–539.

Paul, G. L. (1967). Strategy of outcome research in psychotherapy. *Journal of Consulting Psychology, 31,* 109–119.

Plous, S. & Zimbardo, P. G. (1986). Attributional biases among clincians: A comparison of psychoanalysts and behavior therapists. *Journal of Consulting & Clinical Psychology, 54,* 568–570.

Prochaska, J. O. (1984). *Systems of psychotherapy: A transtheoretical approach.* Homewood, IL: Dorsey Press

Prochaska, J. O. & DiClemente, C. C. (1984). *The transtheoretical approach: Crossing traditional boundaries of therapy.* Homewood, IL: Dorsey Press

Prochaska, J. O. & Norcross, J. C. (1983). Contemporary psychotherapists: A national survey of characteristics, practices, orientations, and attitudes. *Psychotherapy: Theory, Research & Practice, 20,* 161–173.

Rosenzweig, Saul (1936). Some implicit common factors in diverse methods of psychotherapy. *American Journal of Orthopsychiatry, 6,* 412–415.

Schact, T. E. & Black, D. A. (1984). Epistemological commitment of behavioral and psychoanalytic therapists. *Professional Psychology: Research and Practice, 16,* 316–323.

Schafer, R. (1976). *A New Language For Psychoanalysis.* New Haven, CT: Yale University Press.

Simon, R. M. (1974). On eclecticism. *American Journal of Psychiatry, 131,* 135–139.

Strupp, H. H. (1955a.) An objective comparison of Rogerian and psychoanalytic techniques. *Journal of Consulting Psychology, 19,* 1–7

Strupp, H. H. (1960). *Psychotherapists in action.* New York: Grune & Stratton.

Sundland, D. M. (1977). Theoretical orientations of psychotherapists. In A. S. Gurman, & A. M. Razin, (Eds.), *Effective psychotherapy: A handbook of research.* New York: Pergamon Press.

Wachtel, P. L. (1977). *Psychoanalysis and behavior therapy: Toward an integration.* New York: Basic Books

Yager, J. (1977). Psychiatric eclecticism: A cognitive view. *American Journal of Psychiatry, 134,* 736–741.

8

Implications for Training

Consideration of the optimal program for the training of psychotherapists cannot be approached without recognition of fundamentally divergent views as to the essential nature of the therapeutic enterprise. In the final analysis, is the practice of psychotherapy an art, with all that implies for the emphasis on individuality and inspirational specificity (Storr, 1979)? Or is psychotherapy a science, more specifically, the application of technical procedures derived from scientifically established principles (Singer, 1980)? Is the conduct of psychotherapy a technician's craft, or is it a professional discipline? These questions are debatable and there are strong voices on both sides. The uncertain and often critiqued scientific bases for psychotherapy are a source of stress for the therapist in training (Archer & Peake, 1984).

If psychotherapy is mostly an art, of which the essential products (successfully treated patients) are the outcomes of highly individualized if not unique endeavors, it would follow that the crucial preparation of the therapist would be found, as in other art forms, in extended periods of apprenticeship, in mentorships under master practitioners. If, on the other hand, psychotherapy is the technical application of scientific principles, then an extended period of formal study and didactic instruction is appropriate. "The position that psychotherapy is an 'art,' taken to imply that neither the skills nor the effects of psychotherapy are predictable, reproducible, or objective, is clearly a minority position among clinical practitioners, theorists, and consumers of psychotherapy" (Archer & Peake, 1984). (p. 63) Those who address the issue usually stand on reasonable middle ground and argue that psychotherapy is both science and art and that successful treatment draws upon both the therapist's knowledge *and* very personal skills. It has been suggested that therapists are drawn initially to a particular orientation (a guiding theory of psychotherapy) because of its particular intellectual appeal coupled with techniques that are congenial to their personalities (Schwartz, 1978). However, with accumulated experience, professed adherents of a particular theory practice in widely divergent ways because of the influence of their individual personality characteristics (Ellis, 1978).

Does effective psychotherapy result primarily from the curative or corrective processes released by an ideal therapeutic relationship as provided by the therapist? Or, is it a result of the therapist's judgment and skill in selecting and applying those specific techniques of intervention that have established efficacy for the client's problems? If the former, the personality of the therapist would appear to be crucial. If the latter, the therapist's fund of empirical knowledge is of primary import.

Are psychotherapists *born* or *made*? Is there some complex of innate qualities of perceptive acuity and temperament that, stimulated by early life experiences and opportunities, lead the individual to become self-selected for a career as a therapist? Or, is it a high level of intellectual curiosity coupled with attraction to disciplined study of complex phenomena that draws one to medicine (and later psychiatry) or to psychology? The former is consistent with the notion that some individuals are "natural born" therapists. The latter is reflected in the experience of supervisors who find some therapists-in-training to be limited by their predilection to intellectualize and to lack the spontaneity requisite for effective therapy. "One sometimes feels that there are two kinds of clinicians: the 'natural' psychotherapist and the 'forced' therapist—cognitively prepared but affectively awkward with patients" (Reiss, 1975).

Words of comfort skillfully administered are the oldest therapy known to man.
Louis Nizer

This observation by the noted attorney combines the two basic elements of the competing views as to the essential process of therapy and the role of the therapist. "Words of comfort . . ." implies caring and relating, while "skillfully administered . . ." suggests technical knowledge.

Self-Selection

As is true for all vocations and careers, the path on which the individual eventually is led to choose to become a professional therapist is a long one and is marked both by relatively self-determined options at critical mileposts and by the vagaries of exigencies, special opportunities, realistic limitations, inspirational experiences, and a gradually growing knowledge of self. Theories of career choice express a variety of emphases.

Some psychoanalytic writers have argued for the role of unconscious factors in the determination of vocational choice, for the choice of work as an adaptive compromise to the demands of the reality and pleasure principles, and for the significant role of sublimation (Brill, 1949; Forer, 1953). Super (1953, 1957) outlined the developmental stages in the building of the individual's self-concept and viewed self-concept as a primary determiner of vocational choice and career evolution within a vocational field.

Another theory assigns a role to genetic determinants of individual differences in basic aptitudes (response readiness and energy channelization) that interact with very early childhood experiences (Roe, 1953; Roe & Siegelman, 1964).

Still other theories postulate eventual career selection as a product of the interaction between the individual's knowledge of self (interests, aptitudes, attitudes, and values) and of the nature of specific occupations (Holland, 1959, 1973). All theorists acknowledge the role of experiences in contributing to development of that part of the individual's personality that is expressed in interests (attractions and aversions to settings and activities) and values (the assignment of more significance and worth to certain objects and goals and less to others). Theory aside, both general observation and detailed research support the finding that well-adjusted, satisfied workers in very different occupations express very different interest patterns and value orientations. It is this fact that underlies psychological methods of deriving objective indexes of individual interest patterns as a basis for vocational counseling (Osipow, 1983).

Individuals such as psychotherapists, who are drawn toward and select "social service" occupations, are characteristically different in their interests and values from individuals who choose less personal work (e.g., engineers and physical scientists) (Roe, 1953). In broad terms, psychotherapists are more person-oriented, more "psychologically minded" and less thing-oriented. To the extent that psychiatrists, clinical psychologists, and clinical social workers give evidence of a commonality of attitudes and interests, it is pertinent to inquire whether such a shared value structure arises from similarity of early life experiences.

A comprehensive sociological survey of the backgrounds of large samples of the major mental health professions (psychiatrists, psychoanalysts, clinical psychologists, and clinical social workers) reveals that, at least for the older generation of therapists, all four reveal a remarkable similarity in their cultural-ethnic-intellectual roots. "Compared to the natural history of a wide variety of other professions, the pattern of increased homogeneity in the sociocultural origins of mental health professions is extremely atypical" (Henry, Sims & Spray, 1971, p. 25). In addition to marked similarity of early family influence in regard to broad cultural dimensions, a further homogeneity is found in the preponderant tendency of persons who become psychotherapists to have moved away from the more religious and politically conservative values of their parents and toward apostasy and liberalism. "In short, the liberal composition of the mental health profession reflects conversion rather than a life-long adherence to a liberal political tradition" (Henry, Sims, & Spray, 1971, p. 77). For a significant number of eventual therapists, their developmental movements toward a shared *Weltanschuung* are a part of their upward social mobility (see Schofield, 1986, chap. 6). To the extent that the personality of therapists, including their basic value orientations, has a potent role in psychotherapy, as has been increasingly argued by many experts, the fact of a high degree of homogeneity of applicants for training has important implications for training centers. If the regnant attitudes and beliefs characterized by Judeo-Christian ethic and both political and religious liberalism are an inherently salutory complex for the therapist to bring to the distressed client, training centers need not address the issue of personal values either in selection or instruction of those candidates to be prepared for the practice of therapy. However, if the applicants to the training programs of the different mental health professions have a large degree of sociocultural and religiopolitical attitudinal commitments that are undisturbed by their training experiences, the possibility for the four disciplines to afford the basis for a differential treatment modality—where reeducation of values may be either indicated or counterindicated—is seriously diminished.

Institutional Selection

While there are marked similarities in the basic values and work orientations of would-be psychotherapists at the start of formal, professional training, there are particulars of subpatterns of interest, self-knowledge of aptitudes, and reality limitations (most notably "science" aptitude and finances) that determine whether application is made successfully to medical schools or to university graduate programs in psychology or in social work. The screening process for admission means that *some* would-be psychiatrists (physicians) enter psychology training, and some would-be psychologists enter schools of social work. However, the differential admission requirements and subsequent training regimens do not result in three groups of professional therapists who are significantly different in their motivations and personal values as they achieve full status as practitioners. Accumulated evidence suggests that "equalitarianism and humanistic values in general are a modal ideology of mental health professionals over the last decades" (Vardy & Kay, 1982).

The official selection process imposes a large degree of homogeneity in regard to basic intellectual ability and motivation for academic pursuit.

This is accomplished by appraisal of undergraduate college grades and by scores on one or more standardized measures of general aptitude for advanced study (e.g., Graduate Record Examination, Medical College Aptitude Test, etc). Some programs, especially in clinical psychology may use additional standardized tests of personality and interest patterns.

Where interviews are part of the selection process, they are focused on obtaining an impression of those therapy-relevant facets of personality for which objective measures are not available. The literature suggests that most programs, and their faculty representatives in the screening process, have a set of similar, core desiderata for the aspiring therapist. These include such qualities as tolerance for individual differences and respect for the integrity of persons; sensitivity to minor cues to the emotional states of others; and capacity to respond empathically. The American Psychological Association's Committee on Teaching in Clinical Psychology, (APA, 1947) specified 15 personality criteria for clinical psychologists. Rogers (1951) recommends that the student bring to therapy training the experience of having lived and worked with people of a very different background from his/her own and a "deep knowledge of the dynamics of personality." The research of Strupp, Fox and Lessler (1969) led to a description of the therapist whose patients make positive response to treatment as being "warm, attentive, interested, understanding, and respectful." It appears that regardless of the mode of therapy to be taught and practiced, there is a consensus across schools as to the desirable persona of therapists-to-be. In brief, they should manifest aptitude and skill for effective interpersonal communiction and relationship formation.

Beginning in 1954, Whitehorn and Betz reported a series of studies aimed at identifying therapists who were particularly effective in the treatment of schizophrenics. Subsequently, they extended their research to tease out personality variables that distinguished "successful" from "unsuccessful" therapists. Using the Strong Vocational Interest Blank (SVIB) they isolated a number of variables that differentiated the A-therapists (successful with schizophrenics) from unsuccessful B-therapists and derived a set of 23 SVIB items (reflective of interests, activities, and personal preferences) that could be scored to identify A and B therapists (Betz & Whitehorn, 1956). Using this scale to identify therapist-types, later research (McNair, Callahan, & Lorr, 1962) indicated that B-therapists were more successful than A-types with *neurotic* patients. With psychotherapy not regarded generally as "therapy-of-choice" for schizophrenia but, on the other hand, considered the primary form of intervention for a wide range of psychoneurotic disturbances, the promise of an objective method to identify those therapists ("personality types"?) with particular aptitude to treat neurotics generated a spate of studies, both analogue and clinical, to confirm and extend the promise of the A-B typology. An early review of the accumulated literature (Razin, 1971) pointed up serious methodological weaknesses in the laboratory studies of the A-B differential, called for further clinical studies to confirm the "interaction hypothesis," that is, that A-therapists do better with schizophrenics and Bs with neurotics, and pointed up the difficulty of replicating the original Whitehorn-Betz work due to the increased role of drugs in treatment of hospitalized schizophrenics. A further and later review of studies of the A-B distinction (Cox, 1978) ended with the devastating conclusion that the great promise of the A-B typology was essentially fictional because of gross deficiencies in the original Whitehorn-Betz studies. Geller and Berzins (1976) surveyed a sample of 95 nationally prominent psychotherapists with a 19-item version of the A-B scale. The therapists were categorized as to their major orientation: insight, relationship, or action. A-B scores were essentially equal for the three groups, contrary to an expectation that the "action" therapist should be reliably lower (more B-like) than the other two groups. The ardent pursuit of the typology reflected both the potential value of any method that would identify patient-specific therapist aptitudes and the naive expectation that crucial elements of therapist personality could be identified via a brief psychometric scale. The discouragingly small yield of the A-B researches has not diminished the readiness of training programs to utilize interview-based ratings to identify prospective therapists.

Beyond the limited use of some personality tests by some programs, all graduate programs usually seek to assure that students will be person-oriented and interpersonally effective. This goal is sought largely via an admission interview or series of screening interviews. An exemplary itemization of desirable personality characteristics (14 in all, exclusive of intellectual ability) was provided in the American Psychological Association's recommendations for training clinical psychologists. The list includes, among others, "originality, resourcefulness, and versatility," "insight into own personality characteristics; sense of humor," "sensitivity into the complexities of motivation," "tact and cooperativeness," "integrity, self-control, and stability" (APA, 1947). In brief, a "reasonably well-adjusted and attractive personality." The report did not suggest how the presence of these qualities was to be ascertained!

A conviction that they have some degree of ability to "read people" is common among the laity. It is even stronger among those individuals who make their living, in part, by assessing individuals and predicting future behavior (psychiatrists and psychologists, for example). There is solid evidence of the very *limited* inter-judge reliability and the very limited validity of judgments of future behavior based on interview and other observational assessments (Hobfoll & Benor, 1984; Holt & Luborsky, 1958; Kelly & Fiske, 1951; Kelley & Goldberg, 1959; King, Beehr, & King, 1986; Komives, Weiss & Ross, 1984; Milstein, Wilkinson, Burrow, & Kessen, 1981; Rickard & Clements, 1986). Beyond that, there is evidence from controlled studies that when interview input is added to the applicant's dossier, it does not overpower the data on academic aptitude. For example, interviewed and noninterviewed medical school admittees are homogeneous on prior academic achievement and MCAT scores, and their subsequent careers (specialty choices) are undifferentiated (Schofield & Garrard, 1975; Schofield & Merwin, 1966). Most graduate training centers persist in using the interview (or believe they are using the interview) to select candidates for training. Persistence in this practice, which has no convincing evidence of validity, rests upon the interviewers' apparent conviction that they can predict future competencies (e.g., ability as a therapist) and the fact that faculties are generally more comfortable about their public responsibilities when they have made "sighted" rather than "blind" actuarial selections, (i.e., quasi-clinical or cryptoclinical) based on past academic achievement and tested aptitudes.

Graduate Education of Psychotherapists

In considering the appropriate formal and extended training of professional psychotherapists, one must acknowledge an overarching assumption of such obviousness that is has rarely been questioned. It is assumed that our educational programs are essential to assure the preparation of effective therapists. A few studies comparing professionals with relatively untrained or quasi-trained "paraprofessionals" do not convincingly establish the validity of the assumption (Strupp & Hadley, 1979). Review of studies comparing trained and untrained therapists suggests that the former may be somewhat more effective with older patients and with brief psychotherapy; the differences are not large (Berman & Norton, 1985). The cognitively compelling nature of the assumption that more and better training produces better therapists, coupled with the ethical constraints on research using seriously distressed patients with untrained, control therapists, means that the professional education of therapists enjoys a "functional autonomy" like that noted for the practice of therapy itself in the face of earlier, serious doubts about its effectiveness (Astin, 1961).

General Principles of Instruction

The overall graduate school preparation of psychotherapists *ideally* has two complementary, overlapping dimensions. Frequently, and unfortunately, these dimensions are distinct, separate, and uncoordinated. The first of these is didactic, that is, formal classroom instruction. This is essentially a process of information transmission. Through lectures, seminars, and readings, the student is introduced to basic knowledge relevant to the practice of psychotherapy. This involves review of basic theories of etiology and pathology of mental disorder, principles and structures of differential diagnoses, and the theory (theories?) underlying specific techniques of therapeutic intervention. The primarily didactic phase of the therapist's preparation may or may not include some limited exposure to actual clinical material, via films, audio or videotapes, live demonstrations, and short-term "practice" (practica) periods in clinical settings.

The major mental health disciplines that provide a majority of our psychotherapists are differentiable with respect both to the content of their didactic instruction and to the relative emphasis each places on formal education versus supervised "hands on" experience in the total program of preparation, after which, with degree in hand, the graduate is ready to start his or her professional career. Clearly, the pregraduate preparation of the psychiatrist, who must be first a graduate physician, is extremely different from that of the psychologist or social worker, and moderately similar in the extent of medical knowledge to that of the graduate nurse (R. N.) who goes on to advanced training in psychiatric nursing. The prespecialization preparation of both the psychiatrist and the nurse is alike, and different from that of the psychologist and social worker, in that it entails a considerable exposure to limited practice under supervision or at least observation of clinical cases. Early on this gives the medically oriented therapist a "maturational edge" in clinical experience that the psychologist and social worker may be slow to overcome.

At the level of specialized graduate instruction, the mental health professions show both intraprofessional and interprofessional differences in the content and extent of didactic instruction in relation to the amount of supervised clinical experience. Allowing for program-to-program variations, it may be fairly said that the training of psychiatrists is predominantly an apprenticeship, with emphasis on learning by doing. Formal, didactic instruction is commonly limited to a few seminars over the course of the 3-year residency (for adult psychiatrists) with much emphasis on regular, "full dress" case conferences (Grand Rounds) under the oversight of senior professionals.

By contrast, the "standard" 4-year graduate study program for the clinical psychologist is composed of 3 years that provide a heavy concentration of formal lecture classes in advanced psychology and seminars on topics relevant to clinical matters (e. g., psychopathology, psychodiagnositcs, theories of intervention, etc), followed by a full year of supervised internship in a suitable clinical setting.

In brief, it would appear that the typical psychiatrist has been undereducated and overtrained for the role of therapist, while the typical clinical psychologist has been overeducated and undertrained. As models, it would appear that the training of both the clinical social worker and the psychiatric nurse achieve something closer to a good balance between education and training for their practice as psychotherapists, albeit *none* of the current primary practitioners of therapy are efficiently trained for that function (Schofield, 1986, chap. 8).

It must be noted that the discovery of psychotropic drugs has had a striking impact on the training of psychiatrists. Again, allowing for some variation among residency programs, the "remedicalization" of psychiatry has led to a de-emphasis on both didactic instruction and clinical experience with purely psychological interventions (Schofield, 1986, New Introduction).

Figure 7 (chap. 7) is a schematic presentation of three guiding philosophies for the preparation of psychotherapists. (For the meaning and origin of "schools," see chap. 4.) Each encompasses both the educational (didactic) and training (experiential) dimensions of the process. Two of the program types, the monolithic and the eclectic, are presently in operation and readily visible! The third, the pragmatic approach, represents an obvious and desirable evolution from what in recent years has been established about objectively differentiable modes of psychotherapy and their selective effectiveness for specific forms of psychological distress.

A monolithic or unimodal school of psychotherapy is one that has a unified, all-encompassing theory of the etiology of functional mental emotional disorders and teaches a theory-relevant technique of therapy. In point of historical precedence and continuing visibility and prestige, psychoanalysis and the psychoanalytic training institutes provide the premiere example. The psychoanalytic school and the established institutes are probably unparalleled in the degree to which didactic instruction is closely coupled and coordinated with field experience. Each institute's cadre of officially sanctioned supervisors is composed of certified training analysts who have successfully passed through the same educational experience as that of their supervisees. This assures that the eventual independent practitioner will have a firm and *thorough* grounding in a theoretical formulation and well-developed skills with the theory-associated techniques of intervention. The advantages of monolithic training are several and obvious, and not the least of them is the therapist's feeling of confidence in carrying out treatment. This advantage of skill and confidence accrues to the patient when, and *only when,* the patient's problem happens to be one for which the particular approach of the monlithic or unimodal therapist *happens to be* the "therapy-of-choice." The disadvantages, to therapist and client alike, of monolithic treatment, are obvious and arise from the fact that psychological distress is *not* unimodal, neither in etiology nor pathology. Using the psychoanalytic institutes as an example of unimodal training, Frank (1961) drew an analogy to indoctrination and thought reform, and reviewed the advantages and disadvantages of such programs.

While the psychoanalytic school is the most readily perceivable example of the monolithic approach to the training of therapists, a monolithic approach is applicable to any of the major competing schools. A graduate faculty in a psychology program, for example, can choose to present a primarily if not purely cognitive approach—or any other major formulation—to the exclusion of others. Thus, with a degree of sophistication about the competing schools, an aspiring therapist might choose a graduate program that was congenial to his or her predilections. Such a student would be likely to encounter greater difficulty in finding a clinical internship setting in which the supervisory experience would consistently augment and reinforce the particular theoretical orientation. It is typical of public clinical agencies with training programs that supervisory staffs present a multiversity of backgrounds, experience, and viewpoints on therapy. It is possible but more difficult, in contrast with analytic training, for an individual to achieve monolithic preparation as a Rogersian, Ellisian, Wolpeian, Beckian, or other "school" therapist.

Figure 7 indicates that at the level of education, the eclectic approach exposes the trainee to more than one theory and more than one method of treatment. Accordingly, the eclectic model affords potential freedom from the doctrinaire limitations of the monolithic approach. It suggests that because of the variety of theoretical formulations to which the trainee is exposed and, more critically, because of the usual failure of the trainee's supervised experience to be coordinated with and representative of each of the didactically presented schools, the trainee who has not been provided with a differential framework for selectively relating discriminable pathologies to specific intervention techniques is at risk of ending up with a possibly overly rich armamentarium of techniques that he or she applies in largely trial-and-error fashion. The eclectic "seat-of-the-pants," "catch-as-catch-can" therapist will be maintained in practice through experiencing that degree of satisfaction afforded by the modicum of response that most of his or her patients will make to the "common" therapeutic factors in all dialogue conducted with therapeutic intent (see chap. 5).

The pragmatic approach sketched in Figure 7 emphasizes discrimination and differentiation. It assumes the existence of a small number of *valid* theories that formulate the complex of etiology-pathology-treatment for forms of psychological disorder that can be reliably, differentially diagnosed (see chap. 5, and figure 6). Didactic preparation of the pragmatic therapist requires exposure in depth, especially through guided reading, to the basic theory literature of each of the "core" schools. In addition, special attention has to be given to differential diagnosis and the reliable methods of client assessment with integration around the concept of "therapy-of-choice." It is important that didactic instruction not be given in "cafeteria" style, and that each school be presented by an instructor who has scholarly depth and intellectual respect for the school being presented. It is equally, if not more, important that the student's field experience be coordinated so as to provide a reasonably intensive opportunity to practice each of the major interventions respectively under the guidance of a supervisor experienced and skilled in that approach (Winokur & Dasberg, 1983). Paradoxically, with respect to both the didactic and the experiential dimensions of the therapist's preparation, the pragmatic approach requires the existence of nonpragmatic, that is, monolithic instructors! If it is true that all therapists evolve toward a preferred "style" that reflects stable elements of their personality (Schwartz, 1978; Tremblay, Herron, & Schultz, 1986) and the influence of "inadvertencies" (Cummings & Luchese, 1978), at least a sound, pragmatically oriented, basic preparation should enhance their readiness to make appropriate referral of cases that do not "fit" their mode of practice.

The Content of Didactic Education

Inasmuch as there are three primary mental health professions (psychiatry, clinical psychology, and clinical social work) from which the overwhelming majority of psychotherapists are drawn, and inasmuch as the practice of psychological interventions is *not* the *primary* or original training goal of any of the three, it is to be expected that there will be extensive differences in the formal educational experiences of each of the three practitioner types. Obviously, the pre-M. D. medical school curriculum is unique, relatively standard across all U. S. medical schools, and with essentially no overlap with the graduate curricula offered to social workers and psychologists. Unlike the social worker and psychologist, the psychiatrist-to-be, who *may* become a psychotherapist, receives whatever specialized preparation for psychotherapy there is to be, in a postdoctorate residency program that, as noted earlier, is heavily apprenticeship-oriented and light on formal didactic instruction.

Unlike the psychiatrist/therapist, the clinical social worker and the clinical psychologist receive their *formal* instruction as to theories and modes of psychotherapy as part of their graduate degree programs. For the social worker this means 2 years of course work, and supervised practica in clinical settings, leading to a master's degree. The preparation of the clinical psychologist officially recognized by the American Psychological Association (APA) requires a minimum of 4 years of graduate school registration, 3 of which are heavily didactic, with the fourth consisting of a full-time internship in a suitable clinical setting.

To the extent that the preparation of the older generation (still predominant) of psychiatrists and social workers includes theory and technique of psychotherapy, it has historically been unimodal in nature and specifically Freudian or, allowing for neo-Freudian variations, psychodynamic in focus and emphasis. It is relatively recently that the concepts of broader psychological formulations (e. g., cognitive and behavioral) have begun to have even modest absorption into the formal education of these two older and more traditional mental health professions.

The preparation of the clinical psychologist stands in marked contrast to that of either psychiatrist or social worker. Unlike the older professions of psychiatry and social work, with particular regard to the role of psychotherapy, the profession of clinical psychology is not the product of slow evolution but rather of deliberate planning and creation.

At the end of World War II, there was a broad national recognition of the immediate need to train a greatly enlarged cadre of mental health professionals of all disciplines. This was a particular challenge and opportunity for psychology, which prior to World War II was predominantly an academic discipline with only a small number of practitioners, chiefly "mental testers" and industrial personnel consultants. With the availability of federal financial support, the American Psychological Association undertook the design of a doctoral level program to train specialists in clinical psychology. Appropriately, the APA saw the need not only to increase the number of qualified mental health practitioners but to provide for increased research into all aspects of mental illness. In brief, the APA's goal was to draft a curriculum that would produce scientist/practitioners. Because the deliberative bodies that framed what was to be, and still is, the predominant framework for doctoral education in clinical psychology were drawn predominantly from academia, with limited input from practitioners, it is understandable that their "grand scheme" proved to be more idealistic than realistic. To the extent that it was expected that the APA program would contribute significantly, both effectively and efficiently, to the number of well-trained psychotherapists, there is close to a consensus that the scientist/practitioner model has rarely achieved its goal. However, with respect to the needs for both qualified faculty and more and better mental health research, the APA protocol has had definite impact. Certainly it served to draw large numbers of intellectually able persons into the mental health arena. Those who have become effective and dedicated therapists have done so largely by dint of formal and informal postdoctoral training and work experience (for a historical overview of the evolution of clinical psychology, see Schofield, 1982).

Two formal reports provided the structure for what became the nationally recognized standard for the preparation of clinical psychologists. The first of these was the report of the APA's Committee on Training in Clinical Psychology (APA, 1947), chaired by David Shakow. The committee addressed desirable undergraduate preparation and recommended personality characteristics, a "core" didactic program in general psychology (physiological, comparative, theoretical schools, developmental and social psychology), and a "specialty" program including "dynamic psychology" and psychopathology. It is not surprising that in 1947 this report did not suggest specifics as to what theories or methods of intervention should be taught. The relative emphasis on research over practice was suggested in the statement that "we anticipate that *many* will devote a *part* [Emphases added] of their time to some form of psychotherapy . . .

The above report was, in effect, an agenda for a national two-week conference on training in clinical psychology held at Boulder, Colorado, in August 1949 (Raimy, 1950). Of the 71 participants, 42 were representatives of academic psychology departments; the others included supervisors from field training institutions (only seven!), officials from the Veterans Administration, the United States Public Health Service, the Surgeon General's Office of the army, and representatives from related disciplines. The absence of full-time practitioners, who might have been difficult to recruit in 1949, and the predominance of academicians perhaps determined an emphasis that would eventually evolve into vociferous dissatisfaction over a perceived imbalance in the "educational" versus "training" components of the prescribed doctoral program and lack of integration of the two (Hayes, 1986; Peterson, 1985).

With respect to core curriculum, the Boulder conference essentially endorsed the recommendations of the Shakow committee, adding some specifics on sequential content of method courses (e. g., psychometrics). On the subject of psychotherapy training, the conference offered little by way of prescribed didactic courses. Two specific observations are worthy of note:

Integrated [Emphases added] courses which reflect the basic principles of *psychodynamics,* supplemented by adequate and carefully supervised experience in the practical clinical situation, are preferable to a series of single, discrete technical courses.

Except under unusual circumstances, it is expected that final competence in psychotherapy will be achieved at the *postdoctoral* [Emphases added] level. There is a generally felt need for the development of better facilities than now exist for this more advanced kind of training.

One may surmise that if a national conference on training in clinical psychology were held today, professional practitioners would have at least equal representation with academic faculty, the area of psychotherapy would be treated with greater depth and specificity, and any reference to "psychodynamics" would be paralleled by "cognitive psychology" and "principles of behavior modification."

The second report concerned with the training of clinical psychologists focused specifically on psychotherapy (APA, 1971). The product of a committee of the Division of Psychotherapy of the American Psychological Association, this report provided 23 recommended standards for psychotherapy "education" in doctoral-level psychology programs. Recommendations concerning the faculty of the academic program emphasized that teachers in the clinical program should be fully competent, experienced, and currently active practitioners who should be responsible for the didactic instruction in psychotherapy, responsible for students' off-campus training,and skilled in supervision. It was recommended that training experience (practica and internships) should be in settings where "genuine psychotherapy" was practiced at a high level of competence and that students should have training in supervision (!) and opportunity to enhance their self-awareness and personal growth. Ten years later, a follow-up survey was conducted to determine the attitudes of Division of Psychotherapy members toward the recommended standards, in particular as the standards were observed in their own training experiences, and as to whether they should be part of an ideal training program (Rachelson & Clance, 1980). The specific standards had been experienced in their training by a range of 7% (opportunity to observe faculty practicing therapy) to 74% (practica were in settings where therapy by psychologists was accepted) of the respondents. With respect to the presence in an ideal program, there was better than 90% endorsement of the standards except for the requirement of personal therapy for the trainee (62%).

The Substantive Bases for Pragmatic Psychotherapy

General Foundations

If the practitioner of psychotherapy is to express a professional *discipline,* the work of therapy must rest upon a solid foundation of knowledge about human psychology, about how and why human individuals behave, think, and feel in the ways they do. The broader the education of the therapist the better, not only because it will enrich his or her cognitive life (and, perhaps, mental health!) but because a breadth of education will generate a multifaceted persona for stimulation of, and response to, the client. However, practical considerations dictate that the therapist's cultural education must be acquired prior to, and *continue* after, the period of professional preparation. In the period of graduate study preparation for "entry level" competence, formal education must of necessity be focused and limited.

Knowledge of four domains of human psychology is crucial to the practice of psychotherapy. These are developmental psychology, dynamic psychology, the psychology of individual differences (differential psychology), and behavioral psychology, the latter encompassing the psychology of motivation and the psychology of learning.

Developmental psychology teaches that there is a general ontogeny of the individual that begins at birth and is marked by progressive maturation and growth. The modal individual evolves as a unique personality with physical and mental development that is most readily perceived in the period from infancy through late adolescence. There is also growth and change in personality, especially in the development of the individual's self-concept and in the development of social skills and interpersonal relationships. These latter facets may continue to evolve through later years. The ultimate stage in maturation in any of these dimensions may be followed by some degree of regression. Developmental studies tell us the modal or typical age at which certain milestones are reached. These are most clearly established for children, for example, average age to walk, to talk, to have bowel and bladder control, and so on. Developmental psychology also teaches us that there is considerable variation in the rate at which individuals mature and pass through successive stages of the ontological process. For some individuals the trajectory of the growth curve, for example in physical coordination, is steeper than average. For some individuals, acquisition of language facility may be slower than average. Knowledge of the developmental norms and skill with appropriate assessment methods permits the clinician to know whether a presenting problem is one of significant pathology or simply represents a "normal variation" from what is modal. This knowledge protects the clinician from "overpathologizing" and provides the basis for reassurance. Awareness of the transitional stages in individual development in a particular culture helps the clinician to know whether a patient's complaint is something more than the customary stress associated with passage to the next developmental level. Evaluation of the individual's general level of maturation should be a part of the assessment of every candidate for psychotherapy. As is true for formal "skill and knowledge" teaching, psychotherapy may be ineffective if the client is not maturationally ready. Therapy can sometimes stimulate a retarded maturation process but can never substitute for it. A developmental orientation will cause the therapist to look for particular historical circumstances or current situational demands or deficits that may account for the client's retarded maturation and that are maintaining his or her adjustment in an immature pattern.

A second basic domain of substantive concepts critical to the practice of therapy is that of dynamic psychology. This is a field of clinical inquiry, research, and established principles that encompasses the theory of personality development and psychopathology as phenomena crucially determined by early childhood experiences. While having its origins in the seminal writings of Freud, modern dynamic psychology is at once a great deal more and a great deal less than orthodox Freudian theory and its neo-Freudian offshoots and mutations. The significance of dynamic psychology for psychotherapy does not reside in the notion of the "family romance" or of the Oedipal complex, albeit these are valid concepts of limited applicability. Rather, it rests on the basic proposition that personality structure and susceptibility to neurotic coping strategies originate in the individual's earliest life experiences and, in particular, in the quality of parenting received. The experiences of infancy and early childhood play a dominant and formative role in the individual's acquisition of persisting attitudes toward self and toward others, and in the adoption of habitual styles of response. Pathological parenting, for example, overprotection or neglect, projection of parental ambition, inconsistent reward or punishment regimens, neurotic modeling, excessive or deficient affection, by either parent can be the seed of a malignant insecurity as the child is confronted with developmental tasks. The childhood origins of adult maladjustment are found less in the now-recovered, previously repressed instances of one or a few psychic trauma than in pathological indoctrination by defective parental teaching and modeling. Furthermore, it may be that the crippling of adult personality arises as much from the absence of positive childhood experiences as from the occurrence of negative ones (Schofield & Balian, 1959). It is recognized that some of the manifestations of adult maladjustment are a function of unconscious motivation and the operation of repression together with other "mechanisms of defense" against anxiety. Finally, within the corpus of dynamic psychology and with particular relevance to the psychotherapy of dynamically based maladjustment, the pragmatic therapist must be knowledgeable about the operation of transference. The education of the therapist must provide exposure to the field and laboratory validation of those psychodynamic concepts that have been accessible to verification (Fischer & Greenberg, 1977; Kline, 1981; Luborsky et al., 1985).

Differential psychology, the psychology of individual differences, is a third area of factual knowledge that must undergird the practice of psychotherapy. In essence, it teaches that the often and gratuitously cited "average man" or "average woman" is a statistical fiction. It emphasizes the fundamental fact of variation. It provides normative baselines for the appraisal of the individual who is a complex of intelligence (learning ability); temperament; appetites and tastes; interests, skills, and aptitudes; political, religious, social, and economic attitudes; frustration tolerance; ambiguity tolerance; anxiety susceptibility; depression susceptibility; short-term and long-term aspirations; optimism-pessimism; and philosophical values. Study of the range of variation in each of these dimensions and of the characteristically small degree of correlation among them sensitizes the clinician to the meaning of individuality in working with clients. The richness of the complex underlying such individuality supports two potential avenues for psychotherapy: The client may be seriously unaware of important aspects of a fully developed self-concept, and the client may be poorly informed as to where he or she falls on the distribution of one or more of the variables.

Finally, the pragmatic psychotherapist must have a foundation in two of the primary determiners of behavior, especially because of their critical relevance in achieving change. Together, the psychology of motivation and the psychology of learning constitute the domain of behavioral psychology. For the person who is habituated to a self-defeating, inefficient, or potentially destructive pattern of response to particular conflicts or situational stresses, there must be motivation to change before any possible route to change can be evaluated. Capacity to learn new response patterns will be of no consequence if there is insufficient drive to learn. Strong motivation to change will dissipate if positive learning experiences cannot be achieved. Disrupting emotional states, such as anxiety and depression, can be so strong as to interfere or prevent practice of new response modes. Some degree of anxiety can have a facilitating effect on some performances; the therapist needs to know that elimination of all anxiety could result in impaired performance of some acts. The therapist must understand the impact of positive and negative expectancies on motivation. Given adequate motivation for change, the therapist must discriminate whether the primary learning task of the patient is one of extinguishing old response patterns or acquiring new ones. The therapist must know enough about the principles of learning to anticipate plateaus in the acquisition of new responses and not be prone to casually account for such "slow times," or even regressions, as a function of patient "resistance."

To practice a pragmatically sound psychotherapy, the practitioner must have a solid foundation of understanding in each of these content areas—developmental psychology, differential psychology, dynamic psychology, and the psychology of human learning. A deficiency of knowledge in any one of these areas is likely to put the therapist at risk of error—error in assessing the needs of the client and error in choosing an effective modality of therapy.

Special Knowledge

In addition to the above areas of basic education in depth in the psychological processes germane to all psychotherapy, the therapist requires special instruction unique to the practice of therapy.

It is central to the concept of a pragmatically based psychotherapy that the therapist be well versed in the core assumptions, concepts, and specific techniques of intervention associated with each of the *major,* established schools of therapy. (Refer to Chapter 5).

> "Orthodoxy, if it ever had a place in training programs, must give way to greater flexibility and breadth. It is no longer sufficient for students to be trained in only one treatment modality, whether it is psychoanalysis or some form of behavior therapy. Students must learn to tailor therapeutic techniques to the requirements of the patient and his problems rather than forcing patients to fit a particular technique . . . above all, students must realize that a technique which may be appropriate for one patient may be highly detrimental to another." (Strupp, Hadley, & Gomes-Schwartz, 1977)

There may be an optimal sequence for the presentation of the major schools, but this question has not been addressed. It would be appropriate for training centers to experiment with different sequences in a program including carefully designed evaluation to determine an optimal order of presentation. The sequence of didactic instruction should be coordinated with available clinical resources for supervision of the early and later practice opportunities for the student. In order to enhance the probability that students' earliest practice will provide experiences of success it is appropriate that their initial introduction to theory and technique be to those systems which are less complex, for example, the client-centered approach of Rogers and the rational-emotive school of Ellis. These could be followed by instruction in behavioral analysis and modification and by the core principles of psychodynamic therapy. It is crucial that demonstration materials and practice opportunities closely parallel classroom instruction and assigned readings. Generous use should be made of films, videotapes, audiotapes, transcripts of therapy sessions, and especially of opportunities for in vivo observation of ongoing therapy by experienced clinicians (Fiss, 1978).

Didactic instruction in each of the major approaches should be focussed and intensive. Each approach should be presented by a person who combines thorough knowledge of the relevant literature with current and ongoing clinical experience.

> It stands to reason that graduate students who come to an internship or practicum setting in which they will be conducting individual psychotherapy should have a conceptual understanding of this intricate and unique interpersonal process *before* they actually start seeing patients. Without this preparation, which takes many months of intensive, systematic study, the students are not likely to benefit from their field experience, and the student therapists' patients may be hurt rather than helped. (Fiss, 1978, p. 646)

A minimum of a full year devoted to didactic instruction, with coordinated practica, would allow for at least 3 months of focussed attention to each of the major schools. Students are served poorly by cafeteria-like instruction that offers a broad but superficial introduction to a multiplicity of techniques. At the close of this phase of preparation, the student should have read in depth, and have been examined, in selective primary sources that exposit the psychoanalytic-psychodynamic, cognitive, behavioral, and client-centered views of etiology and intervention.

Also important to the education of the therapist is knowledge of the broad realm of psychopathology. This will require at a minimum a sound course in what may be titled descriptive psychiatry, abnormal psychology, or differential diagnostic psychopathology. Such a course should include careful study of the extant, official system for psychiatric diagnoses— DSM III (American Psychiatric Association, 1980).

Finally, the specialty curriculum for the training of the psychotherapist should provide at least an introduction to the psychology of assessment and the methodology for personality assessment and behavioral observation. This instruction should teach the student the sources and significant extent of error (unreliability) in raw observation of human behavior and provide orientation to the techniques and methods that are available to reduce the ubiquitous observational-conceptual errors to which the clinician is subject. In the case of the psychologist, this will usually include extended orientation and practice in the use of specific assessment techniques and instruments (Crivollio, Burns, & Benson, 1985). Therapists trained in other disciplines should be educated in the appropriate use of referrals for objective psychological assessments. In the ongoing observational-inferential processes of therapy, the clinicican needs sophistication in the sources of and reduction of judgmental errors (Watts, 1980). Since

processes of communication are the essence of psychotherapy, the therapist must be taught the principles and modes of interviewing—how to talk,
how to listen, how to record.

The Critical Role of Supervised Experience

The didactic phase of the education of the psychotherapist provides an
essential foundation for *thinking about* all the complexities and subtleties
of the special interpersonal relationships of psychotherapy. It provides
concepts and principles and exposure to the relevant research literature.
Apart from more or less opportunity to practice, as afforded by clerkships,
practica, and laboratory exercises, the formal instruction does not teach
the student "how to do" psychotherapy, or "how to be" therapeutic. For
the development of initial therapeutic competencies, the student is critically dependent on the opportunity to practice for an extended period
under consistent supervision.

The focus of the didactic education of the psychotherapist should be
primarily on how to *think about* the nature of the therapeutic endeavor,
with secondary but more than casual attention to basic principles of *how
to* carry it out. The therapist needs to be stimulated toward the development of a secure philosophical basis for perception of therapy as an
inevitably social process in which he or she is a social agent (see chaps. 2
and 3). Introduction to the core schools of treatment, with particular
attention to their theoretical bases, will serve to protect the future therapist
from naive hubris and the expectation of providing successful treatment
by a single formula (prescription) (see chaps. 4 and 5). The conclusion of
the phase of formal instruction should see the therapist-to-be with an
appreciation of the rich complexity of human maladjustment, knowledge
of the demonstrated applicability and limitations of existing therapeutic
modalities, a tolerance for ambiguity, and a strong motivation to put
principles to practice.

Two aspects of supervised clinical experience for the psychotherapist-
to-be are notable and present something of a paradox. The first is the fact
that when established practitioners are surveyed, they indicate that their
development as therapists was more significantly affected by their supervised practice experience than by their classroom instruction. "Among
the various specific experiences that are considered important by mental
health professionals supervision stands out as being the single most
important experience" (Henry, Sims, & Spray, 1971, p. 150). The second
is the fact that little research has been devoted to the process of supervision (Matarazzo & Patterson, 1986, Matarazzo, Wiens, & Saslow, 1960).

On average, *less than one fourth* of a broad sample of psychotherapists (including analysts, psychiatrists, psychologists, and social workers) rated their graduate school or medical school courses as "very relevant" to their work as therapists. By contrast, all four professional groups gave positive evaluation (60 to 82%) to the value of their supervised clinical work during their residency or internship (Henry, Sims, & Spray, 1971). It is pertinent to note that, at least among psychologist/therapists, there is no broad recognition of "classic" texts to be read by all therapists-in-training. A sample of 83 experienced therapists produced a list of 178 books "helpful in the training of psychotherapists"; only 3 books were nominated by as many as 7, or less than 10% of the judges (Katz & Hennesey, 1981). In a study of psychologist/therapists, only 10% indicated graduate school as where they learned most "about being an effective therapist" (Rachelson & Clance, 1980).

Garfield (1977) noted that more attention had been devoted to the techniques of training subprofessionals or "auxiliary" therapists than to the preparation of professional therapists, but that there had been very little study of methods of supervision. A decade later, Matarazzo and Patterson (1986) observed that "there had been little empirical study of the actual process of supervision." (p. 249)

Although there is little research data on the effectiveness of particular modes of supervision, there is a rather large rhetorical literature on goals, methods, and processes (Tousley & Kobberger, 1984). Several authorities have outlined customary stages in the development of the supervisee. Grater (1985) suggested four stages of passage for the therapist/trainee: (1) developing basic skills (interviewing and data collection) and adopting a therapist role; (2) expanding the range of skills and roles; (3) developing skill in assessing client needs and selecting an intervention mode; and (4) learning to use his or her self in assessment and intervention. Ralph (1980) suggested somewhat similar stages: (1) investigative, information gathering; (2) adopting a theoretical stance; (3) learning to appreciate the reality of transference; and (4) learning to use his or her self as a therapeutic force. With respect to a comfortable theoretical stance at early stages of experience, Ralph wrote, "A student at a given level of sophistication in his functioning as a clinician can best understand and use theoretical constructs that match his own conceptual level. Ideas which are too complex will make the student either bewildered or anxious, and ideas which are too simplistic will not enhance development." (p. 249) Erskine (1982) suggested five stages of learning by the student therapist: (1) acquiring skills; (2) building confidence; (3) gaining identity as a therapist; (4) learning to refine treatment plans; and (5) resolving countertransference issues. Wagner (1957), reflecting on experience in a seminar on supervision at the Menninger Clinic (see Ekstein & Wallerstein, 1972) identified three modes of supervision: (1) patient-centered; (2) therapist-centered, and (3) process-centered, reflecting developmental stages of the supervisee. In the first, focus is on the patient's reactions and problems; in the second, attention is given to the trainee's blind spots and problems of countertransference; and in the process-centered stage, the supervisor/trainee relationship is used to help the therapist/trainee become sensitive to his or her relationship with the patient.

As guidance primarily for supervisors, but equally helpful to supervisees, Watters, Rubenstein, and Bellisimo (1980) have provided an excellent outline of "learning objectives" in psychotherapy. They specify 10 categories of objectives, each classified as a perceptual (P), conceptual (C), or executive (E) skill, with each category accompanied by delineation of specific behavioral goals. For example, under the category of "Patient's Affect" they suggest:

> Demonstrate the ability to: (a) identify accurately the overt emotional component of the patient's communications—accessible, undefended affect (P), (b) label empathically, where appropriate, accessible, undefended affect (E), (c) identify accurately defenses against deeper feelings, inaccessible affect (PC), (d) label empathically where appropriate, defenses against inaccessible affect (E.C.). (p 114)

From the category of "transactions," the recommended goal for the trainee is to "Demonstrate the ability to help the patient identify how he/she contributes repeatedly to unsatisfying transactions with others (P.C.E.)." (p 116)

Logistics and modes of supervision have also been addressed. An excellent outline of practical issues regarding setting, content, and process of supervision has been provided by Tousley and Kobberger (1984). They reviewed the advantages and disadvantages of four methods by which the trainee's work can be presented for supervision: process notes, audiotapes, videotapes, and "live," that is direct observation by the supervisor. It is desirable for supervisors to be able to observe directly the trainees conduct of therapy, especially in the beginning stages of trainee experience. "Live" supervision can entail observation exclusively, via one-way observation windows, with provision of immediate postsession feedback. Trainees noted "direct and straightforward feedback from the supervisor" as an element in 90% of their best supervisory experiences; it was present in only 5% of their worst experiences (Allen, Szollos, & Williams, 1986 p. 95). Technology also permits ongoing suggestion or direction of the trainee during a therapy session via an intercom/telephone system (Goodman, 1985), or use of radio transmission via a hearing aid type receiver worn by the trainee (Gordon, 1975). Use of such techniques may have limited utility in relieving some of the anxiety of the beginning therapist/trainee. However, they are more interventive than supervisory, have great potential for abuse, and must be used with restraint by supervisors if the learning experience of the trainee is to be facilitated rather than impeded (Goodman, 1985).

There is no longer any justification for a supervisor to rely *solely* on the trainee's note-based recollection of what transpired in a therapy session (Goldberg, 1985). Supervisors who rely exclusively on verbal reports of what took place in therapy sessions are given poor ratings by their supervisees (Allen, Szollos, & Williams, 1986). The role of fallible memory and defensive motivation by the trainee in seeking to put a "best foot forward" has been noted (Ward, Friedlander, Schoen & Klein, 1985). A study comparing actual therapy sessions with the supervisory conferences on the same treatment hours concluded that the "more immediately involved the therapist appeared to be in the patient's production (i.e., to have provoked or in some way be responsible for a portion of the subsequent patient material), the less likely he was to report it in supervision" (Muslin, Burstein, Gedo, & Sadow, 1967, p. 430). Students are rarely instructed in efficient methods for recording therapy notes. Presser and Pfost (1985) have suggested a simple yet functional format for creating a record of therapy sessions. (See Appendix A) The supervisor should see to it that the trainee develops skill in taking adequate notes and using them effectively in communicating about the patient and the therapy process (see Chap. 6, re: note taking). However, the responsible supervisor will insist on periodic if not continuous electronic taping, either audio or video. (McGovern, 1985) With the availability of such tapes, the supervisor will not allow the trainee to passively present the tape, but will insist that the trainee "set the scene" with an oral synopsis and be responsible for selecting portions of the tape relevant to specific procedural questions.

Traditionally, most supervision of psychotherapy has been one-on-one, one supervisor with one trainee, an hour-for-hour, an hour of supervision for each hour of trainee therapy. While some amount of such supervision may be desirable in the earliest stages, it is expensive and inefficient, especially as it deprives the trainee of the amplification afforded by group supervision, in which the trainee's cases and the inputs of the supervisor can be shared with other trainees and their cases. If adequate time is provided for supervision of a group of two to three trainees, there can be a reduction of the tension common to the one-on-one setting, together with facilitation of a "learning together" atmosphere.

It is as important to the supervisor-supervisee relationship as it is to psychotherapy that there be a formal contract in the beginning. This should include not only the provision for logistics (frequency and duration of conferences) but also an outline of the supervisor's specific expectations as to how the trainee should prepare for supervision and what materials should be available (Archer & Peake, 1984). In drafting the contract, it is desirable for the supervisor to be aware of his or her distinctive administrative, instructional, evaluative, and professional roles (Tousley & Kobberger, 1984; Worthington, 1984).

It is especially important that both supervisor and supervisee have an explicit understanding of the bases or dimensions on which the latter's performance is to be evaluated. "Receiving a low grade on the practicum has more impact than receiving a low grade in any other course" (Yogev, 1982 p. 239). In one study, it was found that three out of four clinical psychology trainees did not know what criteria would be applied in evaluation of their psychotherapy performance (Rosenbaum, 1984). This is perhaps reflective of the finding in another study that nearly a third of supervisors had received no training in the role of supervision (McColley & Baker, 1982). Salvendy (1977) made the important point that the supervisor should have a role in the selection of cases for trainees; it is important that trainees' earliest cases be chosen for the likelihood that they will provide him or her an experience of at least modest success.

The supervisor, willy-nilly, is a role model, especially as a therapist. A common complaint of beginning therapists is that they have had limited or no opportunity to directly observe "expert" therapists engaged in therapy. In the earliest stages of supervision, it is highly desirable for the supervisor to share his or her work, via either audio or videotapes, or better yet, where facilities permit and clients are willing, by direct observation (Nelson, 1978). In later stages of the supervisory relationship, it is desirable for supervisors to periodically share the current status of their work with selected patients, especially as such sharing helps trainees to learn that the course of therapy is rarely smooth and that the best of "experts" are frequently perplexed. Effective therapy modeling is also possible through role-playing with the trainee assuming the role of his or her patient and the supervisor responding as therapist (Fleming & Hamburg, 1958).

Supervisors are also role models in the broader context of professional identity. In that role, they have a responsibility to be continuously informed about significant professional developments and in touch with the current literature on research and practice, sharing their information and encouraging the habit of professional reading by supervisees. Survey data indicate that psychologist/therapists are not heavy readers of the relevant research studies; "zero" was the modal number of research articles and chapters read per month (Morrow-Bradley & Elliott, 1986). It is probable that therapists from other disciplines are equally negligent. This disregard appears to be a function of the perceived nonrelevance or nonapplicability of much therapy research, such a view being more characteristic of dynamically oriented therapists and less so of cognitive/behavioral therapists. Although published research may have small impact directly on practice, it is possible that it influences therapists at a conceptual level, that is, in the way they think about the complex phenomena of psychotherapy (Cohen, Sargent, & Sechrest, 1986). In contrast to marked neglect of therapy research, survey respondents (psychologists) placed a high value on discussion with colleagues as a source of useful guidance. Supervisors can model the desirable role of consultation by sharing their consultation experiences with their supervisees and in so doing help to counteract any tendency of supervisees to view the supervisor as "all-knowing."

A critical element of the supervisor's role is attention to the ethical principles and rules governing the practice of therapy. Trainees must be alerted to ethical and legal issues relevant to the cases they present. The fact of supervision itself presents the possibility for violation of the principles of confidentiality and vitiation of the client's informed consent if the client is not explicitly told of the status of the supervisee and of the fact that the client's confidences will be shared with a specific supervisor (APA, 1984).

Redlich and Pope (1980) found no publications on the ethics of "mental health training". They noted that the Hippocratic Oath spoke directly to the ethics of teachers of medicine in relation to their students. They then examined the application of five of the Hippocratic principles to the teaching of medical students by psychiatrists. Their admonitions have relevance for all supervisors of psychotherapists in training: 1) Primum non nocere - not to do harm through indoctrination or by behavior that belies teachings; 2) Competence - to safeguard patients by assuring adequate supervision of trainees whose responsibilities do not exceed their level of competence; 3) Not to exploit students sexually or financially; 4) To encourage respect and dignity by helping the student to accept fallibility and ambiguity; 5) To be sensitive to the heightened possibility for violation of patient confidences in teaching contributions, and to protect student confidences. Redlich and Pope added the principle of informed consent, noted above, and that of equity, i. e., the need for teacher/supervisors to be concerned that all patients, regardless of sex, race, creed, or social class have equal access to and quality of care.

The effective supervisor-supervisee relationship is ideally one that grows in mutuality, warmth, and acceptance over time (Carkhuff & Truax, 1965). It entails the sharing of confidences and allows the operation of many of the factors common to the relationships of therapist-client (see chap. 5). As is true for psychotherapy, the supervisory relationship holds the potential for exploitation. In supervision, the "lack of integrity and maturity may lead to 'psychonoxious' . . . supervision" (Rozsnafszky, 1979, p. 190). Of greater probable risk than obvious sexual exploitation is the risk of subtle seduction, by supervisor or trainee, that transforms supervision into or contaminates it with therapy. While some authorities hold that supervision is a form of psychotherapy (Truax, Carkhuff, & Douds, 1964), supervision should not become therapy. The supervisor should hold assiduously to the role of trainer and teacher, not therapist (Greben, 1979a, b.). If a legitimate need for personal therapy for the trainee is perceived by either trainee or supervisor, it is the responsibility of the latter to avoid a dual relationship and to assist the former in finding a suitable therapist.

Consistent with the pragmatic concept of therapy, it is desirable that trainees have the opportunity for supervised experience with a variety of supervisors, each of whom is a model and expositor of one of the basic forms of therapy. The supervisor should seek to communicate the assumptions and principles of his or her school, recognizing it as one among others, and not strive to make converts. Supervisors who seek to indoctrinate may be responsible for part of the "deterioration" of self-concept found in some trainees (Abramowitz, Weitz, & James, 1974).

While *supervision* is the term used universally to describe the process of providing oversight of the early practice of therapist-in-training, it is a word with unfortunate connotations, one of which is the implication that the provider of the oversight has "super-vision." This may encourage an undesirable degree of dependency and passivity on the part of the supervisee. The learning process will be facilitated if in some part of the clinical training experience, the student is oriented toward "consultation." The following illustrates an approach to trainee orientation (in this instance, for psychiatric residents) to the weekly case conference, presented as part of the training contract.

> Although the general notion of supervision is pertinent to the group conference, the concept of supervision is objectionable on several grounds: (1) it encourages a degree of passivity on the part of the resident—i.e., they come to be "overseen," exposed to the "super-vision" of the leader, etc.; (2) it encourages a tendency to unselective "blow-by-blow" accounts of what transpired in the therapy session—some therapy sessions can be essentially repetitive, unchallenging, in a word—boring; detailed reports of such sessions are even more boring; (3) with rare exception, residents are at a level of general maturity and experience where they do not require supervision in the strict sense of that term; in fact, the notion of supervision can be subtly insulting.
>
> Accordingly, for purpose of our group conference, the term *consultation* is preferred. This means that you should attend our meetings *not* to be supervised (passively) but rather to seek consultation (actively). In the context of active

consultation rather than passive supervision, you will necessarily have to give some time and thought to preparation for each meeting.

(For an example of further, formal preparatory instructions to trainees regarding group supervisory conferences, see Appendix B.)

A survey of the distinctions between supervisees "best and worst" experiences in supervision supported the following summary:

> Good supervisors modeled respect of both their and their trainees' differences in values, experiences, and personal privacy. From this nonintrusive and pluralistic base, they provided useful, theory-based conceptual frameworks for understanding psychotherapeutic processes; taught practical skills; and encouraged trainees to experiment with using novel strategies. Good supervisors also were tolerant of mistakes, provided clear and direct feedback,and confronted supervisees' resistances in an atmosphere of safety. They also invested more time in the process and monitored the psychotherapeutic activities of their charges by some means other than trainees' self-reports. Finally, they were open to feedback about their own styles of relating. (Allen, Szollos, & Williams, 1986, p. 97)

The Question of Personal Therapy

Psychologically distressed persons enter psychotherapy in search of insight, information and instruction, improvements in behavior, and, sometimes, inspiration. The probability of their receiving effective assistance is jeopardized if their therapists suffer unresolved psychological "hang-ups" of their own. It is for this reason that, as noted earlier, personality appraisal plays a prominent role in the process of selection of candidates for graduate training. However, as noted previously, the use of interviews and "character references" is of limited power in selecting for positive indexes of mental health.

The earliest stages of close supervision in the practice of therapy are especially stressful and likely to bring to light underlying, pervasive insecurities, immaturities, or value biases that will handicap some future practitioners and their clients if they are not recognized and confronted forthrightly. Supervisors have a vital role in being alert to such factors and in sensitively encouraging the trainee to such personal counseling as may be indicated. As noted above, supervisors must avoid the conflicts of interest that will arise if they seek to play dual roles of supervisor and therapist.

Although the insistence that all therapists have personal therapy would seem to serve a generally prophylactic goal, such a policy involves the risk of iatrogenic pathology when imposed on trainees who are well balanced to begin with. Only orthodox psychoanalytic institutes have a policy of requiring a personal analysis for trainees; the potential detriments of such a requirement have been recognized by thoughtful critics of psychoanalytic training (Frank, 1961). The fact of having been "in analysis" or having been "analyzed" may engender a degree of hubris that is antithetical to the experiencing and communication of empathic therapist response considered by many experts to be a sine qua non of effective therapy. Psychologist/practitioners report only a 4 to 10% incidence of personal therapy as a requirement in the graduate programs in which they were trained (Allen, Szollos, & Williams, 1986; Rachelson & Clance, 1980).

The possibility of significant personal problems for therapists does not end with the period of their formal training. Both anecdotal accounts and surveys of practicing therapists indicate that their work entails particular stresses that may increase the likelihood that they will experience emotional distress and personal problems; prominent among these are relationship disturbances and depression (Deutsch, 1985). Among stresses experienced by therapists are difficulties arising in their relationships with patients (e. g., "internalization of patients' difficulties"; and "slow and erratic pace of . . . work") (Hellman, Morrison, & Abramowitz, 1986). Various surveys suggest that at least 50% of all therapists have sought personal therapy at some time. The percent who need and would profit from some counseling is probably considerably higher (Deutsch, 1985; Farbert & Heifetz, 1981; Garfield & Kurtz, 1975; Prochaska & Norcross, 1983). A number of factors, including embarrassment and humiliation at accepting the role of "patient," may account for the fact that "the majority of experienced psychotherapists appear to resist entering personal psychotherapy, even during times of distress when it may be both useful and appropriate" (Guy & Liaboe, 1986). This potential resistance should be anticipated by supervisors who can alert trainees to the stresses of therapeutic work and to their responsibility to seek appropriate professional help at such times that their psychological state may impair their practice. Beyond that, experienced therapists should be willing to be available to troubled colleagues as part of their adherence to the ethical injunction to do some work without the expectation of customary reward. The possibilities for mutual aid are clearly enhanced when therapists practice in groups and are reduced for the solo practitioner. The need for personal therapy is tersely suggested by a remark, presumably facetious, attributed to Rudolph Dreikurs, "When I am thoroughly cured I will no longer need to be a therapist" (Schwartz, 1978). It is of interest that behavior therapists take their personal problems to nonbehavioral therapists (Grunebaum, 1983; Huber, 1984). It is disturbing that the limited research available indicates an *inverse* relationship between the amount of personal therapy received by therapists and their effectiveness with their patients (Clark, 1986).

Continuing Education

None of the existing standard programs for the preparation of the professional psychotherapist entail a sufficient period of required time to allow for adequate orientation to the core processes (modes) of therapeutic intervention outlined in chapter 5. At most, such programs require some equivalent of a year's full-time supervised, intensive experience in the practice of psychotherapy. At best, and only if specifically planned, the trainee can hope to achieve a foundation in two modes. This means that the conscientious student who seeks preparation for a pragmatic approach to therapy must plan for not less than a year of postdegree supervised work in one or more settings carefully selected to round out his or her foundations.

Beyond this earliest period of preparation, the acquisition of increased conceptual clarity and mode-specific skills can be realized by taking advantage of the advanced workshops, conferences, and seminars offered by leaders of the major schools. Within the limits of time and finances, the learning opportunities afforded by such offerings will be most stimulating for the pragmatic therapist who attends, in any one year, advanced presentations by advocates/experts of at least two different "schools."

Upon completion of the period of formal training, the therapist is able to return to the dimensions of a broad, general education that were closed off upon entering professional preparation. Now there is time for avocational pursuits and intellectual interests that were suppressed during graduate training. ". . . there is no doubt that one of the most powerful stimuli for professional learning emanates from a satisfying personal life outside the professional situation" (Whitaker, 1960 p. 168). The completion of pre-scribed training frees young therapists to begin renewed contact with all the facets of the culture of which both they and their patients are members and through that increased exposure to gain an ever enlarging capacity for understanding.

References

Abramowitz, S. I., Weitz, L. J., & James, C. R. (1974). Supervisor self-concept and self-concept deterioration among psychotherapy trainees. *Journal of Clinical Psychology, 30,* 300–302.

Allen, G. J., Szollos, S. J. & Williams, B. E. (1986). Doctoral students' comparative evaluations of best and worst psychotherapy supervision. *Professional Psychology: Research & Practice, 17,* 91–99.

American Psychiatric Association (1980). *Diagnostic and Statistical Manual of Mental Disorders, Third Edition.* Washington, D.C.: American Psychiatric Association.

American Psychological Association Committee on Training in Clinical Psychology (1947). Recommended graduate training program in clinical psychology. *American Psychologist, 2*, 539–558.

American Psychological Association, Division of Psychotherapy, Psychotherapy Curriculum and Consultation Committee. (1971). Recommended standards for psychotherapy education in psychology doctoral programs. *Professional Psychology, 2*, 148–154.

American Psychological Association (1984). Committee on Scientific and Professional Ethics and Conduct. Memorandum: Informed consent and the use of supervision. January 30, 1984.

Archer, R. P., & Peake, T. H. (1984). Learning and teaching psychotherapy: Signposts and growth stages. In R. P. Archer and T. H. Peake (Eds) *Clinical training in psychotherapy.* (pp. 61–74) New York: Haworth Press.

Astin, A. W. (1961). The functional autonomy of psychotherapy. *American Psychologist, 16*, 75–78.

Berman, J. S., & Norton, N. C. (1985). Does professional training make a therapist more effective? *Psychological Bulletin, 98*, 401–407.

Betz, B., & Whitehorn, J. C. (1956). The relationship of the therapist to the outcome of therapy in schizophrenia. *Psychiatric Research Reports (No. 5,* pp. 89–105).

Brill, A. A. (1949). *Basic principles of psychoanalysis.* Garden City, NY: Doubleday.

Carkhuff, R. R., & Truax, C. B. (1965). Training in counseling and psychotherapy: An evaluation of an integrated didactic and experiential approach. *Journal of Consulting Psychology, 29*, 333–336.

Clark, M. M. (1986). Personal therapy: A review of empirical research. *Professional Psychology: Research and Practice, 17*, 541–543.

Cohen, L. H., Sargent, M. M., & Sechrest, L. B. (1986). Use of psychotherapy research by professional psychologists. *American Psychologist, 41*, 198–206.

Cox, W. M.(1978). Where are the A and B therapists, 1970–1975? *Psychotherapy: Theory, Research & Practice, 15*, 108–121.

Crivollio, A. J., Burns, W. J., & Benson, C. (1985). Towards a model for practicum training in clinical psychology. *Clinical Supervisor: 3*, 51–55.

Cummings, N. A., & Luchese, G. (1978). Adoption of a psychological orientation: The role of the inadvertent. *Psychotherapy: Theory, Research & Practice, 15*, 323–328.

Deutsch, C. J. (1985). A survey of therapist's personal problems and treatment. *Professional Psychology: Research & Practice, 16*, 305–315.

Ekstein, R. & Wallerstein, R. S. (1972). *The teaching and learning of psychotherapy.* New York: Basic Books.

Ellis, A. (1978). Personality characteristics of rational-emotive therapists and other kinds of therapists. *Psychotherapy: Theory, Research & Practice, 15*, 329–332.

Erskine, R. G. (1982). Supervision of psychotherapy: Models for professional development. *Transactional Analysis Journal, 12*, 314–321.

Farber, B. A. & Heifetz, L. J. (1981). The satisfaction and stresses of psychotherapeutic work: A factor analytic study. *Professional Psychology: Research & Practice, 12*, 621–630.

Fischer, S. & Greenberg, R. (1977). *The scientific credibility of Freud's theories and therapy.* New York: Basic Books.

Fiss, H. (1978). A dynamic conceptual approach to the teaching of psychotherapy in the classroom. *Professional Psychology: Research and Practice, 9*, 646–649.

Fleming, J. & Hamburg, D. (1958). An analysis of methods for teaching psychotherapy with description of a new approach. *Archives of Neurology & Psychiatry, 79*, 179–200.

Forer, B. R. (1953). Personality factors in occupational choice. *Educational & Psychological Measurement, 13*, 361–366.

Frank, J. D. (1961). *Persuasion and healing: A comparative study of psychotherapy*. Baltimore: The Johns Hopkins Press.

Garfield, S. L. (1977). Research on the training of professional psychotherapists. In A. S. Gurman & A. M. Razin (Eds.), *The therapist's contribution to effective psychotherapy: Empirical assessment*. New York: Pergamon.

Garfield, S. L., & Kurtz, R. (1975). Clinical psychologists: A survey of selected attitudes and views. *Clinical Psychologist, 28*, 7–10.

Geller, J. D., & Berzins, J. I. (1976). A-B distinction in a sample of prominent psychotherapists. *Journal of Consulting & Clinical Psychology, 44*, 77–82.

Goldberg, D. A. (1985). Process notes, audio, and videotapes: Modes of presentation in psychotherapy training. *Clinical Supervisor, 3*, 3–13.

Goodman, R. W. (1985). The live supervision model in clinical training. *Clinical Supervisor, 34*, 43–49.

Gordon, D. A. (1975). A mobile, wireless "bug-in-the-ear" communications system for training and therapy. *Behavior Therapy, 16*, 130—132.

Grater, H. A. (1985). Stages in psychotherapy supervision: From therapy skills to skilled therapist. *Professional Psychology: Research and Practice, 16*, 605–610.

Greben, S. E. (1979a). The influence of the supervision of psychotherapy on being therapeutic: 1. Introduction and background to the supervisory relationship. *Canadian Journal of Psychiatry, 24*, 499–506.

Greben, S. E. (1979b). The influence of the supervision of psychotherapy on being therapeutic: 2. Modes of influence of the supervisory relationship. *Canadian Journal of Psychiatry, 24*, 507–513.

Grunebaum, H. (1983). A study of therapists' choice of a therapist. *American Journal of Psychiatry, 140*, 1336–1339.

Guy, J. D., & Liaboe, G. P. (1986). Personal therapy for the experienced psychotherapist: A discussion of its usefulness and utilization. *Clinical Psychologist, 39*, 20–23.

Hansen, J. C., & Barker, E. N. (1964). Experiencing the supervisory relationship. *Journal of Counseling Psychology, 11*, 107–111.

Hayes, S. C. (1986). A training model in search of a rationale. *American Psychologist, 41*, 593–594.

Hellman, I. D., Morrison, T. L., & Abramowitz, S. I. (1986). The stresses of psychotherapeutic work: A replication and extension. *Journal of Clinical Psychology, 42*, 197–205.

Henry, W. E., Sims, J. H., & Spray, S. L. (1971). *The fifth profession*. San Francisco: Jossey-Bass.

Heppner, P. P., & Roehlke, H. J. (1984). Differences among supervisees at different levels of training: Implications for a developmental model of training. *Journal of Counseling Psychology, 31*, 76–90.

Hescheles, D., & Kavanagh, T. (1976). Technical eclecticism and open-case consultation: A psychotherapeutic training model. *Psychological Reports, 39*, 1043–1046.

Hobfoll, S. E., & Benor, D. E. (1984). Selection of medical students with emphasis on interpersonal intervention potential. *Journal of Community Psychology, 12,* 74–80.

Holland, J. L. (1959). A theory of vocational choice. *Journal of Counseling Psychology, 6,* 35–45.

Holland, J. L. (1973). *Making vocational choices: A theory of careers.* Englewood Cliffs, NJ: Prentice-Hall.

Holt, R. R., & Luborsky, L. (1958). *Personality patterns of psychiatrists: A study of methods for selecting residents* (Menninger Clinic Monograph Series No. 13). New York: Basic Books.

Huber, H. (1984). More about where behavior therapists take their troubles. *Behavior Therapist, 7,* 98.

Katz, J. F., & Hennessey, M. T. (1981). Which books are perceived as helpful in the training of psychologists? *Journal of Clinical Psychology, 37,* 505–506.

Kelly, E. L., & Fiske, D. W. (1951). *The prediction of performance in clinical psychology.* Ann Arbor: University of Michigan Press.

Kelly, E. L., & Goldberg, L. R. (1959). Correlates of later performance and specialization in psychology: a follow-up study of the trainee in the VA Selection Research Project. *Psychological Monographs, 73* (12, Whole No. 482).

King, D. W., Beehr, T. A., & King, L. A. (1986). Doctoral student selection in one professional psychology training program. *Journal of Clinical Psychology, 42,* 399–407.

Kline, P. (1981). Fact and fantasy in Freudian theory (2nd ed.). London: Methuen.

Knoff, H. M., and Prout, H. T. (1985). Terminating students from professional psychology programs: Criteria, procedures, and legal issues. *Professional Psychology: Research and Practice, 16,* 789–797.

Komives, E., Weiss, S. T., & Ross, R. M. (1984). The applicant interview as a predictor of resident performance. *Journal of Medical Education, 59,* 425–426.

Kurz, R. B. (1984). The future of clinical training in psychotherapy. *Clinical Supervisor, 2,* 117–124.

Levine, S. P., Barzansky, B., Blumberg, P., & Flaherty, J. H. (1983). Can psychiatrists be recruited in medical school? *Journal of Psychiatric Education, 7,* 240–248.

Levy, J. (1985). The supervision of the experienced psychotherapist. *Psychiatric Journal of the University of Ottawa, 8,* 133–138.

Luborsky, L., Mellon, J., vanRavenswaay, P., Childress, A. R., Cohen, K. D., Hole, A. V., Ming, S., Crits-Christoph, P., Levine, F. J., & Alexander, K. (1985). A verification of Freud's grandest clinical hypothesis: The transference. *Clinical Psychology Review, 5,* 231–246.

Matarazzo, R. G., & Patterson, D. R. (1986). Methods of teaching therapeutic skill. In S. L. Garfield & A. E. Bergin (Eds.), *Handbook of psychotherapy and behavior change* (3rd ed). New York: John Wiley & Sons.

Matarazzo, R. G., Wiens, A. N., & Saslow, G. (1966). Experimentation in the teaching and learning of psychotherapy. In L. K. Gottschalk, & A. Auerbach, (Eds.), *Methods of research in psychotherapy.* New York: Appleton-Century-Crofts.

McColley, S. H., & Baker, E. L. (1982). Training activities and styles of beginning supervisors: A survey. *Professional Psychology: Research and Practice, 13,* 283–292.

McGovern, M. A. (1985). The use of video in the self-evaluation of speech therapy students. *British Journal of Disorders of Communications, 20,* 297–300.

McNair, D. M., Callahan, D. M., & Lorr, M. (1962). Therapist type and patient response to psychotherapy. *Journal of Consulting Psychology, 26,* 425–429.

Milstein, R. M., Wilkinson, L., Burrow, G. N., & Kessen, W. (1981). Admission decisions and performance during medical school. *Journal of Medical Education, 56,* 77–82.

Morrow-Bradley, C., & Elliott, R. (1986). Utilization of psychotherapy research by practicing psychotherapists. *American Psychologist, 41,* 188–197.

Muslin, H. L., Burstein, A. G., Gedo, J. E., & Sadow, L. (1967). Research in the supervisory process: 1. Supervisor's appraisal of the interview data. *Archives of General Psychiatry, 16,* 427–431.

Nelson, G. L. (1978). Psychotherapy supervision from the trainee's point of view: A survey of preferences. *Professional Psychology: Research and Practice, 9,* 539–550.

Osipow, S. H. (1983). *Theories of career development* (3rd ed). Englewood Cliffs, NJ: Prentice-Hall.

Peterson, D. R. (1985). Twenty years of practitioner training in psychology. *American Psychologist, 40,* 441–451.

Presser, N. R., & Pfost, K. S. (1985). A format for individual psychotherapy session notes. *Professional Psychology: Research and Practice, 16,* 11–16.

Prochaska, J. O., & Norcross, J. C. (1983). Contemporary psychotherapists: A national survey of characteristics, practices, orientations, and attitudes. *Psychotherapy: Theory, Research and Practice, 20,* 161–173.

Rachelson, J., & Clance, P. R. (1980). Attitudes of psychotherapists toward the 1970 APA standards for psychotherapy training. *Professional Psychology: Research and Practice, 11,* 261–267.

Raimy, V. C. (Ed.). (1950). *Training in clinical psychology.* New York: Prentice-Hall.

Ralph, N. B. (1980). Learning psychotherapy: A developmental perspective. *Psychiatry, 43,* 243–250.

Razin, A. B. (1971). A-B variable in psychotherapy: A critical review. *Psychological Bulletin, 75,* 1–21.

Redlich, F. C. & Pope, K. S. (1980). Ethics of mental health training. *Journal of Nervous and Mental Diseases, 168,* 708–714.

Reiss, N. B. (1975). Problems in the teaching of psychotherapy. *Psychotherapy: Theory, Research and Practice, 12,* 332–335.

Rickard, H. C. & Clements, C. B. (1986). An evaluation of interviewed versus noninterviewed clinical psychology students. *Professional Psychology: Research and Practice, 17,* 78–79.

Roe, A. (1953). A psychological study of eminent psychologists and anthropologists and a comparison with biological and physical scientists. *Psychological Monographs, 67,* No. 2 (Whole No. 352).

Roe, A. & Siegelman, M. (1964). The origin of interests. The APGA inquiry series, No. 1. Washington, D. C.: American Personnel & Guidance Association.

Rogers, Carl R. (1951). *Client-Centered Therapy: Its Current Practice, Implications, and Theory.* Boston: Houghton Mifflin Company.

Rosenbaum, D. N. (1984). Evaluation of student performance in psychotherapy. *Journal of Clinical Psychology, 40,* 1106–1111.

Rozsnafszky, J. (1979). Beyond schools of psychotherapy: Integrity and maturity in therapy and supervision. *Psychotherapy: Theory, Research & Practice, 16,* 190–198.

Salvendy, J. T. (1977). Education in psychotherapy: Challenges and pitfalls. *Canadian Psychiatric Association Journal, 22,* 435–440.

Schofield, W. (1982). Clinical psychology in transition: The evolution of a profession. In J. R. McNamara & A. G. Barclay (Eds.), *Critical issues, developments, and trends in professional psychology.* New York: Praeger Publishers.

Schofield, W. (1986). *Psychotherapy: The purchase of friendship.* New Brunswick, NJ: Transaction Books.

Schofield, W., & Balian, L. (1959). A comparative study of the personal histories of schizophrenic and non-psychiatric patients. *Journal of Abnormal and Social Psychology, 59,* 216–225.

Schofield, W., & Garrard, J. M. (1975). Longitudinal study of medical students selected for admission to medical school by actuarial and committee methods. *British Journal of Medical Education, 9,* 86–90.

Schofield, W., & Merwin, J. C. (1966). The use of scholastic aptitude, personality, and interest test data in the selection of medical students. *Journal of Medical Education, 41,* 502–509.

Schwartz, B. D. (1978). The initial versus subsequent theoretical positions: Does the psychotherapist's personality make a difference? *Psychotherapy: Theory, Research & Practice, 15,* 344–349.

Singer, J. L. (1980). The scientific basis of psychotherapeutic practice: A question of value and ethics. *Psychotherapy: Theory, Research & Practice, 17,* 372–383.

Smith, H. D. (1984). Moment-to-moment counseling process feedback using a dual-channel audiotape recording. *Counselor Education & Supervision, 23,* 346–349.

Storr, A. (1979). *The Art of Psychotherapy.* New York: Methuen.

Strupp, H. H., Fox R. E., and Lessler, K. (1969). *Patients View Their Psychotherapists.* Baltimore: The Johns Hopkins Press.

Strupp, H. H. & Hadley, S. W. (1979). Specific vs. nonspecific factors in psychotherapy: A controlled study of outcome. *Archives of General Psychiatry, 36,* 1125–1136.

Strupp, H. H., Hadley, S. W., & Gomes-Schwartz, B. (1977). *Psychotherapy for better or worse: The problem of negative effects.* New York: Jason Aronson.

Super, D. E. (1953). A theory of vocational development. *American Psychologist, 8,* 185–190.

Super, D. E. (1957). *The psychology of careers.* New York: Harper & Row.

Tousley, M. M., & Kobberger, K. (1984). Supervision in psychotherapy: A systems viewpoint. *International Journal of Psychiatry in Medicine, 14,* 133–152.

Tremblay, J. M., Herron, W. G. & Schultz, C. L. (1986). Relations between therapeutic orientation and personality in psychotherapists. *Professional Psychology: Research & Practice, 17,* 106–110.

Truax, C. B. & Carkhuff, R. R. (1967). *Toward effective counseling and psychotherapy: Training and practice.* Chicago: Aldine.

Truax, C. B., Carkuff, R. R. & Douds, J. (1964). Towards an integration of the didactic and experiential approaches to counseling and psychotherapy. *Journal of Counseling Psychology, 11,* 240–247.

Vardy, M. M. & Kay, S. S. (1982). The therapeutic value of psychotherapists' values and therapy orientations. *Psychiatry, 45,* 226–233.

Wagner, F. F. (1957). Supervision of psychotherapy. *American Journal of Psychotherapy, 11,* 759–768.

Ward, L. G., Friedlander, M. L., Schoen, L., & Klein, J. G. (1985). Strategic self-presentation in supervision. *Journal of Counseling Psychology, 32,* 111–118.

Watters, W. W., Rubenstein, J. S., & Bellisimo, A. (1980). Teaching psychotherapy: Learning objectives in individual psychotherapy. *Canadian Journal of Psychiatry, 25,* 111–117.

Watts, F. N. (1980). Clinical judgment and clinical training. *British Journal of Medical Psychology, 53,* 95–108.

Whitaker, C. A. (1960). The on-going training of the psychotherapist. In N. P. Dellis & H. K. Stone (Eds.), *The training of psychotherapists: A multidisciplinary approach.* Baton Rouge: Louisiana State University Press.

Whitehorn, J. C., & Betz, B. (1954). A study of psychotherapeutic relationships between physician and schizophrenic patients. *American Journal of Psychiatry, 111,* 321–331.

Winokur, M., & Dasberg, H. (1983). Teaching and learning short-term dynamic psychotherapy: Techniques and resistances. Bulletin of the Menninger Clinic, 47, 36–52.

Worthington, E. L. (1984). Empirical investigation of supervision of counselors as they gain experience. *Journal of Counseling Psychology, 31,* 63–75.

Worthington, E. L. (1984). Use of trait labels in counseling supervision by experienced and inexperienced supervisors. *Professional Psychology: Research & Practice, 15,* 456–461.

Yogev, S. (1982). An eclectic model of supervision: A developmental sequence for beginning psychotherapy students. *Professional Psychology: Research and Practice, 13,* 236–243.

9

Overview

As the complexities and capabilities of the human psyche have evolved over the milleniums, so too has the human's susceptibility to psychic pain. As the capacity for communication has evolved, so too has the human's readiness to express psychic pain to others and to experience relief from the response of others. In the beginning, perhaps, the only relief from stark terror came from the comforting touch of another human. Later, with the crudest of speech, touch could be augumented with "words" that conveyed a "feeling with," a sharing that brought some relief from the isolating experience of pain.

With the development of societies and the flowering of culture, the healing power of touch was assumed by individuals sanctioned by the group. In time the healing touch was incorporated into the rituals of healing words. For a time, the treatment of psychic pain and disorder was the prerogative of priests, later priest/physicians, and still later, with the founding of "medical" lore, treatment of all diseases fell to the physician. The earliest tensions between belief in the physical (touch) or the mental (words) as the *media rex* for relief of emotional distress persist to this day.

Those who would offer relief to the mentally miserable are divided by their conceptions that man suffers either from a primary susceptibility to irrationality or from a thoroughly deterministic conditionability. The human is seen by some intervenors as the victim of biological inheritance, by genetically determined electrochemical vagaries; by others, the human who is maladjusted is seen as the victim of pathological indoctrination. There is an intellectual and a professional tension between those who would provide rescue by chemistry and those who would heal by compassion and counsel.

Until the mid-20th century, study and treatment of mental disorders was a branch of medicine and psychiatry held an unchallenged monopoly. The preeminent role of psychiatry evolved naturally from the responsibility of physicians to provide at least nominal care if not active treatment of individuals who were so seriously deranged as to require institutionalization. With growing awareness of milder yet no less socially significant forms of psychological disorder and with Freud's discovery of psychic etiology, the rationale for psychiatry's hegemony was open to challenge.

With the massive social and personal dislocations of World War II, the demand for mental health services reached a magnitude that greatly exceeded existing medical resources. The national response was to mount a massive program to train not only more psychiatrists, but also more psychologists, clinical social workers, and psychiatric nurses. Both by training and by numbers, the nonmedical mental health professionals were better situated than psychiatrists to provide the demand for psychotherapeutic services. By dint of history, professional prevalence, and lack of reality contact, organized psychiatry sought to maintain or restore at least administrative control of the practice of psychotherapy. Its efforts toward this end have waxed and waned, ranging from attempts to have psychotherapy defined legally as the practice of medicine to efforts (via state laws or service contracts) to require that all psychotherapy be under medical supervision. In such efforts, psychiatry has achieved only limited and unstable islands of success. Such is the nature of conversation with therapeutic intent that its market can never be cornered by any single profession, at least not by any of those presently engaged in the enterprise.

The success of the post–World War II training programs resulted in an increasing number of clients being served by an increasing number of professionals with diverse backgrounds of preparation for the practice of psychotherapy. This provided a greatly enhanced resource for research that was also supported by generous funding. Out of this matrix, and with the pressure to find more effective treatment modalities, we have witnessed the founding of new theories and associated techniques. At present there is an active competition for exclusivity and spirited claims of "best." Time should bring the reasoned acceptance of the essential complementarity of the major schools.

Early in the period of rapid expansion of psychotherapy resources, there was recognition that none of the primary professions had quite adequate or appropriate programs to train practitioners specifically for the tasks of psychotherapy. Over 30 years ago, a prominent psychiatrist, Lawrence Kubie (1954) made a strong plea for the establishment of a new profession. He argued for the recruitment of young persons who would be trained intensively and specifically for the practice of psychotherapy. He proposed a detailed curriculum of formal studies and graded clinical experiences and a new title, Doctor of Psychological Medicine or Doctor of Psychotherapy. Kubie concluded, "Society needs a new profession, based on a new curriculum, which will enable more men to become competent practitioners of psychodiagnosis and psychotherapy at an earlier age. (p. 710)" In 1969, a psychologist, Robert Holt, presented a review of the specifics of Kubie's proposal and countered the dissents and oppositional arguments that the proposal had elicited. Holt concluded with the prematurely optimistic appraisal that "Kubie's dream has indeed had a considerable impact on reality . . . it is a great deal nearer actualization today than it was a decade ago." (p. 205)

Some 20 years ago this writer offered a "modest proposal" for the education and training of a new professional—the psychotherapist (Schofield, 1964, rev. ed. 1986). This recommendation envisioned a logistically feasible curriculum of approximately 2 years of postbaccalaureate study and training, considerably more modest than the 7 to 9 years required by Kubie's proposal, and likely to have greater recruitment potential. It was suggested as a socially desirable entry-level career from which individuals might choose to go on to future graduate study in one of the established mental health professions.

It is not only rational analysis that supports the concept of a single program to train psychotherapists. Upon review of the experiences and evaluations of their preparation as therapists provided by samples of analysts, psychiatrists, clinical psychologists, and social workers, Henry, Sims, and Spray (1973) offered the following observations:

> "Graduates of each of the professional training programs evaluated clinical experience as being much more important than course work. Since each of the professions has an elaborate structure of formal course work, the practitioners were, in effect, criticizing a large segment of the training system." (p. 5).

> Since there is considerable uniformity in the types of training experience evaluated negatively and positively, these considerations raise the possibility that the process of becoming a psychotherapist might be more effectively organized into one program stressing the positive and most relevant experiences rather than, as now, be found as subparts of four different training systems. (p. 6)

Both the Kubie and Schofield proposals were logical and reasonable, but—sad to say—unrealistic. Society was not about to establish a new and competing profession so soon after the establishment, almost overnight, of another one—clinical psychology. The necessary cooperation and energies of psychiatry and social work and their clinical teaching facilities were not likely to be dedicated to the creation of another professional group that would demand their time and attention intially, and later become competitive with them for clients. Furthermore, the interests and resources of psychology had been drawn to the notion of specialized training for psychotherapy with the creation of a professional degree

(Doctor of Psychology) and the establishment of professional schools as distinct from academic departments (Peterson, 1985).

Given the improbability in the foreseeable future that the relevant social forces will cooperate in the development of a new profession of psychotherapy—although that would be a rational clarification of the present professional and public confusions—and given the natural motives of professional identity, the best that can be hoped is that each of the primary mental health professions will work for optimal complementarity. Beyond that, in the practice of therapy by each of the professions, the interests of clients and patients will be served best if the principles of pragmatic psychotherapy are observed.

The review of the evolution of schools of psychotherapy (chap. 4) indicates the growth and changing perspectives that have arisen through the interplay of clinical experience, research, and changing social expectations. Given the limitations on the dimensions and mechanisms of human response that can become psychologically disordered, it seems unlikely that there will be discovery of any further major new approaches to psychological treatment. Rather, the basis exists for a more systematically individualized practice of therapy than has existed heretofore. Whether the potential for an efficient practice of differential psychotherapy is realized hinges on whether the training programs of the three major mental health professions undertake to design didactic curricula and coordinated clinical training experiences so that their graduates will have the foundation to offer a therapy that is pragmatically adapted to the individual needs of their client. It is to be hoped that monolithic (unimodal) and technique-focused eclectic approaches to psychotherapy training will be replaced by instruction and supervision that emphasizes the principles of a pragmatic approach. It is relevant to note the results of a Delphi poll of senior therapist/researchers requested to predict future developments (Prochaska & Norcross, 1982). The respondents expected that therapy would become more cognitive-behavioral, problem-specific, briefer, and focused on the here-now, with a decrease in treatments that are cathartic, aversive and long-term.

In a provocative paper, Magaro (1985) outlined a "fourth revolution" in the treatment of mental disorders. With a focus on the chronically mentally ill, he anticipated further erosion in the "fee for service" practice of therapy and argued for therapists to have "performance contracts" with fees adjusted to the difficulty of the rehabilitative goals and payment contingent upon achievement of the goals. Under such a system (which obviously would face strong resistance), Magaro saw the possibility for enhanced rewards for the "entrepreneurial motive of the private practitioner" and reduced reward for the salaried therapist who lacks "financial incentive to produce behavioral change." (p. 540)

It is already clear that extraprofessional developments are impinging upon the practice of psychotherapy and are likely to have increasing impact. Among these are the increasing prominence of biological treatments, the increasing role of insurance coverage for treatment of mental disorders, and the growth of corporate medicine. Furrow (1983) has reviewed these developments with particular attention to the potentials for malpractice suits, and Kurz (1984) has noted that these developments will cause training programs to "find it increasingly difficult to train therapists in traditional ways with traditional clients." (p. 120)

In closing a work on psychotherapy a conservative note is in order. Not all candidates for treatment can be significantly helped. Of those who respond positively some do so only very slowly and the therapist must be very patient and very persistent. In his seminal volume, Ellis (1962) devotes a final chapter to the *limitations* of psychotherapy. He argued that the very elements of "humanness" (biology and earliest learnings) which dispose the individual to become emotionally and psychologically disordered are the same elements that make for resistance to change, for slowness to respond to treatment, for persistence in maladaptive patterns, and for susceptibility to relapse. While biological inheritance cannot be totally reversed, the nature of early environment and experience (learning) is open to direction. Our best hope is to bring the understandings from clinical experience to bear upon education in the principles of mental hygiene so that parents and children are better equipped mentally and emotionally to be adults who can adjust with reasonable equanimity to an imperfect social order, who maintain adequate morale as they strive to achieve their personal goals, and who are more ready for constructive effort, less ready for passive complaint as they accept responsible roles in working toward improved communities and a more rational society.

References

Ellis, A. (1962). *Reason and emotion in psychotherapy*. New York: Lyle Stuart.

Furrow, B. R. (1983). Will psychotherapy be transformed in the 1980s? *Law, Medicine and Health Care, 11*, 96–117.

Henry, W. E., Sims, J. H., & Spray, S. E. (1973). *Public and private lives of psychotherapists*. San Francisco: Jossey-Bass.

Holt, R. R. (1969). Kubie's dream and its impact on reality. *Journal of Nervous & Mental Diseases, 149*, 186–207.

Kubie, L. S. (1954). The pros and cons of a new profession: A doctorate in medical psychology. *Texas Reports in Biology & Medicine, 12*, 692–737.

Kurz, R. B. (1984). The future of clinical training in psychotherapy. In R. P. Archer

Magaro, P. A. (1985). Fourth revolution in the treatment of mental disorders: Rehabilitative entrepreneurship. *Professional Psychology: Research & Practice, 16,* 540–552.

Peterson, D. R. (1985). Twenty years of practitioner training in psychology. *American Psychologist, 40,* 441–451.

Prochaska, J. O., & Norcross, J. C. (1982). The future of psychotherapy: A Delphi poll. *Professional Psychology: Research & Practice, 13,* 620–627.

Schofield, W. (1986). *Psychotherapy: The purchase of friendship.* New Brunswick, NJ: Transaction Books.

Appendix A

Illustrative Format for Recording Notes
of a Psychotherapy Session

I. *BRIEF SUMMARY OF SESSION:*

Name
_____

Date
_____

Session #

THERAPIST'S OBSERVATIONS OF:	THERAPIST'S INTERPRETATIONS/ HYPOTHESES
II. *CLIENT*	
III. *THERAPIST*	
IV. *THERAPIST-CLIENT INTERACTION*	
V. *PROBLEMS ADDRESSED*	VI. *PROGRESS MADE*
VII. *PLANS*	

VIII. *OTHER*

Source: From "A format for individual psychotherapy session notes" N. R. Presser and K. S. Pfost, (1985) by *Professional Psychology, 16,* pp. 11–16. Copyright 1985 by the American Psychological Association. Reproduced by permission of the authors.

Appendix B

Illustrative Preparatory Instructions for Group Supervisory Conferences

General Expectations

For each meeting, you will be expected to give an *organized* account of what you perceive as significant *highlights* of your most recent therapy session. These may be new points of information about the patient, new situational developments, new insights by the patient or yourself into pertinent dynamics of the case, specific instances of resistances, evasions or other difficulties encountered. These salient points should be presented, as far as you are able, in the context of the stage of therapy as you perceive it. In presenting this material it is desirable that you develop the ability to be concise, succinct, and highly selective. In those instances, which always occur, when the process is on a plateau, with little movement, you can simply say so in a very few words.

As a second part of each report you should be prepared to comment on how your overall strategy for the case and your choice of specific tactics is reflected in the session and how strategy and tactics are related to the therapy goals.

A third element in each review will consist of how you view the stage of therapy in terms of your perspective on the overall therapy course with the particular patient.

A final part of each presentation will be comprised of the essential *consultation* that is, questions you wish to raise, problems for which you wish suggestions. These questions may be both specific to your case and general in regard to theory of therapy.

As outlined above, this may sound like a very complex and lengthy oral report. Keep in mind that, on average, you will have 30 minutes or less to cover these elements. This will demand selectivity and an effort at precise communication. Preconference preparation will be necessary; you will be unable to meet the above expectations without taking at least 10–15 minutes for preparation.

Beyond responsibility for the presentation of your own case, you will be expected to participate actively in the review of the cases presented by your colleagues—raising questions, making suggestions, offering to role-play, etc.

Specific Expectations

You will be expected to have an *audiotape* of *each* session. You will be responsible for determining beforehand which part of the tape you wish to review and having the tape wound to that section.

At least once in the course of each case, you should arrange to make a videotape of a session and share it with the group.

As soon as a case has been selected by you for conference presentation, you should provide a copy of the clinic intake interview summary, and any laboratory data, including psychological test results.

Appendix C

Selected General References

Colby, Kenneth M. (1951). *A primer for psychotherapists*. New York: Ronald Press.

Ellis, Albert (1962). *Reason and emotion in psychotherapy*. New York: Lyle Stuart.

Garfield, Sol L. and Bergin, Allen E. (1986). *Handbook of psychotherapy and behavior change*. (3rd edition) New York: John Wiley & Sons.

London, Perry (1964). *The modes and morals of psychotherapy*. New York: Holt, Rinehart and Winston.

Meichenbaum, Donald H. (1979). *Cognitive-behavior modification: An integrative approach*. New York: Plenum Press.

Monroe, Ruth (1955). Schools of psychoanalytic thought: An exposition, critique, and attempt at integration. New York: The Dryden Press.

Rogers, Carl R. (1942). *Counseling and psychotherapy*. Boston: Houghton Mifflin.

Wiener, Irving B. (1975). *Principles of psychotherapy*. New York: John Wiley & Sons.

Yalom, Irvin D. (1970). *The theory and practice of group psychotherapy*. New York: Basic Books.

Yates, Aubrey, J. (1970). *Behavior therapy*. New York: John Wiley & Sons.

Author Index

Subject Index